SPEAKING
WITH
CONFIDENCE

Scott, Foresman's
Consulting Editor in Speech Communication
Douglas Ehninger
The University of Iowa

Speaking with Confidence

A Small-Group Approach to Speech Communication

KAREN CARLSON and ALAN MEYERS

Wilbur Wright College

Scott, Foresman and Company · Glenview, Ill.

Dallas, Tex. · Oakland, N.J. · Palo Alto, Cal. · Abingdon, England

All hand-drawn illustrations
in this book
are by Ron Bradford.

All photographs are by
Paul Sequeira.

Library of Congress Cataloging in Publication Data

Carlson, Karen.
    Speaking with confidence.

    Includes bibliographies and index.
    1. Oral communication. I. Meyers, Alan, joint
author. II. Title.
PN4121.C244   808.5   76-45355
ISBN 0-673-15022-4

So often students, interesting and engaging in relaxed, unstructured interpersonal exchanges, become self-conscious before an audience and lose sight of their speaking purpose and their listeners. They lose confidence and, with it, their natural ability to communicate. Aware, confident speakers speak best. But how does a speaker develop awareness and confidence? We believe they stem from three sources: (1) thorough instruction and preparation, (2) frequent experience, and (3) successful experience.

Unfortunately, the typical ten- or fifteen-week speech course with its enrollment of thirty to thirty-five students, while often offering sound instruction in speech preparation, cannot provide enough opportunities for students to practice and succeed at speaking to an audience. *Speaking with Confidence* is an attempt to overcome the limitations of the traditional classroom organization through a program which uniquely utilizes class time. On frequent occasions the book provides for dividing the speech communication class into three or four small groups. This allows several students, each with his or her own small-group audience, to speak simultaneously, and all of the students in the respective groups to speak during one fifty-minute class period. By term's end, each student will have benefitted from actively participating in thirty or more communicative experiences, delivering short speeches to small-group and whole-class audiences, and engaging in a wide variety of other speaking activities.

All students will have benefitted, too, from the individualized attention and guidance that the instructor, working with each small group frequently during the term, can provide. Additionally, the groups—when working without the instructor—can offer the student speaker advice and encouragement and provide the instructor with brief, written reactions to the speeches they've heard. Above all, in this relaxed, small-group atmosphere students discover their own successful communication traits and talents and discover experientially that all communication is an interchange of reactions, both verbal and nonverbal, between a speaker and a listener.

As critical listeners, students are encouraged to look for positive traits in each other because novices require encouragement if they are to discover and develop their communicative skills. To this end, the text focuses early and sharply on the "I'm OK—You're OK" philosophy of Transactional Analysis, the self-revelation model of the Johari Window, and the skills of listening, questioning, and criticizing constructively. Additionally, since the group setting frequently involves the student in group problem-solving situations, the book directs early attention also to the practical aspects of group function and format.

Speaking with Confidence assumes that good speakers are effective, in part, because they talk about subjects they know well. So it encourages and assists students to prepare a personal interests-inventory from which to choose, narrow, and develop topics for the speeches they will subsequently give. Further, the book stresses the need for the student to speak from personal experiences and perceptions, emphasizing that the most interesting and memorable moments from a speech frequently are those individualized stories and anecdotes which enliven and illustrate the speaker's point. Thus the book moves from an emphasis upon the telling of personalized events and experiences to building upon them through research in interviews and in the library.

The overall structure of the work also is aimed at maximizing the opportunities for student success in speaking. Part One is centrally concerned with the basics of interacting with others, Part Two with the commonsense goals of communicating with *interest, clarity,* and *usefulness.* Part Three guides the student through the successive stages of preparing and presenting an effective speech: choosing a subject, finding and verifying materials, analyzing the audience, organizing and humanizing the speech, rehearsing it, and—ultimately—delivering it. Part Four extends these speechmaking skills to the strategic planning, preparation, and presentation of persuasive speeches; and Part Five deals with some practical, real-life problems of locating and landing a job and the need to cooperate with and lead others in work situations.

Throughout, carefully selected aspects and concepts of communication lead directly into communicative *action.* Each chapter is interlaced with activities and exercises which encourage the student to discover, test, or apply a useful principle in a speaking experience. More than eighty of these experiential/participation exercises, progressing from the relatively easy and simple to the less easy and more complex, are also aimed at ensuring opportunities for student success in speaking. Each activity or experience emphasizes the understanding and development of a specific, clearly defined skill. All enable the student to discover his or her communicative strengths in short interactions or brief, informal speeches, then progress to longer, more fully developed speeches to inform and persuade, and—finally—to role-play the application of sound communication principles to the workaday world of job-getting and job-holding. A complete list of exercises for all chapters appears on pages 293–296. A few of these activities involve tape recording and videotaping, the necessary equipment for which is often found in the speech classroom or laboratory; but such equipment is by no means a requirement for using this text-book.

In addition to making the text as useful and workable as possible, we've tried to make it *readable* — enjoyably so. We've aimed steadily at a style that is fast-paced, often touched (we hope) with a bit of humor, and addressed directly to the student reader. These same criteria have also influenced our choice of excerpts from speeches, a number of which have never appeared in print before, and some of which are from students themselves.

We wish to thank the many people who have guided us through our first voyage into book-writing. First, we owe special thanks to Ken Macrorie, whose common sense and humanistic program of instruction in *Telling Writing,* published by the Hayden Book Publishing Company of New York, has strongly influenced our efforts in this volume, especially Parts One and Two. We also thank Professors Roy M. Berko, Lorain County Community College, Elyria, Ohio; Kenneth E. Fountain, Miami-Dade Junior College, Miami, Florida; Jo-Ann Graham, Bronx Community College of the City University of New York; Deldee Herman, Western Michigan University, Kalamazoo, Michigan; and Patrick O. Marsh, California State University, Sacramento, California, who read successive versions of the manuscript and offered many helpful suggestions.

We are grateful, too, to the many people who have consented to allow excerpts from their speeches to appear in our text, and we wish to thank them all. We also thank those who provided copies of their speeches, but which we could not include because of space limitations. Also deserving of our gratitude and appreciation are Orlando Ponzio and Eugene Gawlick, whose Forum Program at Wilbur Wright College, Chicago, served as the source of many of the speech tapes and manuscripts from which we have drawn extensively. We are grateful also to the many students whose performance in our classrooms inspired us to write this book.

Finally, we thank our spouses, Edward and Ann, who have put up with us for the more than two years we've worked on this project and whose love and encouragement have lessened our occasional pain and increased the joys of creating a textbook.

KAREN CARLSON

ALAN MEYERS

Contents

What Persuasion Is, 197: How it "works"—and doesn't "work";
Aristotle's advice. What Persuasion Is Not, 203. Gearing Up for Your
Persuasive Speech, 205: Looking for persuasive topics inside and
outside yourself

Audience Feelings and Attitudes, 211: Positive, neutral or indifferent, and
negative or hostile audiences. Audience Needs as Factors in Persuasion,
212: *Physiological-survival, safety, love and belonging, esteem,* and *self-
actualization needs;* How needs may affect audience response. Audience
Beliefs as Factors in Persuasion, 220: *Peripheral, authority,* and *core*

Strategy: The "Available Means of Persuasion," 226. Emotion, Your
First Big Gun, 227: Using emotional appeals; Misusing emotional
appeals; Reason, Your Second Big Gun, 235: What evidence is; What
reasoning is—and is not; Some characteristics of logical arguments;
Key elements of a persuasive argument—the Toulmin model modified

Planning Your Strategy One Step at a Time, 244: Establishing your
credibility; Establishing the problem; Presenting your solution to the
problem; Moving your audience to action. Organizing Your Persuasive
Speeches, 250: Climax order; Anticlimax order: *The shock tactic, Direct
onslaught, Reinforcing your reinforcers, Advancing from signpost to
signpost*

What You Should Know About the Interview, 261: Your purpose and the
employer's purpose; Physical circumstances; Expectations; Needs and
biases. Preparing Your Strategy for the Interview, 265: Your physical
appearance; Researching the company's background; Anticipating
questions; Preparing a resumé

Observing the Rules, 274. Dealing with Clients, 277. Leading Others in
Their Work, 278. Conducting and Participating in Meetings, 280

Of Speech and Speakers

MUMBLERS, PRODUCERS, AND OTHER STRATEGIES FOR SURVIVAL

In high school, Art Schmutz was, according to the idiom of the times, a "skag"—a bum, a hood, a punk—and, therefore, of course much admired by classmates. The customary hard-guy attire bedecked his 6'5", 135-pound frame: white tee shirt or Italian knit buttoned all the way up to the neck, pants with reverse pleats, silver-studded belt, heavy leather boots, and the inevitable black motorcycle jacket with 5,000 zippers, snaps, and pockets, which he wore indoors and out, warm weather or cold, its thirty-six-inch sleeves exposing two or more inches of bony wrists. Every thirty seconds—or if he was careless, every forty-five—Art combed and teased his towering Elvis Presley pompadour, glued down with two pounds of shimmering goose grease.

Art was beautiful. He was also the star of the speech class. While others observed decorum with the usual presentations on how to draw Donald Duck, how to decorate a homecoming float, and why one candidate for Student Council was preferable to another, Art had his own ideas. Wide pant cuffs flapping against angular legs, he would jive-step to the front of the room, plant his feet apart like Clint Eastwood dueling at high noon, and—with thumbs hooked into his silver-studded belt—fire off a speech on subjects that counted for him and his audience: Chuck Berry as the king of rock 'n' roll; taking a girl to the beach parking lot to watch the "submarine races"; installing the necessities on a hot rod: four-barrel carburetor, mag wheels, and jagged racing stripes.

Fully prepared, in command, Art would capture and captivate his audience immediately, then lead them directly to his point. "Greetings, culture lovers," he would drawl. "I want to talk about Beethoven—that is, 'Roll Over, Beethoven,' which, like the rest of Chuck Berry's compositions, is finely crafted, superbly orchestrated—and it's got a good beat; you can dance to it. No lie." Unlike his classmates, who gazed abstractedly or fidgeted as they spoke, punctuating their pauses with "um's" and "uh's," Art would grin, wink, and joke; he would roll off his words like dice in the washroom. And everything came up seven—a winner. "Sure, the old folks complain about our music," he'd say. "But what do they know? My mother thinks Lawrence Welk is too racy." The class would roar and whoop. The speech teacher, though pretending outrage, would grin along with the rest. And Art, triumphant, would fire his remaining ammunition on target, saving his most direct shot for last, then return to his seat like a cowboy riding off in the sunset.

Not surprisingly, his classmates dropped their inhibitions and picked up Art's example. They recognized that Art knew how to communicate. He knew his audience, knew what they liked, and knew what he did best. He was confident, animated, surprising, funny, vivid, detailed, unafraid to take chances. He was prepared, yet casual; never lengthy, but always clear. He realized the only rebels worth following are good at their trade, and so he was.

Perhaps, memories of people like Art, or expectations of meeting similar characters, help account for the full enrollment in college speech courses. At registration, students may weep at the thought of foreign language and memorizing three hundred irregular verbs, or tremble at the prospect of freshman composition with its themes and grammar and term papers, or shudder at biology and tests on the eight thousand bones in the body. But many rush to sign up for speech class. There, they think, they'll get to talk a lot, laugh a little, listen, and participate. And what could be easier? Everyone can, after all, talk.

Their assumptions carry some truth. Some students — the natural comedians, debaters, or storytellers — not only enjoy but also excel at speechmaking. They welcome the challenge of going before an audience. They can charm, persuade, elucidate, and argue easily. They can sense and satisfy their audience's needs and expectations. And, in turn, the members of their audience laugh, or nod their heads, or ask questions, or argue back. In short, they listen because they hear something worthwhile; they react because the speaker has sparked their interest.

But how about *you?* Do you have the guts of an Art Schmutz? Or, for you, is speech class fearsome, intimidating? Publicly, in front of strangers or even friends, do you dread exposing yourself to inspection, criticism, even ridicule? Do you fear you'll struggle to select a topic, struggle to say something about it, struggle to contain nervousness and dejection or even tears as the instructor tells you what you already know — that you didn't do very well? If, in answering these questions, you find that the emerging portrait looks familiar, odds are you don't speak in *any* class, and haven't in years. To find out why, let's return to grammar school for a moment and examine what you as students often had to do to survive.

Strategies for Survival

Typically, even today, in first grade, second grade, sometimes all the way through fifth or sixth grade, every hand in class shoots up when the teacher asks a question. Kids are normally curious about the world and enjoy pleasing adults in question-and-answer games. But, gradually, students discover the rules are rigged against them. The teacher frowns (or maybe smiles) at their answer, says "No-o-o" gently, and calls on someone else. Though they mean well, teachers communicate that rewards go to right answers only.

So, to survive without embarrassment, humiliation (classmates might laugh at your "stupidity"), or sense of failure, at some point you, like most students, became cautious. You learned to outguess teachers, to detect danger signs, to keep a low profile. School became a daily obstacle course—assignments, homework, questions to answer in class, punishments, and boredom which you felt you must overcome or avoid. Everyone, even the best of students, encountered and learned to cope with these feelings.

Looking back at those early years, you may realize that occasionally you took the most extreme measure for coping—*avoidance.* You didn't turn in homework or attend class. Nothing ventured, nothing lost. Better to say you failed because you didn't care, didn't try. But, since complete avoidance is neither possible nor practical most of the time, you may have developed what John Holt, in his book *How Children Fail,*[1] calls "strategies" for surviving in the classroom each day. You may have rushed through written assignments, for example, employing what Holt calls the "one-way, don't look-back, it's-too-awful" strategy. After all, why prolong an unpleasant experience needlessly? In the middle of an examination period, you may have handed in a short, error-filled, sometimes unsigned paper, returned to your back-row seat, and buried your head in your arms or a comic book.

Mumblers, guessers-and-lookers, avoiders, ostriches, producers, and thinkers.   Let's examine these strategies for coping with class discussions because they're particularly relevant to a speech course. First, in Holt's terminology, you could have been a "mumbler." When the teacher called on you, you had to say something; so you mumbled, hoping that no one would hear or that someone would rescue you. "How do you find the lowest common denominator in these fractions?" a teacher might have asked you.

"Moldiply," you managed to gulp, your eyes riveted to your desktop.

"That's right," the teacher would say, smiling. "You take the four in the first denominator and multiply it by the three in the second. And you multiply the first numerator by three and the second by four." Your vague mumble worked. You approximated what the teacher wanted to hear, and the teacher did the rest.

---

[1]John Holt, *How Children Fail* (Belmont, California: Pitman Publishing Corporation, 1964), pp. 3-4.

Holt calls another common strategy for surviving in class-discussion situations "guess-and-look." When using it, you began a statement, hesitated, checked the teacher's expression for approval or disapproval (a sophisticated communication skill, by the way), and changed or continued your answer on that basis. To the same question on common denominators, you may have responded: "You add *(uncertain pause)* . . . no, wait, you multiply *(pausing, then brightening)* . . . the three *(pause)* . . . by the four *(pause)* . . . and then you, um . . ."

But we've observed that far and away the most common strategy is another form of avoidance, simply to "shut up." What you don't say can't hurt you. Silence is golden. Children should be seen and not heard. If you kept a low profile, by high-school graduation day you may have left only scraps on the lunchroom table and cigarette butts in the washrooms as evidence that you attended.

You shouldn't be ashamed if you recognize these strategies in your behavior, past or present. Everyone uses them, good students as well as "failures." In fact, we admire your ability to survive through high school and into college without serious damage. Unfortunately, however, these strategies obviously can interfere with learning. They are symptomatic of what Holt labels the "producer" mentality. Fearful of failure and anxious to please, "producers" mostly concentrate on following the teacher's orders instead of their own instincts. Unlike those Holt calls the "thinkers," who enjoy resolving a problem, "producers" panic if left to their own devices. They need explicit directions. "Where should I say my thesis statement?" "Should I use the lectern?" "How big should my visual aid be?"

School shouldn't bear all the blame. Everyone is born with the "producer" impulse. As helpless babies, you depended on bigger, older people for all your needs—food, shelter, transportation, advice and instruction for guidance, a hug and consolation for moments of insecurity. Growing up, you never completely overcame your dependency needs, and a "right-answer"-oriented school may have nurtured them. Consequently, as students you may do or say the most dumb-headed things, contrary to all common sense, because you want to follow instructions. Once, for example, an instructor—on examining a college freshman's outline for a six-minute speech—expressed surprise that the plan had made no provision for a beginning or an ending. "But," the student protested, "you didn't *tell* me I had to have a beginning and an ending!" Most instructors, in fact, have heard students panic at nonprescriptive directions for an assignment. The students obviously suspect the instructor isn't playing fair, that the instructor is concealing standards which the students will be judged against later. "What do you want?" they beg. Or, afterwards, as they tentatively shove a speech outline at the instructor, they ask, "Is this all right?"

"Trust your own judgment," the instructor may say. But "producers," trained otherwise, throw up their hands in frustration.

So, armed with this assortment of "survival" strategies, you enter college speech classes. What are the consequences? Some of you, like Art Schmutz, may defy your earlier impulses and genuinely *think* about communication and how it works. Some of you, using the avoidance strategy, may cut class—especially on days you are scheduled to speak. Others among you may mumble through an entire speech, padding it with vague and thoughtless generalities. And some of you, no doubt, will try to follow orders with the utmost rigidity. You will assume (1) there is a single "correct" way to give a speech, and (2) you can learn this technique *only* from the teacher or the textbook. Mechanically, you'll choose your topics ("How to Bake a Cake" or "How to Ski"), never considering the possibility that your audience—the other students—neither care nor are listening. You may ramble on monotonously, without organization or point, addressing yourself to the teacher sitting in judgment ("guess-and-look," again) and ignoring your classmates sitting in boredom. Or, like an ostrich seeking safety, you simply may not look up at all, reading your fully written-out speech as you hold it in trembling hands. If you can't see anyone, you figure, no one can see you. And you'll be right. No one will be looking. Your classmates will slump in their chairs, staring at the clock, or out the window, or at the good-looking female or male in the next seat. If the instructor has required that they evaluate your performance, like good "producers" they will dutifully and dully fill in questionnaires about your thesis statement, organization, posture, delivery, use of visual aids, etc., even though they—also like ostriches—won't bother to glance up to verify your existence.

As the hour ends, in fact, you and they will scamper out of the room to grab a cigarette and a few minutes of conversation before the next class. Ironically, you could not or would not talk freely inside. Like wooden soldiers, you marched to the lectern, recited your speeches, and retreated to your seats. Only outside—in the halls, the johns, the lunchrooms, or on the lawns—could the wood turn to flesh. There, you feel, you can be real without risk, at ease with yourself and your friends. As orators, Winston Churchill you probably aren't; but you certainly relate better out from under inspection, official scrutiny, or threat of disapproval.

If you are an "avoider," a "mumbler," an "ostrich," or a "producer," obviously, to speak well in the classroom you must break your habits. Freshman psychology texts claim that within a year you forget ninety percent of the material you memorized. *Real* learning, therefore, involves not memorization but a change in your habits and attitudes—things that affect *behavior*. Altering the habitual strategies and deeply fixed attitudes requires both persistent work and practice. It requires viewing speech primarily as a behavior, as a skill, as much more than a body of theoretical information—though some theory is certainly necessary.

Therefore, let's share our assumptions about speech and about you. *First*, we assume that you already speak fairly well in most circumstances. *Second*, we assume that you probably have some talents and charms that others don't—humor, dignity, glibness, vigor, an analytical mind, a disarming smile, a facility with serpentine syntax, a homespun freshness, or a little child's vulnerability—and that each of you brings to the class a varied set of experiences, opinions, prejudices, and hangups which make you respond differently to the same stimuli.

This leads to our *third* assumption—that there are as many ways to give speeches as there are speakers, subjects, audiences, and occasions. We can only describe the way the communication process works; we can show you the interaction between a speaker, a subject, an audience, and an occasion. We can—and will—lay out what we consider to be some useful guidelines; we can't—and won't—prescribe a bunch of inflexible "rules." What's appropriate to one situation—never use poor grammar or profanity, for example—may be unsuitable for another. Our parents and friends, fourth-graders at recess, grocery clerks and bus drivers, bank presidents and priests, firemen and policemen, TV repairmen, waitresses, and seventy-year-old aunts—all speak with different styles and mannerisms. Joshing with people in the locker room isn't the same as interviewing for a job.

Consequently, our *fourth* assumption is that you must discover your own seeds of talent before cultivating them in new soil. You must speak informally for a while, without lectures of either the teacher or student variety. Don't search for the rules; discover *first* what works best for you, in an atmosphere free of fears and the crippling strategies they create. Let's eliminate those strategies by eliminating their causes. Just starting out in the course, you need encouragement. Encountering the unknown is scary business. Later, when you feel at ease, having discovered or reaffirmed your speaking strengths, you can refine them, add to them, accept and even welcome criticism. Later, without strategies interfering as frequently, you can rise to challenges, not merely duck obstacles.

Art Schmutz was a natural communicator who needed very little guidance. Perhaps you may need more. But you can learn to speak as freely and effectively as Art if you'll allow yourself to take a few risks, develop new habits, and stop worrying about obeying—or avoiding— inflexible rules. So let's begin by talking to each other. And let's be supportive, pointing out what others do right rather than wrong. Let's pull the ostrich's head from the hole in the sand, transform producers into thinkers, make success a many-laned highway. That is what communication is about, and that is what this book will try to communicate.

". . . Now, class, let's all be supportive and pull
the ostrich's head from the hole in the sand."

Part One

Interacting with Others

9

THE COFFIN, THE WINDOW, AND THE OK SEAT

1 Understanding Yourself and Others

Let's face it. The idea of speaking publicly intimidates all of us a bit. Though it rarely happens, we're afraid we'll look foolish or be hurt. Consequently, you, like everyone else, are almost sure to feel uncomfortable sometimes: in school, when your liver drops into your stomach as the teacher unexpectedly calls on you, or when you try to be suave and aren't with a cute girl or good-looking guy in the cafeteria, or when you stand behind a lectern and "um" and "you know" your way through a public speech. You'll feel uncomfortable outside school, too, when you're trapped in a conversation with five friends of a friend, or when you shrink before your presumed social or intellectual superiors, or when in a job interview you "yes, sir" and "no, sir" to a man in a double knit suit sitting behind a mahogany desk—in your mind a picture of an impersonal, indifferent antagonist.

A speech course should, in part, help you overcome that discomfort, should build confidence in the you that you are. In it you should learn, if you don't know already, that everyone suffers from insecurities and bleeds from similar wounds. Everyone, even an Art Schmutz, no matter how seemingly mature and self-possessed, must placate secret fears of being disliked, of being incompetent, of being dumber, slower, less charming, less good looking, less articulate than the next person. You will never destroy these fears, but you can learn to minimize or ignore them. When a voice inside you says, "You can't do it, you dummy," you can learn to reply, "The heck I can't." You can learn, in short, to like yourself.

I still don't know the people; I just can't seem to get in and start talking with them like everybody else does. I wish that I could be like them. It's terrible being unable to just jump in and start talking with everybody. I feel dumb, but I just don't seem to know what to say.

—from a Student's Communication Journal

Of course, in a tough, unpleasant, often hostile world, some sticks and stones can break your bones, but words need not cripple you when you understand their purpose. If you know that someone is trying to club you verbally to mask a sense of insecurity, you can bite back the impulse to retaliate. You can't avoid some pain, but what worthwhile relationship carries no bruises? Life involves—indeed requires—risks. You can't dodge every unpleasant situation; you must face some head-on. And you can, if you overcome your hang-ups. To an extent, at least, a speech course can help you initiate the process.

A speech course isn't—and shouldn't try to be—amateur group therapy. Most likely, neither you nor your instructor is a trained psychologist. Nevertheless, within the course you can learn to know yourself better and communicate more confidently and openly. You can be honest, refreshing, alive. No one's requiring you to confess every one of your crimes and sins. But why not share opinions, experiences, and occasionally admit to a foible or two? In short, why not discover and share the strengths in your personality?

EXPLORING YOUR INTERPERSONAL COMMUNICATION WITH TRANSACTIONAL ANALYSIS

Your self-confidence comes from self-understanding and self-acceptance. Probably the best-known method for developing an understanding and acceptance of yourself as a person and as a communicator is *Transactional Analysis,* or TA, as it's often called. Created by Eric Berne and popularized by Thomas Harris, both psychiatrists, TA describes, analyzes, and labels the attitudes you reveal toward yourself and others each time you communicate. As a basis for understanding these attitudes, let's begin by defining what we mean by *communication.*

Communication as transaction

Communication itself is a *transaction,* a process of exchange. You send me a message, and I send you *back* a message, to which you respond with *another* message, and so on — back and forth. Each of us continually switches roles from sender to receiver; and in this process, each of us *adapts* the other's message. Moreover, you and I send messages in many different ways, since a message is whatever one of us says and does and whatever the other interprets to have meaning. Our words send out potential messages; but so do a great many other things, including our tone of voice, our rate of speech, our pauses, and the volume and pitch of our voice. We also communicate unspoken, or nonverbal, messages with our body: through our facial expressions, hand movements, posture, through how close we get to each other, and how often and how long we maintain eye contact.

Our *perceptions* further affect the speech communication process. We can only communicate what we *perceive* — what our senses "tell us." At this moment, can I see you without distortion? Can you hear me clearly, without distraction from "external noise" — the stereo in the next room or the traffic sounds outside? Naturally, then, our perceptions greatly depend on how well we pay attention. The more we *focus* on something — whether a single word, a whole speech, or a traffic accident — the more likely we'll perceive and understand it clearly. Just as important, our perceptions depend on our *memory.* The more we associate something we now see or hear with past perceptions or feelings, the more quickly we'll recognize and understand (or, in some cases, *mis*understand) it in the present. In fact, we would probably perceive very little without the benefit of our recall and memory.

Of course, a great many stimuli bombard us simultaneously—in, for example, a classroom. We feel our clothes against our body and the pinch of our too-tight shoes. We hear the sounds of footsteps in the hallway, or a radio outside an open window, or a clock ticking in the room, or three separate conversations in small groups. We see twenty-five people sitting, standing, pacing, gesturing; we see chairs, tables, the chalkboard, the green painted walls, the green grass and the trees outside the window. We detect subtle smells and tastes like, for example, cigarettes and chewing gum. Since we couldn't perceive and remember all of these stimuli, we narrow our focus to a few, sometimes intentionally and at other times unintentionally. To demonstrate a few of the problems of perception in only one very important part of the speech communication process—*listening*—let's try a little test. See how well you perceive word sounds and retain what you hear.

1 Whole-Class Exercise
Testing Your Perception of Spoken Language

Your instructor will rapidly read aloud a list of one hundred words provided in the *Instructor's Manual* for this book. Immediately afterwards, take a pencil and a sheet of paper and write as many of those words as you can remember. Then, your instructor will read each word again, asking for a show of hands from those who've included the word on their lists. When you've completed the initial rereading and checking, discuss why some words appeared on many of your classmates' lists and others appeared on only a few lists or not at all. Consider your own reasons for including words, too. Did some words shock you or seem unusual? Were some close to your interests and experiences? How did this affect your ability to perceive and remember? Were some the last words the instructor read?

As a class, draw some conclusions about perception and perceptual skills under these circumstances. What circumstances would increase the possibility of people's hearing and remembering each word?

Our *relationship to others* affects the messages we send and perceive. Are we employer/employee, husband/wife, teacher/student, old friends, new acquaintances? Do we share common interests? The *physical circumstances* also partially determine how and what we communicate. Are we alone on a couch before a crackling fire, crushed against each other in an elevator, shouting across a meadow, eating dinner in a fancy restaurant?

Finally, our *state of mind,* our *psychological makeup,* and our *physical health* can strongly shape what we say and do. Am I too upset from the argument I've just had with my father to listen to you? Or do you, in fact, remind me of him? On the other hand, do you usually respond angrily to inattention from people like me? We could call such psychological/emotional distractions "internal noise."

2 Whole-Class Exercise
Observing a Communication Transaction

The instructor will ask for two volunteers to hold a five-minute conversation about all of the ways people communicate. The rest of you in the class will observe the conversation; it will also be videotaped or tape-recorded.

Using the tape as reference and guide, participate in a whole-class discussion analyzing all the elements of the transaction. Here are a few questions to consider:

1. What nonverbal gestures communicated messages?
2. Did the speaker's tone of voice communicate any messages? Did the other speaker respond to them?
3. Did the postures of the speakers change during the discussion? Why?
4. What did the pauses and silences communicate? Why did they occur?
5. Did one speaker imitate the other's mannerisms? Why?
6. Did one speaker dominate the conversation? Why?
7. Did the setting—speaking before an audience and being recorded—seem to affect the transaction? How?
8. Do you think the sex of the two speakers affected their interaction? How?
9. In addition to ideas, what feelings did the speakers communicate?
10. Did the speakers' involuntary gestures communicate feelings their words didn't clearly reveal?

In short, a speech transaction is a complex *inter*action, where we shift continually from the role of sender to receiver, where we exchange verbal and nonverbal messages, where the physical context and our personal physical and psychological limitations affect our perceptions. And, finally, it is an interaction where the relationship—whether formal or informal, primarily physical or psychological—between you and me determines the messages we send and (think) we receive. In each transaction, then, we exchange more than information, ideas, or opinions; we exchange feelings and establish *emotional* relationships as well.

And in doing so, we reveal certain *attitudes* crucial to communication. Let's examine these relationships and attitudes a bit further.

The "Tape Recorder" inside your head

In his book, *I'm OK—You're OK,* Dr. Thomas Harris describes some useful and fascinating research concerning our memory of past events and feelings.[1] He tells how—in brain operations on epileptics—Dr. Wilder Penfield, a neurosurgeon, applied a mild electrical shock to areas of the temporal cortex, the part of the brain which stores memories. Since the brain feels no pain, Dr. Penfield's patients were awake on the operating table. To his surprise, each time he stimulated the cortex, the patients began discussing a past experience and, even more surprisingly, expressing the emotions associated with it. In fact, Penfield observed, the patients apparently often felt the emotions first, and only with some effort could they verbally reconstruct the experience.

Penfield's experiment, says Harris, proves that your brain is like a high-fidelity tape recorder, with great capacity for playback. You really "exist" in both the present and past, experiencing earlier fears, joys, anxieties, and angers if an event in the present presses the replay button. Buried deep within your brain is a rusty old coffin of dead memories and feelings; and a casual or rude remark, a smile or a smirk, a resemblance someone bears to your father or mother, an event in the news or the next room can resurrect them. Your inner life is as important as your outer life.

Harris divides this inner life into three "ego states"—*Parent, Adult,* and *Child,* as illustrated in the diagram on page 16.

The **Parent** *"Tapes"*   The first of these "tapes" records all memories and feelings you associate with your parents. Their actions and words, good and bad, especially those you accepted uncritically in your first five years, return in the present as a permanent lecturing, directing, moralizing agent. Such feelings and memories make up your *Parent* "ego state" and influence your attitudes toward yourself and the others you communicate with. The *Parent* in you always looks over your shoulder, counseling and advising you, whether you wish to obey or not: "Be sure you clean your plate." "Associate only with your kind." "Stay away from strangers." "Keep your opinions to yourself." "Get drunk every Saturday night." "Remember that a woman's place is in the home." "A penny saved is a penny earned." "You are better dead than red." Obviously, your *Parent* "tapes" offer both excellent guidance and sheer nonsense. The maxims and sanctions may be contradictory (parents, like everyone else, often say one thing and do another), outdated, or simply wrong—full of prejudices and misinformation. Nevertheless, as you transact with another person and your memory recorder begins to replay these "tapes," you may find yourself repeating their messages. You'll therefore be expressing the attitude: "I'm OK—you're not OK."

The Child "Tapes"   In addition, Harris claims, you carry a second set of "tape recordings" from your youth, called the *Child.* Especially in the first five years the conflicting demands of parents, the physical world, and your own body are overwhelming. An infant, explains Harris, is "dependent, he is inept, he is clumsy, he has no words with which to construct meanings." In short, as a baby you can do nothing on your own. You must depend on others to satisfy all needs, physical and emotional. Furthermore, your desires to explore, to investigate, to bang

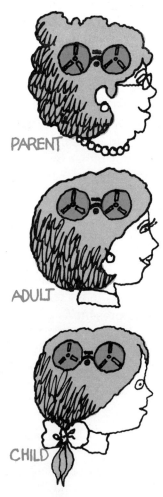

The Three Ego States.

forks against the table, to fill your mouth with objects or diapers with urine—all clash against your wish to win parental approval, which often requires restricting yourself. "No, no, no," you hear. "Take that out of your mouth." "Don't touch that," and "Use the toilet." On one hand, your infant and childhood desire for approval leads to the "producer" mentality described earlier in this book. On the other, your constant exposure to restrictions makes you feel incompetent and insecure. You can't do anything right. Both the desire to be a conforming "producer" and a dependent incompetent are inseparably recorded on your *Child* "tapes." And replayed in the present, as you transact with another person, they are expressed in the position: "You're OK—I'm not OK. You can do it, but I can't, so I won't, or I'll just try to follow orders." Everyone feels this way often, since everyone experiences childhood.

Consequently, even as a grown-up, your *Child* ego state sometimes makes you feel shameful and timid. Or, frustrated by restrictions, your *Child* may urge you to act childishly, wanting attention and expecting punishment. Your insecure *Child* may insist that you seek protection and acceptance. At the same time, fortunately, your *Child* "tapes" record the positive, happy memories of your youth, and are largely responsible for much of your charm, creativity, and spontaneity. Allowed free play in your communications, this aspect of your *Child* makes you endearing, vivacious, and clever.

The Adult "Tapes"   As should be obvious, *Parent* and *Child* have differing and conflicting interests. The *Child* in you whispers, "Go on and cut class; it's too nice a day to be inside." Your *Parent* "tape" admonishes, "Don't you dare, you evil, irresponsible brat; school will make you rich and wise." This kind of internal civil war between both "tapes" could destroy you if a third ego state, which Harris calls the *Adult,* did not serve as peacemaker. The *Adult,* weighing both the *Parent's* advice and the *Child's* impulses against its own data recorded over the years, regulates your actions. Your *Adult* "tapes" help you accept or reject the *Parent* in you while suppressing or encouraging the *Child,* or blending the two. In short, your *Adult* is, in Harris's words, a "data-processing computer" and practical design-making apparatus. Though often inefficient and error-prone, the *Adult* in you decides not only how to act but also how to feel.

Whereas at times the *Child* may insist, "I'm not OK—you're OK," in some cases it may also take the reverse position, "I'm OK—you, and everyone else, are not." This second attitude develops in people consistently abused or battered by parents or the world. To survive emotionally, these people may conclude that in an irrational, hostile environment where everyone is out to get them, they can trust no one but themselves. They become defensive, suspicious, tense, humorless, incapable of friendships or love. "Why concern yourself with others," their *Child* questions, "since they aren't OK?"

If you are aware that neither the "I'm not OK—you're OK" nor the "I'm OK—you're not OK" attitude leads to healthy, productive behavior, you can allow your *Adult* to suppress both of them. Consciously, willfully, you can ignore—though never destroy—them by taking the only positive, fruitful attitude: "I'm OK—you're OK." It's positive because it means accepting yourself and others. It's fruitful because it helps you trust yourself and others—to act freely, without intimidation. To be sure, everyone you encounter has hang-ups; but like you, most people are basically OK. To demonstrate how you can learn to be positive and supportive in your dealings with others, let's further examine the influence of your *Parent, Child,* and *Adult* "tapes" on your transactions.

The Nine Basic Transactions.

The nine basic transactions

Each time you and I transact in speech communication, I address one of your ego states through whatever ego state dominates my personality at the moment, and you respond through whatever ego state dominates yours. Since internally each of us carries all three ego states, my personality could begin by addressing yours in nine different ways, as the accompanying diagram illustrates. Note that the heads represent the three ego states, and the nine lines represent each of the possible relationships among our ego states which my words to you establish.

Although the diagram makes the process of interaction appear static, it never is. In transacting, neither of us is likely to stay within the same ego state throughout a conversation. Each of us can—and frequently will—switch from one ego state to another with each statement we make, with each verbal and/or nonverbal message we send.

For example, if with a pouting face and whining voice I say to you, "Do I have to wear a tie tonight?" I'm probably talking through my *Child* to your *Parent.* I'm showing my "I'm not OK—you're OK" attitude. I'm expecting either your permission to leave my tie at home or your order to put one on. You can respond as the *Parent* to my *Child,* reinforcing my original attitude and fulfilling my expectation. Or you can choose instead to address my *Adult* through your *Adult,* showing that we're both OK, and say without irritation, "It's up to you." Now I must choose which ego state I will use in responding to you. I can continue in my role as not-OK *Child,* or switch to an OK *Adult* and say, "OK, I won't wear one; I don't think it's necessary." A diagram of this complete transaction appears on page 20.

3 Whole-Class Exercise

Demonstrating Supportive Behavior in a Speech Transaction

To show how to be supportive and encouraging to someone transacting as a not-OK *Child,* one member of the class should volunteer to role-play the not-OK *Child,* while the instructor assumes the supportive role. The two will introduce themselves, then discuss their feelings about the class. Here's how part of their conversation might go:

INSTRUCTOR: Why did you decide to take speech, Harry?

HARRY: Only because it was required. I really hate speaking in public. I'm no good at it and never will be.

INSTRUCTOR: You're doing all right so far. Did you take speech in high school?

HARRY: Yeah, and I thought it was really dumb. I felt like I was making a fool of myself when I spoke before the class.

A Communication Transaction.

INSTRUCTOR: Well, my impression is that people only feel foolish when they take themselves too seriously. If you just relax and enjoy it, you won't feel so self-conscious.

The other members of the class will observe and tape-record the conversation. Later, with the tape as a reference, discuss the transactions you observed, suggest ways to improve the supportive behavior in the transactions, and predict responses from the student's not-OK *Child* if the instructor had made non-supportive remarks.

DEVELOPING SELF-CONFIDENCE AND SELF-AWARENESS

As you see, then, through word choice and other means we often communicate a great many insecurities and hang-ups. Only by becoming aware of them in ourselves and others can we begin to develop the confidence to let our OK *Child,* OK *Adult,* or OK *Parent* attitudes emerge. So now let's look for some answers to the question: *How can we become aware?*

Adopting a "Why Not?" attitude

Self-confidence begins with positive thinking; more importantly, it results in significant *behavioral* changes. Rather than asking yourself, "Why take a chance?" you might ask, "Why not? It could be wonderful." Instead of moping at home on Saturday night, for example, you could be taking in a movie or the vibes at a party; you could be cavorting, dancing, falling in love, having fun. You could be learning to ski, to bowl, to make your own furniture, to work for pay or for free. You could be making friends instead of excuses. Asking "Why not?" involves some risks, but it also allows you to learn more and accomplish more. It frees you to grow and to adapt to change.

These personal reasons in themselves would warrant adopting a "Why not?" attitude. But "Why not?" is equally valuable for success in a speech course and in daily communication. The wisdom of your OK *Adult,* combined with your OK *Child,* frees you to *be* yourself and therefore *speak* like yourself, without pretensions or needless fears. Your confidence can lead to self-revelation—to acknowledging honestly and openly both who you are and what you feel. Remember that your "me" has many aspects. The "me" you generally present for official inspection is only *one* level of a complex self. If you refuse to reveal any of the other levels, or refuse to let others see them, your day-to-day speeches and conversations will be safe—but dull and unimaginative. If you concern yourself only with the safe and the non-controversial, you seriously limit what you say. You can't discuss your religion, your politics, your hang-ups, or even your pleasures—partly because you do not want to take a risk and partly because you may not even know what you think about them. To play it safe, you'll stick to the orthodox and the non-controversial, the trite and true. You'll keep a coffin full of past feelings and experiences buried in a graveyard completely separate from your own consciousness, and you'll kill any impulse to give them life and expression.

Looking through the Johari Window

Instead of thinking of your inner self as a coffin interred in a graveyard, though, why not consider yourself a *window*—a window through which both you and others can see some of the many aspects and facets of your "you"? Two psychologists, Joseph Luft and Harry Ingham, have designed a self-revelation model they call the *Johari Window* (a combination of their first names, Joe and Harry).[2] They divide it into four sections—or windowpanes—each indicating proportionately how much you and others know about your self: your emotions, your ideas, your habits, your appearance. The relative size of the areas or windowpanes changes with each of your encounters with another person. You may reveal more to your best friend than to strangers, for example. And some people can see more in you than others can. The areas on the left (areas 1 and 3) contain information that you *know* about; those on the right (areas 2 and 4) contain information that you do *not* know about.

The Open Area As you can see in the accompanying diagram, Section 1 is a clear glass for both you and others. It consists primarily of obvious and "safe" information about you, your motivations, and your behaviors: your long blond hair is parted on the right; you dress casually in jeans and tee shirt or a halter top; you are fine, thank you, but overwhelmed with homework; you like the Dodgers' chances this year, and so on. You may feel free to admit to your friends (but not to your parents) that you failed a math exam. You may discuss your sexual interests with friends in bull sessions, but not with strangers. You may philosophize about your ambitions in life with almost anyone, but reserve talking about your personal problems for your closest friends or your parents.

The Hidden Area When you wish to conceal things from others, therefore, whether accurate or not (remember, your beliefs about your inadequacies, for example, may be groundless), you place them in Section 3, the *Hidden Area*. Here, you pull down the shades to the outside world, refusing to reveal or admit to *anyone* that you think Nixon was terrific, despite all that furor; or that you don't read well; or that you dislike blacks, Jews, Catholics, and assorted minorities; or that tall, sexy men turn you into mushroom soup; or that rather than a doctor, you'd really like to be Mick Jagger. We know two girls from a religious family who dress up each Sunday in their finest clothes presumably to attend church. Actually, however, they walk aimlessly for hours in snow, rain, or hot weather rather than tell their parents they have forsaken the church and be told that they will burn in hell.

The Blind Area   Sections 2 and 4 in the Johari Window contain information you *don't* know about yourself. Section 2, the *Blind Area,* is a one-way glass, transparent only to others. They see through your calm exterior, detecting the nervousness in your trembling hands, in your fingernails jagged and bleeding from constant biting, or in your

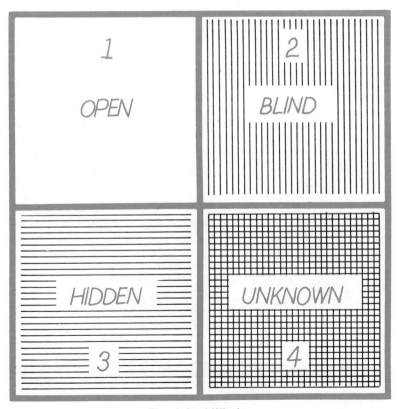

The Johari Window.

darting eyes. They see the insecurity your sarcasm masks. They notice your physical defects and unpleasant mannerisms: your body odor or slouch, your nervous lip-biting or hair-twirling. But they notice positive traits as well: an attractive vulnerability, a cute little giggle, an infectious grin, an expertise in auto mechanics which you consider unimportant or undignified, a sensitivity and capacity for caring.

The Unknown Area Section 4, the *Unknown Area,* is boarded up not only to you, but to everyone else. You can only discover the motivations and behaviors that lie behind it—your unique but unused talents or depths of personality—by accident, or by continual self-

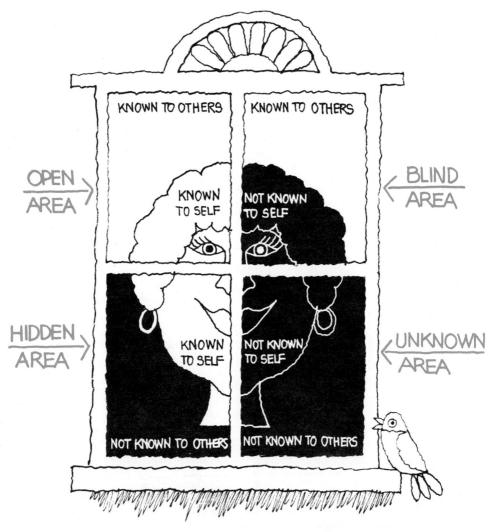

Seeing Yourself in the Johari Window.

examination and a willingness to be open. As in the other panes of the window, you may find some good things here, too.

Opening up the areas of your awareness

If you make a genuine effort to understand yourself, you can shift information from your Unknown and Blind Areas into your Open Area. You may want to withhold some information in your Hidden Area from certain audiences, but release it into your Open or Free Area for others. That's fine. You're entitled to privacy, and every casual exchange need not be a confessional. "How are you?" doesn't really require a full medical report. Let your common sense—coupled with your awareness of the circumstances of the communication—guide you in determining what you will and will not reveal to others. But don't be over-cautious. Be real. And be willing to take a few risks. Be willing to trust others with some glances through your Hidden or Unknown windowpanes.

Openness does yield benefits. If you demonstrate a willingness to talk freely and openly, others will probably follow your example and reveal more of themselves, too. Your relationships with others, consequently, can grow deeper, warmer, more sharing. You may discover that others share your hang-ups, your opinions. Expect them to disagree with you on certain things, of course. But remember that you can learn from their disagreements, too, including more about yourself. Trusting you, feeling your warmth and openness, others may sincerely and directly reveal their impressions about your Blind Area. Finally, when others realize you trust them and want to share your experiences and insights with them, you'll have their sympathetic ear.

As a public speaker, you'll find that openness also yields positive results. You'll have more to say. You'll get a better reception, too. Admitting your nervousness or biases often disarms possible critics and reduces hostility. "OK," your audience may think, "so you've got the jitters. That's normal and understandable, and I'll forgive you." Or, "OK, so you're a warmonger, but at least you don't pretend not to be. I don't have to challenge you on that."

So take an "I'm OK—you're OK" position. On occasion, your *Adult* can stifle the not-OK *Parent* in you and let out your playful *Child*. If you think genuinely of communication as transactional, you can pull the shades off almost all the windowpanes of your Johari Window and learn to say, "Why not?" You can be yourself, the best self you can be.

Introducing Yourself in the OK Seat

As a way of getting to know each other, place the chairs or desks of your classroom in a circle, but leave one chair unoccupied. We'll call it the "OK Seat." Then, in turn, you and each of your classmates will take a few minutes to sit in it, introduce yourself, and make five or six statements about things important to you. Try to go quickly past the surface stuff — where you live, where you went to high school, what you do for a living. Talk instead about a few "deeper" issues: what you most want out of life, what you value most in people, what you'd like to be doing ten years from now (the last topic comes up often in job interviews, incidentally). Don't be pretentious about your remarks; just be yourself. You won't be making a "speech," since at any time others in the class will be free to ask you questions and chat with you a bit. Your goal is to relax and be OK. Try to be supportive of each other. And don't be afraid to joke either. This is no funeral. You're discarding your Coffins for Awareness Windows and OK Seats.

Reference Notes

[1]Based on Chapters 1, 2, and 3 of *I'm OK — You're OK* by Thomas A. Harris, M.D. Copyright © 1967, 1968, 1969 by Thomas A. Harris, M.D. Reprinted by permission of Harper & Row, Publishers, Inc.

[2]Joseph Luft, *Group Processes: An Introduction to Group Dynamics,* 2nd Ed. (Palo Alto: Mayfield Publishing Company, 1970), pp. 11–12.

2 Group Function and Format

Speaking with confidence requires the right attitude, but it also requires experience — and time. You'll never *automatically* feel comfortable and in command standing before listeners who stare at you silently, waiting to be informed, persuaded, entertained. You must practice facing them, learn to relax, work at being yourself. You must experiment, develop new skills, refine old ones. And, to learn how your listeners respond to you, you should hear their comments, encouragement, and advice. You should hear their praise and their suggestions for improvement. In short, you should speak often, gain experience, and consequently gain confidence. Yet, in the typical fifty-minute class period, at best, ten people can talk for five minutes each. At that rate, you'd have few speaking opportunities on center stage. There must be a better way.

SETTING UP YOUR WORKING GROUPS

There is a better way. By dividing the class into smaller groups of six or seven people, in a single class period each of you can deliver a five-minute speech and still have time to hear reactions from your audience. You'll get to speak often and, within the intimate atmosphere of a small group, gradually and easily develop confidence in yourself and trust in your audience. You'll experiment and gain experience in an atmosphere of friendliness and mutual acceptance.

"There's safety— and harmony— in numbers."

Probably, as a practical matter, your instructor will change the composition of the groups regularly—maybe each week or even each class period. In this way, the group's work won't be hindered by absences; and in a short time, you'll get to know all your classmates fairly well. Occasionally, however, your instructor may prefer that you remain with the same group for a longer time to promote greater unity and mutual trust. Or occasionally a particular group activity might require that the group keep the same membership for a few days or weeks. Either way, whether you change groups often or rarely, the operating procedures we're about to describe will be equally effective.

Since you talk more easily in informal, small groups, you'll begin that way, sitting in a circle, giving little speeches, holding short discussions. Later, you'll stand before your small group to speak; and, finally, you'll speak in front of a larger group—your entire class. But, even then, in your preparations for longer speeches to be given before the whole class, the members of your group can help you. They can serve first as a sounding board for your ideas, later as a rehearsal audience for practicing and presenting the speeches, and always as counselors, friendly critics, and models to imitate. To ensure that the group works well, however, let's first examine what a *group* is, how it operates, and what your role as a group member will be.

Defining a group

A *group,* as we're using the term here, is a small number of persons who meet, talk, and work together to accomplish something. Four conditions distinguish the members of a group from any other collection of people: (1) they must share a common purpose or goal; (2) they must feel a sense of unity; (3) they must work together over a period of time; and (4) each member must contribute.

At a rock concert, department store, or during registration for classes, hundreds—perhaps thousands—of people congregate for a short time. But they don't work together, help each other, feel that they belong. Indeed, few of them even look familiar to each other. It's a small world—some of the time—and occasionally the passing parade makes you stop and look, but most often it only makes a traffic jam. It's a *crowd,* just a big gathering of people who don't know each other and have little in common except being in the same place at the same time.

An example of a group: Your class

On the other hand, you and the other members of your speech class are changing from a crowd into a group. First, you share common goals and purposes: learning something, surviving the course, avoiding boredom. You may have enrolled for any number of reasons: you needed the GI benefits; you heard the instructor was terrific; your girl friend or boyfriend was taking it; it was the only class open at the hour you wanted; you like speech; your counselor insisted; you thought it would be easy. But now that you're here, you have in common the desire to succeed in or survive the course.

Second, you're beginning to feel some sense of unity. You're gradually coming to know each other. On the first day of class, you waited silently and stoically for the instructor to arrive. Now, the congeniality-level and the noise-level have increased. You talk outside the door and joke and smile in your seats.

Third, you're interacting over time. You remember what happened during the last meeting of your speech class. You anticipate meeting in future classes. You think about the class when you're away from it, probably discuss it with friends, perhaps even look forward to coming to class. The longer you're with the members of the group, in fact, the greater the chance you'll like them and be like them. To put it another way, the longer you're with them, the more you'll adapt to them. In a crowd, you might move back to let others pass, but you wouldn't change your beliefs or the way you think. Here, in your group, you're discovering, shaping, and conforming to the norms. You're testing the climate the instructor establishes, using your classmates as a barometer—are they silent, questioning, docile, aggressive? Then you're adjusting your behavior. If nobody talks, neither do you. Group pressure is strong. Finally, you're all beginning to contribute, some more than others, and of course in different ways, but everyone has taken a turn in the OK Seat.

In the SMALL-GROUP APPROACH . . . first, probably, you'll want to think about your speech, its ideas, and materials *alone.* You'll want to "discover for yourself."

At times, you'll interact with a friend or some other person on an interpersonal, one-to-one basis in conversations, interviews, and mutual-help situations.

Since you talk more easily in informal, small groups, you'll begin that way, sitting together, holding short discussions, giving little speeches.

Later, you'll stand
before your small
group to speak.

And, finally, you'll speak to a larger group—your entire class.

1 Discovering for Yourself
Testing the Definition of a Group

On a sheet of paper indicate which of the following meet the four criteria for a group:

1. An open house to celebrate your birthday.
2. An elevator crammed with fifteen people.
3. A PTA meeting called to discuss a new school-bond referendum.
4. A tenth-year reunion of your high-school graduating class.
5. A gynecologist's waiting room filled with pregnant mothers.
6. A class of thirty-five elementary school children on a field trip to the zoo.
7. A convention of Shriners in San Francisco.
8. The eighteenth annual meeting of the Birdwatchers' Society.
9. The first official session of the United Nations meeting in San Francisco in 1945.
10. A street gang standing on the corner.

Consider under what circumstances each of the "non-groups" not on your list would become a group. Consider also under what circumstances each of the groups you've included on your list would *not* qualify as a group.

Now bring your lists to class for comparison and discussion. Did the other members of the class agree unanimously with your choices? Did you discover in some cases that you lacked sufficient information to decide?

As you can see, your class has already met or will soon meet the four criteria *all* groups have in common. However, in the small groups you'll be working with this term, each time you'll be starting more or less afresh. You won't know each other very well in the beginning; you'll need to adjust and readjust, to establish new roles: Who talks? Who keeps silent? Who readily accepts leadership responsibilities? Who is more willing to follow? This process of establishing new roles occurs as every new group forms, even where members are good friends.

2 Small-Group Speaking
Letting Your Group Reintroduce You

Your instructor will divide your class into small groups of five, six, or seven persons each. These groups will then move to designated sections of the classroom, each group physically removed as far as possible from every other group. To speed up the getting-to-know-each-other process, try the OK Seat exercise again (see page 26), but with two changes: (1) Place your chairs in a circle, but this time stay in your own seat. Every chair can be OK. And (2) let the *other* members of the group recall as much about you as they can from the first OK Seat exercise. Don't volunteer any information unless you have to, but tell the others if they are correct or incorrect, and give occasional hints. Continue until everyone has been reintroduced.

WHAT MAKES SMALL GROUPS WORK BEST

Not all groups operate successfully, if we define "success" as the accomplishment of the group's goals to the satisfaction of all of its members. Remember, however, that success depends less on the method than on *you.* By our definition a group requires that each member contribute, so you can't merely occupy a chair throughout the term. You can't be unenthusiastic, unprepared to speak, and unwilling to take risks in what you say, or you'll simply encourage others to act that way, too. You must try to communicate your reactions, ideas, and thinking to others in the group. Though you needn't speak every minute of every class period, you must get involved. *Producers* cherish non-involvement. They want the instructor to tell them what to think, what to do. But you're not a *producer;* you're a *thinker;* and *thinkers* can operate independently, can take a "Why Not?" attitude.

Your role as a participant in small-group interaction

Your involvement can take many constructive and productive forms, the most common of which lies simply in *giving your information and ideas to the group.* When you make a speech to the group, momentarily you'll be the principal supplier. And when you participate in information-gathering or problem-solving discussions, you must continue contributing facts or information which the others don't know. Often when the group lacks information, as a member you can *ask questions* to elicit it. "Wait a minute," you might say. "Can't we find more than three kinds of nonverbal communication?" Or, "Your response to Jack's speech was interesting, Mary, but why do you think it would succeed only with college students?"

Groups can easily be led onto side issues, too, especially if they're more fun than the main task, so you may occasionally be *guiding the discussion back on course.* You might find yourself saying, "I'm enjoying this; but with only a few minutes left in the hour, shouldn't we reach some conclusions about Jack's speech?"

In discussions, you will often find that you must be sensitive to the feelings of other members, too. Thus, occasionally, you must *lessen conflict* between members, make a joke to *relieve the tension* or monotony, or *negotiate a compromise between two or more differing ideas.* You'll watch for verbal or nonverbal signs of problems between people—name-calling, raised voices, grimaces, withdrawal—and you'll make an effort to find a solution. "I know you're angry, John, but hear Marty out before you jump in." Or "Look, Sue, you and Diane both have valid points. Let's identify the areas in which you mostly agree."

Of course, the fact that these negotiating and tension-reducing functions are necessary suggests some of the potential *pitfalls* in participation and involvement, risks which can prove destructive, especially when they lead the group away from its task and into personality conflicts. Carl R. Rogers, an eminent psychologist who has spent much of his career working with groups, believes the primary cause of ill will and unproductivity in groups is the tendency to judge a person's remarks through one's own biases rather than trying actively to understand the person's own point of view. Rogers explains:

> When someone expresses some feeling or attitude or belief, our tendency is, almost immediately, to feel "That's right"; or "That's stupid"; "That's abnormal"; "That's unreasonable"; "That's incorrect"; "That's not nice." Very rarely do we permit ourselves to *understand* precisely what the meaning of his statement is to him.[1]

According to Rogers, we remain fixed in our judgments because understanding is "risky." As he puts it, "If I let myself really understand another person, I might be changed by that understanding. And we all fear change." Yet Rogers feels we must make the attempt and by our "own attitudes create a safety in the relationship . . . where feelings can be expressed, where people can differ."[2]

Those attitudes, as Rogers points out, include being yourself, being honest, being trusting, and in all cases being aware of the example you set for others. In short, you and the members of your group must maintain the "I'm OK—you're OK" position. You needn't love each other, but you should respect each other. You can agree to disagree and still work together. Real trust means allowing all members the freedom to be their OK selves. Too much pressure to conform can stifle creativity.

Note, however, that we've said "the freedom to be their *OK* selves." Don't judge too harshly, but be vigilant. Be on the lookout for the intrusion of less creative and positive attitudes. Be alert to the people communicating an "I'm not OK" attitude. They tend to joke when they should be serious; they're overly aggressive; they seem to want to win arguments, not work for compromise. Rather than communicating to solve problems, they want to grab the limelight, or they don't want to talk at all. If you spot such behavior, discourage it diplomatically. We realize this advice is easier written than followed, but trust your common sense. You're OK. You can handle things.

"The whole is only equal to the sum of its parts."

Your role as a leader in small-group interaction

None of you will assume the throne by divine right. In fact, your group will function most productively when you think of leadership as a responsibility which you all must assume and share. But at various times—when you ask for reactions after your speech, or when the group discusses an issue you've raised—you'll find yourself in an informal leadership role.

Traditionally, researchers have described three types of leaders: the *authoritarian,* the *democratic,* and the *laissez-faire.* The first probably has no place in your group. The *authoritarian* leader is the BOSS, the drill sergeant, second in command to the deity: Do it my way—no questions, no complaints, love it or leave it. In the military or in some businesses, authoritarians lead efficiently as long as they have legal or economic power to back them up. But among your classmates, a group of equals, no one should or will conquer and build an empire.

Which of the other two types of leadership—democratic or laissez-faire—will be appropriate to your small group depends on the nature of the discussion and the personalities of the people in the group. Both types, however, are merely more formalized extensions of the positive attitudes and roles we've already described for all group members. As a *democratic* leader you (1) treat the others as equals, (2) allow everyone to speak, (3) respect everyone's opinions and feelings, (4) guide the discussion, (5) summarize occasionally, (6) try to effect compromise, and (7) arbitrate disputes.

On the other hand, a *laissez-faire* leader (French for "let it happen") leaves the leadership and maintenance functions to the group itself. He or she merely presides over the meeting. Successful laissez-faire-led groups require the right mix of sensitive and sensible, responsive and responsible people who can operate without supervision. Most likely, you and the other members of your group will practice both the democratic and laissez-faire types of leadership, even in the same discussion. No matter how you lead, however, be sensitive both to the *task* and the *feelings* of the people involved.

In short, as a leader you should be a participant in group interchange, too. You should offer information, ask questions to elicit it, keep the discussion on the topic, summarize occasionally, help to work out compromises and resolve conflicts. But don't feel you must perform all of these tasks all of the time. A group straying off the topic for a while may be feeling the need to ease off a bit, inject a little humor, relax. This may serve to bind the members more closely together and in the long run make them more productive. If you see that the group is trying to proceed without adequate information—which you don't have—perhaps you can help someone else notice and supply it. In those instances where you are serving as a *leader* in the interaction of the group, show patience, sensitivity, an awareness of subtle differences and variations in ideas and opinions. Good leaders listen to the words the group members exchange and sense the feelings behind the words. They look and feel, as well as speak and listen. If you see Mark grimace, ask him what's on his mind. If Judy shakes her head, ask her why she disagrees. Don't force an issue, though. A skillful leader respects the rights of others to be silent. If each of you in the group considers yourself responsible not only for involvement and participation, but also for assuming these positive leadership tasks, you will find that your group will function smoothly and productively.

The trouble with getting good advice is that it gets in the way of all our other plans.
—Bits and Pieces

MAKING YOUR IN-CLASS GROUPS MORE EFFECTIVE

To this point we have defined groups in the broad sense and used your class as an example of our definition and of how a group is formed. We have suggested some specific practices you might follow, both as a participant and leader, to help your small groups of six or seven students function effectively. (Remember, of course, that these same practices could help *any group anywhere* come closer to achieving its objectives.) So, while much of your work and many of the recommended activities for this course are *group centered* or have a *group origin* and *orientation,* they needn't occur only in your small groups. Remember that *the entire class* is also a group. You can perform some or most of your work and the various activities in that larger context, too. Regardless of the class format your instructor may choose, two specific procedures may help to maintain the stability of the group, reflect progress, and measure success. These are (1) appointing the *group secretary* and (2) keeping the *personal communication journal.*

Appointing a Group Secretary

When the class divides into small groups, your instructor will visit your group often, sometimes staying the whole period, at other times visiting every group during the hour. Because your instructor can't be in all places at once, he or she may want someone to take notes on your group's activities. This note-taking and record-keeping will be the responsibility of the group secretary. Your group will probably appoint a different person for this task at each class meeting. Or perhaps the same person will serve in this capacity for a week or for the duration of a particular ongoing activity. Whatever option you or your instructor may choose, when all of you make short speeches, the group secretary will write down who spoke, a brief summary of what the person said, and comments about how the other members reacted and responded to each presentation. When you're holding a group discussion, the secretary will record the major ideas mentioned and any conclusions the group reached. Your instructor may provide additional guidelines. The secretary will turn in to the instructor the notes and written comments at the end of each class period.

Even when you're not the group secretary, you will probably find jotting down a few notes for your own use helpful. Nothing elaborate — just keep a brief record of each presentation and your reactions to it, so that you will have something to refer to in the follow-up discussion, and also as a record of the progress of your group.

Keeping a Communication Journal

We know an editor who always says, "I'll have to run this through my typewriter to see if it makes sense." He can examine his and others' thoughts most critically once they're committed to paper. A personal communication journal will allow you to observe in this same way your thoughts and feelings about the group's activities.

Your journal is a confidential communication between you and your instructor. No one else will read it. You'll make entries on separate sheets of paper, keep them either in a folder or loose-leaf notebook, and from time to time hand some of them in. You'll make three kinds of journal entries. *First,* each week after class, you should merely record your reactions to *two* presentations you've heard in your group. Simply

summarize the presentation and then repeat or expand on the follow-up comments which you shared with the group. Note what, if anything, particularly caught your ear or fancy. This part of the journal will serve as source material for assignments later in the term.

Beyond this short record of your reactions to two speeches, however, the journal can also serve a *second* function—as a vehicle for exploring responses you have *not* shared with the group. For one reason or another, you may have been reluctant to reveal your thoughts or feelings. But, privately, in the journal you can commit them to writing. Your instructor will read them only as an aid to adjusting the operation of the classroom, but will never grade or discuss them with others. You may mention anything you think is important, for example, any of the following matters:

1. Your own progress as a speaker and as a listener. What exercise has taught you the most, or let you discover the most? What are

your difficulties, your hang-ups, your fears? Are you reluctant to speak or respond to others' speeches?

2. *Your frustrations or satisfactions with the method.* What seems most productive? What doesn't work for you? Are you feeling bored, insulted, trivialized? Is the instruction progressing too slowly, too fast, or just right?

3. *Your relationships with the group,* including your frustrations with or complaints about the group. Are you fitting in? Have you little in common with the other members? Are their values or their responses to each other different from yours? Why?

4. *Your reactions to a particular speaker.* Who seemed most interesting? Who seems unable to adapt to the interests and needs of the group? Is the person failing to improve? What might help the person to grow and develop?

5. Your reactions to a person as a group member. Does he or she seem sensitive in drawing others out? Is he or she monopolizing the group's time unproductively? Is the person exploiting the freedom and seeming lack of supervision which the small-group format provides? How could the group control or redirect the person's activities?

6. Your reactions to an assignment. Do you understand its goals? Is it too easy or too difficult? Do you see no reason for it?

Finally, the journal will become a *repository of source materials you gather for future speeches.* This part of your journal should begin with a PERSONAL INTERESTS-INVENTORY. What turns you on? What makes you mad? What makes you laugh? Cry? What incidents from your present experience or your past memories are especially meaningful to you? Why? We'll return to this use of the journal in later chapters.

However you use the journal, don't think of it solely as a gripe collection. And it isn't for playing CIA on your classmates, either. It is an ongoing record of your feelings and judgments and an aid to your instructor in continually evaluating the work and progress of the course.

3 Small-Group Discussion
Problem Solving in Your Small Group

This exercise should allow you to compare your individual work with a group's work in solving the problem: *how best to prevent burglaries in your home.* Listed below are a police department's suggestions. On a separate sheet of paper, rank-order each suggestion according to your personal assessment of its effectiveness in preventing burglaries. List the most effective suggestion first and the least effective one last. Then, bring your list to class. Participate in a discussion with your group. Compare your ranking with those of the other group members. Arrive at a list which reflects the consensus of your group.

Possible Solutions:
1. Put "dead bolt" locks on your doors.
2. Ask the police to watch your property.
3. Paint your address on your garbage cans and your back fence.
4. Construct a large stockade fence around your backyard.
5. Ask the neighbors to watch your house when you're away.
6. Keep lights burning at all times.
7. Install burglar alarm systems.
8. Have a friend remove mail when you are out of town.
9. Floodlight the yard.
10. Remove garbage cans from near the house.
11. Buy a big watchdog.
12. Secure lower windows permanently.

13. Remove your keys from the locks inside the house and hide them.
14. Install locks on all windows.
15. Buy a gun.
16. Buy a baseball bat.
17. Hire a protection service.
18. Remove all ladders from outside.
19. Store valuables in a vault.
20. Install safety glass on doors.
21. Set squirrel traps.
22. Put a drinking glass over the inside handle of your door and a metal tray beneath it on the floor.
23. Set timer switches to turn lights on and off.
24. Leave a radio on when you leave.
25. Buy several flashlights and distribute them throughout the house.

Did you find that your group spent more time considering the rankings than you did when you worked by yourself? Was the time well spent? Did you discover more insights and information from the group discussion than you did from your own independent analysis? Did the members of your group reach a consensus easily? Perhaps in your journal, you might write down whether in your opinion your small group *functioned* as a group. Was everyone participating? Were there arguments and antagonisms, or did everyone cooperate? Did you feel a sense of unity and a sense of achieving a common goal?

Since your group will be the center of almost all discussion, speech preparation, and speechmaking this term, let's repeat a few key points we've made in the chapter. Keeping at your task and keeping everybody happy require a delicate balancing act. You must take responsibility for keeping the group from falling off the high wire. Participate productively: supply information, ask questions, be willing to compromise, work together, not against each other. Don't monopolize, antagonize, or trivialize. As a leader, shift from *laissez-faire* to *democratic* when the need arises, but trust the group members to contribute. Summarize, ask questions, jump in occasionally, but not to kill the discussion, only to keep it lively and on target.

Reference Notes

[1] Carl R. Rogers, *On Becoming a Person: A Therapist's View of Psychotherapy* (Boston: Houghton Mifflin Company, 1961), p. 18.
   [2] *Ibid.*, p. 19.

CONCENTRATE—INTERROGATE—AND CHEER THE TEAM ALONG

3 Listening, Questioning, and Criticizing

This is a course in speaking. But, more than that, it's a course in communication, and speaking is only part of the communication process. Listening is the other part. If you're to help your classmates open up and discover their speaking strengths, you must listen attentively, ask the right kinds of questions, and offer unbiased, constructive criticism, sympathetic to the speaker's feelings and intentions, dwelling on successes and not failures. Therefore, each of these three skills—listening, questioning, criticizing—deserves a close examination.

LISTENING FOR COMPREHENSION AND EMPATHY

As others speak in your small groups, get involved with what they are saying. Don't blend into the background. Good listeners aren't passive, inanimate targets of messages tossed in their direction. They're *active* receivers. They're like big-league ballplayers; they can field—or at least make a stab at—everything that comes their way.

Active listening is not searching for flaws in another's performance. You've probably experienced that kind of listening often; in fact, we described one such episode earlier in this book. A timid, nervous speaker (an *ostrich*) hides behind the lectern and buries his head in his notes during his presentation; meanwhile, his classmates busily fill out evaluation forms. "Is the thesis explicit?" the evaluation forms ask. "Is the organization logical? Has the speaker defined all unusual terms? Is the evidence ample and convincing? Has the speaker used his voice effectively, varying pitch, rhythm, and volume?" Valid concerns, every one of them. But what's the point in criticizing a speech before you've heard it through? What's the point in distracting yourself so much with form-filling and note-taking that you can't glance up to verify the speaker's existence? In short, whether you fill in forms or not, what's the point of judging a speaker with your *Parent* before you've listened for understanding with your *Adult*? Judgments are fine and necessary, but they should be secondary to understanding what the speaker has to say. So keep your eye and mind on the speaker and message *during the presentation or discussion*. Make your notes and evaluations afterwards.

Mental errors don't show in the box score, but they'll lose you the game.
—An Old Baseball Saying

Mortimer J. Adler, in *How to Read a Book*,[1] draws an analogy between baseball and reading; the analogy also applies to speaking and listening. The writer (or speaker) is the pitcher, actively projecting the message. The reader (or listener) is the catcher. But baseball catchers aren't passive receivers. And to be a good listener, you can't be passive, either. Like a pitched ball, a message rarely comes at you straight and soft. It curves in or out, drops or rises, is thrown hard or off-speed. The receiver must follow it all the way, adjust as it changes directions, prepare for some pain if it smacks dead center into the mitt. Speakers, like pitchers, want you to receive their message—they want to throw strikes—but they don't always succeed. However, unless they throw a "wild pitch" and the ball or message completely eludes your reach, you must catch it or you'll be charged with an error. Major-league catchers must snare almost one hundred percent of the balls thrown within their reach. Yet communication research has shown that listeners understand and remember only twenty-five to fifty percent of what they hear. Those sound like Little-League percentages. How, then, as a listener, can you increase your "percentages" in catching and comprehending the messages coming to you from speakers? In short, how can you become a better *listener?* We offer five "ground rules" that may help:

1. *Forget about being an "umpire."* Make sure that you actively attempt to receive and absorb a message before you judge it. Decide to get totally involved in the game. You may think a speech is silly or the whole situation meaningless and absurd, but give it a chance.

2. *Be on your toes.* Many a ball gets away because a receiver isn't concentrating, isn't mentally or physically ready to "field" it. Sit up straight; don't lean on your elbow and allow yourself to fall asleep. And look at the speaker, not out the window or at the clock. The speaker's expressions and body language provide cues and clues to understanding, too. Don't daydream. Sure, you've got problems; maybe you'd rather be somewhere else right now; but you're in the ball game, and you owe it to yourself to play your best.

3. *Don't interrupt.* Pitchers can't throw their best if catchers stop them every second to change signals, offer advice, or check their delivery. The speaker-listener relationship and system will break down under similar conditions. Give speakers a chance to "show their stuff." Hear them out before you ask questions. They'll be less distracted, and their messages more organized and more meaningful.

4. *Don't be fooled by appearances and first impressions.* Be careful not to prejudge. Prejudgment literally means "prejudice." In baseball, the first time a small guy comes to bat, the fielders may assume he can't hit, and move in close—only to watch his long ball fly over their heads. Don't let some guy's crew cut or long hair tied in a bow turn you off. "Uh-oh," you'll be thinking, "he's one of those fascist-reactionary types, or a hippie-commie-pervert freak." Forget about what you've heard the speaker say in the past. Listen to his words, not to what you think he represents. Listen to what the person says, not to what you *think* he is saying. Withhold judgments you can't be sure of.

5. *Finally, try to empathize.* Try to put yourself in the speaker's place and understand his or her assumptions, motivations, and purpose. The best catchers learn to think with the pitchers. They ask themselves: "If I were in their spot in this situation, what would I do?" Empathy is different from prejudice. In the latter you quickly decide to like or dislike, agree or disagree with people, and then ignore or distort their message accordingly. At such times you're really listening to *yourself,* to *your* ideas about what you think the speakers say. Empathy, however, means you consciously attempt to think *along with* the speaker, to understand the speaker's assumptions, purposes, and feelings.

1 Whole-Class Discussion
Seeing What Causes Rumors

In part, rumors develop and escalate because people listen badly. This experiment should prove the truth of that statement. Your instructor will send six people out of the room and then will read a story to the rest of the class. Listen as actively and attentively as possible. The instructor will then bring one of the six people back into the room. Someone from the class will be asked to retell the story to that person. That person, in turn, will retell the story to the second person brought back into the classroom, and so on. Repeat this procedure until all six people in the first group have reentered the room, listened to, and retold the story. Your instructor will then reread the original story. Participate in a class discussion guided by these questions: Has each retelling changed the story? Specifically, how? Can you determine what caused each change? What might have helped to avoid the changes and/or distortions? Which of the five "ground rules" of good listening seem to have been violated most frequently?

Another way to think along with the speaker and try to understand that person's assumptions, purpose, and feelings is to *restate the point* he or she is making. Try to make restating another's point to that person's satisfaction a permanent part of the way you respond to others. Your instructor may remind you about this from time to time, and the following exercise will help you develop this skill.

2 Small-Group Speaking
Improving Your Communication Skills Through Restatement

Here's a way to improve your communication skills by restating *in your own words* what another person has said.[2] Meet with your small group. Each of you should take three or four minutes to talk about an idea important to you. Do you believe in reincarnation? Astrology? Hard work? Three-year-renewable marriage contracts? Free enterprise? The abolition of grades? Legalized marijuana? The others in the group can respond to you in any way they wish—asking questions, disagreeing, supporting, modifying, expanding. But before they can make their own comments, they must *restate* what you have said, and restate it to your satisfaction. In turn, the next person—before making additional comments—must restate what you have said to your satisfaction. He or she should not repeat your words, but should rephrase them completely. The rephrasing will show how well each listener has understood. Your instructor and a volunteer may want to demonstrate how this procedure works before you begin.

Following the experiment, discuss it in your group. In trying to restate another's ideas, did you find that you had originally misunderstood or misinterpreted anything? Try to explain why. Do you think your differing assumptions, vocabularies, or prejudices affected your understanding?

It is not every question
that deserves an answer.
— Publius Syvius, Maxim 581

ASKING QUESTIONS

Words and the messages they form are often imperfect and inexact. Consequently, they often lead to misunderstandings. We'll illustrate the point. While in college, Art Schmutz earned spending money as a piano player in a bar. One day a man came into the bar, sat down, and ordered a beer. To his amazement, Art's trained monkey hopped off the piano, sauntered casually across the floor, climbed the bar, and ambled over to where the man sat. Then, with a yawn and a stretch, the monkey plopped on his haunches and dipped his feet in the man's mug.

Indignant, the man stomped over to Art and demanded, "Do you know your monkey's got his feet in my beer?"

"No," Art replied. "But if you hum a few bars, I can fake it."

The joke's punch line depends on misunderstandings, but good communication does not. Consequently, in order to clarify someone's meanings and understand someone's messages, you can *ask questions.*

"Do you know your monkey's got his feet in my beer?"

Formulating useful questions and useful answers, though, are skills you develop through practice. You must practice them constantly—in conversations, small-group discussions, and from time to time after you've heard your classmates' speeches. Remember, however, that questions, like all communication, can be misunderstood, too. They can appear to seek information, or they can sound like a challenge or a threat. You can demand, *Parent*ally, "Why are you always late?" Or, with your *Adult* in control, you can simply ask, "Why are you late?" In most cases, you gather information best from transacting on an *Adult-to-Adult* level, but maintaining transactions on that level requires patience and a sense of trust. When a questioner seems *Parent*al, you can answer with your *Adult*, ignoring the tone of the question and responding only to its content. Above all, either in asking or responding to questions, you must avoid the position "I'm OK—you're not OK." When you take that position, you'll be reflecting hostility and suspicion; you'll be exchanging unpleasantries rather than information.

Types of questions you can ask

So, keeping in mind that you want to encourage people to reveal meanings and not expose their weaknesses, here are several types of questions that might serve your purpose. These include questions that *mirror* what you believe to be the other person's meanings and intentions, questions that *limit*—redefine and refocus—the subject matter you're considering, questions that *probe* and extend the line of inquiry, and questions that are *open-ended*—encouraging the speaker to enlarge upon a point or a prior answer.

Mirror questions repeat the speaker's words while inviting him or her to pursue a subject. If, for example, someone says she has no major, you can ask what majors she is considering or what subjects she likes. If a guy says he plays baseball, you can ask him where, for whom, what position.

With *limiting questions* you can elicit specific information from people, thereby sharpening a broad statement into a more detailed or focused one. For example, you might ask, "You've said that a number of things about speaking in public bother you. Could you explain what they are?"

With *probing questions,* you can encourage others to provide answers in greater detail and depth. You can probe their comments and motivate them to explore their ideas and feelings more fully. Essentially, probing questions ask *why.* Why did you choose to major in accounting? Why do you think you are nervous now? Why did you choose to come to this school?

You can ask *open-ended questions,* which allow a person free range to speak. "Can you tell us about your experiences in a prep school?" Or, "What was traveling in Europe like?"

Types of questions you should generally avoid

Of course, there are other types of questions which, for purposes of this book, have limited value, so usually you should avoid them. These include the *closed question,* the *leading question,* and the *trick question.* The first, the *closed question,* merely requires a yes-or-no answer or a short reply: "How old are you?" "Are you married?" It does little to draw a person out, to encourage someone to speak, though it serves well when you want a short, factual piece of information. The *leading question* virtually forces people to respond as you would like them to. In effect, it answers itself. "You do like speech, don't you?" "You wouldn't disagree with an authority like Mr. Ruggers, would you?" The final type, the *trick question,* is great for trapping people, for luring them into saying what they don't want to. The most familiar example is, "Do you still beat your wife?" But leave that device to lawyers. You're interested in helping people succeed, not discrediting their testimony.

Listening to and answering questions

Answering questions requires both good listening and good speaking skills. Since how you answer can increase either your group's understanding or frustration, you might consider the following guidelines:

1. *Make sure you understand the question.* If necessary, ask the questioner to rephrase it, or try to restate it in your own words. When you're both satisfied as to the question's meaning, then you can begin to answer it accurately.

2. *Keep your answer brief and to the point.* A fifteen-minute response to one questioner while seven others wait with their questions can transform a friendly group into a lynch mob.

3. *Try to interpret what a questioner REALLY means.* Sometimes you may sense that this questioner is requesting more than information. He or she may, in addition, be seeking emotional support, trying to divert your attention to a minor problem, or issuing a subtle challenge to you. In other words, as you listen to questions, try to determine the *level* on which they are being asked. What real or hidden *purpose* prompts the asking?

Psychologist Eric Berne says that communication transactions sometimes have a *social* purpose and an *ulterior, psychological* one.[3] For example, an *Adult*-to-*Adult* question may mask a *Child's* challenge of the other's *Parent* or a *Child*-to-*Child* flirtation game. To decide whether or how to respond to these ulterior transactions requires some experience, judgment, and skill. In cases where the transaction is a challenge or an enticement, perhaps the best policy is to respond only to the social transaction. Where the ulterior transaction seems to be a sincere request for help, then perhaps you should honor it.

Dr. Domeena Renshaw, a psychiatrist and head of a sex-therapy clinic in the Chicago area, seemed to recognize the existence of these different levels from the question raised by a nervous young man after her speech in a college forum. He asked her whether people should follow the directions of sex manuals. She answered him at first on the *social* level, relating well to the questioner's experiences:

How you filter out what's good and what's rotten from the massive detail of commercial sex books is as hard a job for you as it is for me. . . . I think you are going to have to use judgment. Just like you'd research any subject for school here, you'd find a pile of junk and you'd find something solid. Trust your good, human, common sense.[4]

But the student, apparently dissatisfied with the speaker's answer, then rephrased the question. "If we don't 'live up' to the models of the sex books," he asked, "won't that cause frustration in ourselves?" Dr. Renshaw, perceiving the insecurity the *social transaction* was camouflaging, switched to the *psychological, ulterior level* and responded supportively, as the comforting *Parent.* Her voice softened, became reassuring, though not condescending:

OK, I see what you're getting at. These are not "how to's" as far as you particularly go if it's not right for you. You have to use judgment and say—you know—you have to get in touch with your body. Perhaps that's the essential message I've missed to get across to you tonight. I'm asking you to get in touch with your values, to get in touch with your body and your common sense, that you make judgments about those things. You don't have to follow every silly nonsense in [a sex manual]. You know, it's your life. [The author of a sex manual] is not your guiding daddy, OK? So you pick up what you feel comfortable with and right for you. You don't have to do any of it. You can read it, then say, "Well, that's entertaining." Trust your own basic values for yourself.[5]

Though Dr. Renshaw is a professional psychiatrist, her basic approach to providing answers was not complicated: Tell people they're OK, that they can cope. If, however, in answering an audience's questions, you feel ill-equipped to respond to *ulterior transactions,* don't. As Dr. Renshaw put it, get in touch with your own common sense.

3 Small-Group Speaking
Eliciting Information Through Questions

Meet in your small group. Each one of you should take a minute or so to tell the others what famous person—living or dead, real or fictional—you resemble or would like to emulate. You may mention several people if you wish. Maybe you'd like to look like one, have the career of another, the politics of a third, and the personality of a fourth. Explain the reasons for your choice in very general terms.

Then, the others in the group—by asking mirror questions, probing questions, open-ended questions, and limiting questions—can try to elicit more specific information about why you've identified with the person you've chosen. They can also try to determine what qualities in that person you admire, and whether you feel you possess these same qualities yourself, or merely wish you did.

If time permits, continue this exercise until everyone in the group has had a turn at receiving and handling the questions. Not only will it improve your questioning and answering skills, but you'll also get to know each other better.

A true critic ought to dwell rather on excellence than on imperfections, to discover the concealed beauties . . . and communicate to the world such things as are worth their observation.

—Joseph Addison, *The Spectator*

BEING A CRITIC AND A CHEERLEADER

After hearing speeches in your small group, you'll be expected to comment on them, to criticize them. Naturally, good criticism depends on good listening. You should practice the same behaviors we discussed earlier in the chapter: Make no assumptions about the speaker and what you think he or she represents. Make sure you *understand* the speaker's message before you respond to it. Ask questions. Try restating points in your own words. Try to be sympathetic to the speaker's intentions, to what the speaker is trying to accomplish.

Keep it positive! Walk—and talk—on the sunny side!

If you can listen attentively and empathically, don't worry about your qualifications to criticize. Though few are professional, everyone is a critic. You have opinions about the latest John Wayne movie, the new cops-and-robbers television show, David Crosby's new album, and Kurt Vonnegut's most recent excursion into his fantasy world of granfalloons and foma. You judge everything you see and hear, from the performance of your football team to a blonde's mid-back-length hair, to some guy's crew cut or beard. Making your views known is a different matter, however. Most of us (wisely, it would seem) share our opinions sparingly, only if asked, and then couched in the gentlest possible language.

Negative criticism, however well intended, merely confirms most novices' worst suspicions about their incompetence and worst fears of their eventual failure. It discourages, not encourages. Learning something new is often intimidating, embarrassing, risky. To cite an example, those too afraid to fall will never mount a horse and consequently never learn to ride. Advice from more experienced riders, especially if it centers on faults and mistakes, only feeds that anxiety; it sounds threatening.

Good positive criticism, however, encourages the ascent and cushions the fall. It reinforces the "Why not? It could be wonderful" attitude. Accustomed to competing, most people tend naturally to find fault with others. But competition need not be cutthroat. You can learn from each other and learn to keep trying. You can point out what others do right, not wrong. One success encourages another. In fact, positive criticism creates *mutual successes* and *mutual rewards.* When—through your own efforts and the suggestions of others—you discover your speaking strengths, you'll continue to develop them. When others—through their efforts and your suggestions—discover their own strengths, they'll develop them further, too. Therein lies growth and satisfaction.

So, your task in criticizing will be to look for effective, pleasing practices in others and, with supportive, positive remarks, to encourage maintaining and refining them. You can keep others in the saddle by complimenting their horsemanship. With sarcasm and scorn, they'll quickly dismount; with praise, they'll stay on. Despite their nervousness and self-consciousness, they will learn and improve. Some will improve more slowly than others, but a series of successes, however small, should lead eventually to large successes. You need not point out faults. In time, speakers will drop most practices that win them no praise and hold on to the ones that do win praise.

. . . But call it as you see it

In short, as an effective critic, you're a cheerleader. After actively listening to and carefully observing speakers, you applaud only what you like. *Positive, supportive behavior, however, doesn't necessitate dishonesty.* People around you will quickly spot and reject insincerity. You need only praise what you genuinely like, whether merely a gesture, a phrase, a word, a smile. Be specific. Although saying "Nice" or "I enjoyed that" is better than nothing, try to notice details, too. Say, "I liked your expression 'colder than a North Pole stripper.' " Or, "That wink and joke at the beginning made me feel comfortable." Or, "Your hand movements held my attention." If you keep the speakers on the right track, eventually they'll roll quite smoothly on their own steam. Later on, more confident of their abilities and potentials, they'll listen to and accept some negative observations, especially if these come from a source they trust and respect.

Q. What do you think of the critics?
A. They're very noisy at night. You can't sleep in the country because of them. But, otherwise I like them. I think that's crickets you're talking about, sir. I mean critics.
A. Oh, critics! They're no good.
Q. Why is that?
A. They can't make music with their legs.
— MEL BROOKS, in a Newsweek interview[6]

A wise critic learns also when *not* to talk. *A too-frequently-heard voice soon loses the ears of its listeners.* So limit yourself to the essentials and ignore the trivialities. Small imperfections can be polished later; first, the diamond has to be cut.

You may find that being a critic does not come easily to you—that you feel incompetent to judge others. Perhaps what you're really thinking is that you're slow to speak in class and others usually say what you had planned to say. To avoid that problem, try jotting down a quick note of what you like in a speaker's presentation. Keep it short—don't be an ostrich. Then, after a speech, you can refer to your notes and contribute something positive to the discussion.

. . . And learn to take it—as well as dish it out

Learning to accept your group's criticisms is important, too. Opinions vary among individuals, and you'll find that you'll accept some while rejecting others. If only one or two like something, you may not take their views seriously. If most like it, though, you may feel they have a point. The combined voices of seven or nine people cannot be ignored.

Now let's try to tie together everything we've said in this chapter. *As group members,* you play a significant role in each other's growth and improvement as speakers. You're *critics* who encourage and point out what works. You're *questioners* who help clarify each other's meanings and draw each other out. As both questioners and critics you must be careful *listeners,* stifling your prejudices, sympathizing with each other's intentions, trying to understand rather than judge.

Reference Notes

[1]Mortimer J. Adler, *How to Read a Book.* Copyright © 1940, 1967 by Mortimer J. Adler. Reprinted by permission of Simon & Schuster, Inc.

[2]Adapted from Carl R. Rogers and F. J. Roethlisberger, "Barriers and Gateways to Communication," *Harvard Business Review* XXX, No. 4 (July—August 1952), pp. 46 and 48.

[3]Eric Berne, M.D., *What Do You Say After You Say Hello? The Psychology of Human Destiny* (New York: Grove Press, 1972), pp. 23–24.

[4]Dr. Domeena Renshaw, "Sexual Behavior and Vaiues," speech delivered at Wilbur Wright College, Chicago, Illinois, March 12, 1975.

[5]Ibid.

[6]Mel Brooks, "The 2,000-Year-Old Director." *Newsweek,* February 17, 1975, p. 57.

Part Two

Communicating for Interest, Clarity, and Usefulness

STARTING FROM YOUR OWN EXPERIENCES

4 Creating Interest Through Telling Stories

You'll be speaking many times this term, so of course you'll need something to speak about. But what? You consider the world spinning, wobbly with controversy and problems—ecology, energy, elections, revolutions, starvations, abortions, liberations (women's, gay, etc.), welfare, capital and corporal punishment, cruelty to animals and children—you consider all *that* big stuff and think: "How can I say anything but trivialities? What important ideas do I have? None. What, then, can I discuss? Nothing."

Rubbish. You do know—or can learn—more than just clichés about some of these world-shaking issues and problems. But, for your beginning speeches at least, why look to the big world as your source for material? There's a more interesting and less discussed world to explore instead — the world of your own experiences. So begin with it. Begin with what you know best — yourself. You know more about *you* than anybody else does. Exciting things have happened to you that have happened to no one else in the world. Talk about them. Tell some stories from your past.

GETTING STARTED: TELLING STORIES

Storytelling is the oldest of the speechmaking skills, and it is among the most important. Stories concern people, and nothing interests people more than other people. A story about yourself makes you real, human, and somehow more accessible to your listeners. Moreover, good stories *entertain,* and entertainment is important in virtually every kind of speaking. Even when you deliver a long persuasive speech on a controversial subject, you'll find that the most motivated audience may lose interest and lose track of your argument. To keep their attention and interest, you'll need stories which animate, enliven, illustrate, vivify, and prove a point. A few days after your speech, your audience may have forgotten much of what you've said, but they won't likely forget your good stories — and, as a result, the point behind each. The meat of any speech is its ideas, but stories provide the flavor to make it tasty, digestible, and memorable.

Discussing your personal experiences is often easy, too. Just choose any one of the thousands of small adventures and funny or tearful or embarrassing moments from your past. Potentially, any one of them can develop into a lively and entertaining story. Lecturing around the country at the turn of the century, Mark Twain spun his best yarns about his childhood. Storytellers like Bill Cosby are still doing the same thing. Here's a small section from one of his youthful recollections about street football:

> ". . . Arnie, go down ten steps and cut left behind the black Chevy. Philbert, you run down to my house, and wait in the living room. Cosby, you go down to Third Street and catch the *J* bus. Have them open the doors at Nineteenth Street. I'll fake it to you."
> "You always had one fat kid they never threw to."
> "What about me?"
> "You go long."[1]

Stories needn't be funny to capture and hold listeners, though. The following incident, which happened to someone we know, could — when told to an audience — elicit something very different from laughter:

I was five, or perhaps six, when my brother took me to the playground near our house. All the playground equipment, of hard steel and wood, seemed enormous and threatening. I was especially frightened, yet fascinated, by a contraption I called a "merry-go-round." It consisted of nothing more than a circular bench attached to a metal tubular frame which revolved around a central hub. Kids would scramble for a hold on the frame and whip it around in a circle until the contraption spun—it seemed—at fantastic speeds. Then they would push off and hop on to enjoy the ride. Eventually, as the bench barely spun, they would dismount, dizzy and slightly headachy.

I was too small to run and jump on the bench, but no one would accuse me of cowardice; I was too tough for that. So, during a pause while the contraption lay at rest, I climbed up and sat down, squeezing the frame with my tiny hands before the big kids provided the motion and the speed.

I knew about courage, but not about centrifugal force; I could fight fear, but not the laws of gravity and motion. The machine slung me off, slamming my head against the rock-hard ground.

I awoke at the hospital with my dad and mom over me. My head throbbed from something called a concussion. Within a few days the hair would fall out over the spot where my head hit, and to this day I retain the bump and the bald spot and the memories of the doctor's comments in the hospital: "There are a lot of blows in life, kid," he said, "so you had better get used to them."

This story illustrates the advantage of talking about the past. You remember an event in sufficient detail, but the maturity of years lets you see yourself with fondness or irony or smiling regret. The telling lets your listeners see you better, too. The telling establishes you as a real human being. Not all stories need be from your youth, of course. One from last week will suffice, provided you can detach yourself from your emotions at the time—if, for instance, your genuine anger or real humiliation isn't too painful to share.

So, get started now, telling stories from your own experience. Odds are, you already feel relaxed and natural in *impromptu* speaking— that is, unplanned and unexpected conversations and discussions. Now simply be relaxed and yourself in *extemporaneous* speaking—that is, speaking which you plan (and perhaps rehearse) ahead of time, but for which you don't write out or memorize the exact words. Although extemporaneous speaking requires planning, it doesn't require rigidity. You're free to adapt to your audience, to be spontaneous, and to choose many of your words as you speak. A third kind of speaking—from a carefully planned and written-out *manuscript*—can be equally exciting; but it requires skills in oral reading, maintaining eye contact with your audience as you read, and other communication skills which you probably don't yet possess. So, especially at first, make most of your speaking in this course extemporaneous.

Telling a Story Extemporaneously

Choose an experience from your past—awful or wonderful, painful or poignant—as a subject for a short extemporaneous speech. Then sit in a circle with the members of your small group, and talk about that experience for five minutes. Try to recreate the incident. Move back in time; supply the physical and psychological details of the situation; make yourself and your audience relive the experience. By all means, relax and be spontaneous. Don't plan too much. Concentrate on sharing your story with your audience. Let your dimples show—and your warts, too, if they're honest ones. Your audience will enjoy finding their blemishes on someone else. Joke a little, fool around, acknowledge your emotions. Some things will work, others won't. But you'll get experience, which all good, confident speakers need.

Good words are worth much,
and cost little.
— George Herbert,
Jacula Prudentum

SPICING YOUR STORY WITH DETAILS

Not every story merits the telling. Some will never burn with excitement, though clever narration may warm them a bit. Conversely, however, the most inflammable tale can be snuffed out by a soggy presentation. As we've said, sparking interest and keeping it aglow is a crucial requirement of all effective speaking; and telling stories well usually provides the spark. If your stories aren't generating much heat, though, don't despair. Successful storytellers are *made* as well as *born*. You enter this world screaming; but gradually you learn from others to use language. Art Schmutz began by consciously imitating the stand-up comedians of his day, then discovered and refined his own communicating style. We'll try to help you discover *your* own speaking style, then show you how to refine it through (1) using *details* and (2) adding *metaphors*.

Using details—and more details

In speech, specific details work much better than abstract truths or esoteric ideas. For one thing, details make your ideas more concrete, and hence *clearer*—obviously an important goal in any kind of speaking. For another, they make your ideas *more alive.* Unless your words describe the concrete and real, so people can sense—see, hear, feel, taste, smell—something, your ideas may dissolve into mere sounds, touching no one. You can clarify and vivify any speech, discussion, or chat by fidelity to details. Rather than gushing:

> My trip to New England last summer was one of the most exciting trips of my life

describe what made it so exciting:

> I'm used to the buildings and cement of New York. I had never seen a large hill, let alone a mountain. So when I saw those miles of green mountains covering the entire state of Vermont, I had to look twice. They were everywhere, covered with pine trees, and I drove through them on Route 100, dipping into the valleys and climbing up out of them onto the mountaintops. New Hampshire was even more spectacular. I saw white mountains, twice as high as Vermont's. Their tops rose above the point where vegetation will grow, leaving the grey, naked rock. In each state, the only signs of civilization outside the cities were little white farmhouses and three or four cows.

Effective speakers establish the dimensions and action of a visible, palpable world. Even if fictitious, it seems and feels real. In his essay, "Shooting an Elephant," George Orwell shows the ugly reality of an abstract term—British imperialism—through concrete details. Rather than discussing its evils in generalities, he demonstrates them with a specific story. As the white agent of British supremacy in dark-skinned Burma, he was forced to kill an elephant to demonstrate his power and official status. When you read his story, however, remember that it's from an essay, not a speech. We do not expect you—or even want you—to imitate the polished phrases of a prose selection in a speech. Look instead at the *details;* consider the feelings they create; note how as a consequence you can experience the elephant's death as Orwell did:

> When I pulled the trigger I did not hear the bang or feel the kick—one never does when the shot goes home—but I heard the devilish roar of glee that went up from the crowd. In that instant, in too short a time, one would have thought, even for the bullet to get there, a mysterious, terrible change had come over the elephant. He neither stirred nor fell, but every line of his body had altered. He looked suddenly stricken, shrunken, intensely old, as though the frightful impact of the bullet had paralyzed him without knocking him down. At last, after what seemed a long time—it might have been five seconds, I daresay—he sagged flabbily to his knees. His mouth slobbered. An enormous senility seemed to have settled upon him. One could have imagined him thousands of years old. I fired again into the same spot. At the second shot he did not collapse but climbed

with desperate slowness to his feet and stood weakly upright, with legs sagging and head drooping. I fired a third time. That was the shot that did for him. You could see the agony of it jolt his whole body and knock the last remnant of strength from his legs. But in falling he seemed for a moment to rise, for as his hind legs collapsed beneath him he seemed to tower upward like a huge rock toppling, his trunk reaching skywards like a tree. He trumpeted, for the first and only time. And then down he came, his belly towards me, with a crash that seemed to shake the ground even where he lay.[2]

The concrete description of the elephant's death and the circumstances surrounding it speak more eloquently than a whole dictionary of abstract words. Orwell puts you on the scene. He stirs the senses. He helps you feel the event as he is reliving it. Note how he cowers at the "devilish roar of glee" from the crowd. He watches the elephant he had no wish to kill sink "flabbily to his knees." He sees the elephant's mouth slobber. And then he stands by as the majestic animal seems "for a moment to rise . . . to tower upward like a huge rock toppling, his trunk reaching skywards like a tree." The elephant's collapse, belly forward, demonstrates his loss of majesty in death.

At first you may not easily find such details for your stories. But keep looking. Think about the details before you speak. Plan ahead. Try saying the story silently or aloud to yourself in a spare moment. Orwell's essay makes supplying details look easy, but no doubt he revised it many times before publication.

The more practiced you become at finding details, the more they'll become a part of your natural speaking habits. You can even tell stories with *dialogue* to create a clear and believable scene. For example, Stokely Carmichael has spoken so often before crowds that he can relax, adapt to a situation, and extemporaneously supply a story. In this speech explaining Black Power to a white audience, he ad-libbed a little story complete with dialogue to explain why he was speaking softly:

> Well, I'll tell you why you can't hear me. [*Laughter*]. When I was small, I used to come home, and I'd say to my mother, "Ma, Ma, I'm home." Now she'd say, "Shhh, Negroes are too loud." [*Laughter*]. So since I didn't want to be a Negro, since then I've tried to become soft.[3]

Note that Carmichael's details and real-life dialogue not only captured and held his listeners' attention and drew them psychologically closer, but the details and dialogue also helped him *make a point.*

Drawing from their own experiences, accomplished speakers anywhere, any place, can color a story with precise, detailed brush-strokes, to *illustrate* and *relive* rather than merely talk about. Do the same as you speak. Don't fall back on adjectives like "beautiful," "large," "small," "happy," "fat," or "fantastic"; carry your narrative forward with the details that both suggest and exemplify your words.

But make your details *necessary* and *relevant.* Don't be like the speakers who pad a story with extraneous material and who pause to say, "Wait a minute. Was it Wednesday or Thursday that I broke my foot? Wednesday, I think. No, maybe it was Thursday." Dragging in— and dragging on with—such details merely prompts your listeners to say, "Get to the point." Put meaningful details in your stories and speeches; develop a sense of what is and is not important, relevant, dramatic. Prune out the dull, the trivial, the immaterial. If your purpose in discussing a New England trip is to contrast the natural scenery of the countryside with the buildings of the big cities, don't bother with how long it took, what you ate along the way, or how much it cost.

2 Small-Group Speaking
Adding Details to a Story

Select another story or incident from your past as the basis for a five-minute extemporaneous speech that you will present to the other members of your small group. But as you prepare your speech, think about what details to include. First consider the main idea or impression the story seems to convey. Then decide what you want to emphasize. Try to avoid generalizations—be specific. Don't waste time and energy on the trivial and unimportant. Decide what details should begin and end the story. And include only the details that seem appropriate and relevant to the main idea or impression you want to make. Try to practice giving the speech a few times before you bring it to class. At least try to work out some of the details orally beforehand.

Adding flavor with metaphors

Public speakers, who live by language, respect the *life* of words. Most people deal in dead phrases, taken like lifeless sardines from mass-produced cans. They rarely fish for fresh terms or expressions. But the best speakers keep their hooks baited with metaphors—figurative language. They continuously cast for the unusual, for the vivid. And on occasion, they go for the big one, throwing the harpoon—or even the lampoon—if that's what is called for.

In advising you to flavor your communication with metaphors, we don't mean to get fancy. You needn't be Shakespeare and compose verbal sonnets. All we're asking is that you learn to recognize and utilize the potential *liveliness* in your words. *Metaphors,* discussions of one thing *in terms* of another, will provide some of that liveliness, and they are easy to find or devise. They are inseparable from human thought;

you coin them naturally. ("Coin" is a metaphor, since you can't spend words, and so is the "fishing" metaphor we opened this section with.) Metaphors mark some of humankind's most noble expression; they also abound in slang:

"He grows on you" (like a fungus?); "I'm really into organic foods"(you had better get out before someone eats you); "I'm getting my head together" (it's about time, but while you're at it, replace that nose); "I can really dig that music" (we'd prefer you bury it); "That was some trip" (hope you didn't skin your knee); "I'm getting good vibes from you" (hope they don't tickle).

This passage from Eldridge Cleaver's *Soul on Ice* suggests the frequency with which colorful metaphors appear in black slang:

Wow, that *did me in, cleaned me out,* and I realized that I was standing there *gaping* at her *like a country fool.* I was really confused and embarrassed and I *cut out,* completely *blowing my cool.* And as I *split,* I saw her *cracking up with kicks. [Italics ours.]*[4]

Although many slang terms and colloquialisms are essentially metaphors, your general vocabulary also has many peeping out beneath its words. You can easily spot metaphors since, as figurative language, they're not true *literally.* The following examples, from standard, informal English, should illustrate the point: "My mind's made up" (of what?); "I'm heading over to the park" (your feet will get you there faster); "I've got a splitting headache" (we've noticed the hole); "May I have the floor, Mr. Chairperson?" (take the walls, too); "Why don't you drop over tonight?" (At this point you can anticipate the punch line yourself.)

Unless you have become accustomed to thinking in metaphors, at first you may have difficulty developing clever ones in *impromptu* speeches. You must plan them in advance. Walter Jacobson, anchorman and reporter for WBBM television news in Chicago, used an extended metaphor in a manuscript speech he delivered to a college audience. It summarized and illustrated his argument that news reporting on television cannot easily be biased, because too many people must exercise judgment over what appears on the screen:

The point of all this is that there are so many *cooks in the kitchen,* tossing so many *ingredients into the stew,* that it's foolish to believe, as many insist they believe, that the form and substance of the result can be manipulated by a few *number-one chefs* in New York. *[Italics ours.]*[5]

Metaphor-making is an acquired skill; you probably won't learn quickly or easily to twist and stretch words. Metaphorically, you'll skin your knuckles and strain your muscles for a while. But, in time, if you allow yourself to romp around and enjoy your words, you can learn to create and incorporate metaphors in a speech as you prepare for it.

The most commonly used metaphors lose their sense of surprise — that small charge that shocks or tickles. You can recharge them in many ways, but one way is by taking them literally, as we've done with our examples above. To increase your awareness of metaphors and wordplay, try this little exercise: Write down five common metaphors and play with them until they regain some of their sparkle. "That grass is growing like wild-fire," you can write, and follow it with "but watering won't put it out." Or, how about, "Can you lend me some money? I'm broke," to which you can add, "Is the money for repairs?" Bring your list to class and share your creations with other members of your small group.

In sum, you can achieve two important goals of speaking — to be interesting and clear — most easily and comfortably by beginning in your own world and telling stories from your own experience. But make them detailed; make the details relevant; and make your language lively. Don't just talk about your childhood. Free the *Child* in your personality to play with words and metaphors. Have fun with speaking, and your listeners will, too.

Reference Notes

[1] From Bill Cosby, "I Started Out as a Child." Warner Bros. Records (W.S. 1567). Reprinted by permission of SAH Enterprises, Inc.

[2] George Orwell, "Shooting an Elephant," *Shooting an Elephant and Other Essays* (New York: Harcourt Brace Jovanovich, Inc. and London: Secker & Warburg, 1950), p. 10.

[3] Stokely Carmichael, "Stokely Carmichael Explains Black Power to a White Audience in Whitewater, Wisconsin," *The Rhetoric of Black Power* (New York: Harper & Row, Publishers, 1969), p. 98.

[4] Eldridge Cleaver, *Soul on Ice* (New York: McGraw-Hill Book Company, 1968), p. 28.

[5] Walter Jacobson, "A Free Press, Government, Elections and Politicians," speech delivered at Wilbur Wright College, Chicago, Illinois, September 27, 1972.

5 Improving Clarity Through Language

As you tell stories, we've emphasized, you must be clear. But clarity applies to *every* act of communication. In fact, giving and receiving clear, accurate information is central to human survival. From the moment babies can understand, their parents supply them with the data to help them recognize the world and discover their relationship to that world. They give them the names of things: toy, ball, fork, knife, diaper, chair, eyes, nose. They give them instructions on eating, dressing, asking for help. They give them such simple information as "Don't touch," or something as complicated as an explanation of why someone died. In short, the parents give their children rules and regulations, advice and instructions, facts and opinions, and language to communicate about those things in relation to their wants and needs.

But giving doesn't guarantee *receiving*. Ask any parent who has taught a baby table manners, and has discovered that food, utensils, and patience often scatter in the process. The tradition of rejecting instructions, in fact, traces back as far as Adam and Eve, who paid no attention to advice on a dietary issue; through Moses, who smashed the Ten Commandments; to his followers who ignored them; and on down to the numerous rebels of our own time. In any situation, a great deal of information can and does get lost between sender and receiver. Communication, as we've said before, is often imperfect and inexact. But why?

"Do you mean that you think you can find the answer to it?" "Exactly so," said Alice. "Then you should say what you mean," the March Hare went on. "I do;" Alice hastily replied; "at least I mean what I say—that's the same thing, you know." "Not the same thing a bit!" said the Hatter. "Why, you might just as well say that 'I see what I eat' is the same as 'I eat what I see.'"
—Lewis Carroll, *Alice's Adventures in Wonderland*

THE TROUBLE WITH WORDS

The answer, in no small part, lies in the limitations of language and the ways we must use it. In each of the advantages of language there's a disadvantage. Three of these, in particular, contribute heavily to the "trouble with words" when we try to communicate with them; namely: (1) They can only *symbolize* or *represent* what they stand for— they cannot *be* it; (2) they are frequently highly *abstract* and *lacking in reality;* and (3) often they are *inexact* and *not specific* enough. Let's examine each of these limitations.

1. Words, being merely symbols of the things they name, have no meaning in themselves. The verbal and nonverbal symbols (words, gestures, facial expressions, etc.) can only *represent* or "stand for" objects or ideas. Words—symbolic labels—cannot stand alone, isolated from or independent of the thing they refer to. Hence the expression "Words *in themselves* have no meaning." They are merely sounds which we arbitrarily decide represent a certain something, though we could just as easily have them represent a different something. Try asking a five-year-old, who has been carefully taught the names of things, why a potato is called a potato. "Because it looks like a potato," you might hear, "or because it is brown." But in French a potato is a *pomme de terre* (literally translated, an "earth apple"); in German, a *Kartoffel;* and in Swahili, it's called a *kiazi sena.* Any group of people could agree to call it by another name, like—say, a *plurp*—and communicate perfectly well if the term has been generally accepted and disseminated.

"Pass the mashed *plurps,* please," you might say. Or, "I can't tell the difference between American fried and French fried *plurps.*" Hash-brown *plurps* would be great with eggs; catsup on French fried *plurps* adds flavor; and creamed *plurps* sprinkled with chopped parsley would make a great delicacy.

2. Words, since they may name both tangible and intangible things, often are highly abstract, generalized, and remote from reality. Words, as symbols, are *abstractions* (literally, things pulled away from reality). Semanticist S. I. Hayakawa calls them a map of reality,[1] a map of a tangible reality or an abstract, intangible idea that they either represent or create. While the word *potato* refers to an object in the real world, the word *year* does not. On your birthday do you really feel a "year" older? Of course not, because *year*—unlike *potato*—is not a specific, seeable, touchable object; it is an idea, an invention, something thought up by people: an intangible concept of a time interval created through a word. Consider another word: *Indiana.* The mere word, of and in itself, is a "map of reality," too. But it is just that—a map—not *the* reality. *Indiana*—with apologies to the Hoosiers—does not *literally* exist. The dirt, the grass, the stones, the asphalt, the buildings, the lakes, and streams of Indiana exist; they have reality. The boundary line, however, between Indiana and Michigan exists only in minds and maps. You can't hold it in your hands or see it, although you may see a sign saying "Welcome to Indiana" as you enter.

All sorts of words—*time, justice, democracy, love, heroism, free enterprise, Christianity, marriage, genius,* and *beauty*—do not exist in objective reality. They are names given to abstract, high-level, and broadly generalized processes, ideals, beliefs, relationships, etc. In the isolated and literal sense, they are sounds without meaning. You cannot see, feel, hear, or touch *justice;* you can only observe actions you choose to call just or unjust. Nevertheless, though nothing in the physical world corresponds to these words, the relationships they represent and the feelings they evoke can be experienced and imprinted on your consciousness. In that sense, they do exist; they have what we call "subjective reality." You need words like *Indiana* and *justice* to regulate society. People, in fact, have been known to fight private and public wars over them, to make love for them, to build monuments to them.

   3. Words, by their very nature, are necessarily inexact and—very often—aren't specific enough. A word can, of course, represent any number of different things. Especially when words are quite far removed from reality, they can represent *too many* things and, in turn, can have too many different meanings attributed to them. And the more abstract and general a word is, the greater the likelihood of disagreement among those who use it and receive it in the process of communication. To some, for example, *democracy* "means" the form of government characteristic of our country and of all those in the rest of the "free world." To others, it "means" a government in which all citizens vote directly on all issues, as in some small New England towns. To others, true *democracy* will occur only if all workers participate in decisions now delegated to managers and owners. And finally, to still others, *democracy* "means" merely "rule by the people," its original meaning in Greek. For them, a legitimate *democracy* is whatever form of government the people choose—whether a dictatorship, a kingdom, or a republic.

KEEPING YOUR COMMUNICATION CLEAR

   Since any one of thousands upon thousands of words can be given so many different "meanings" by so many different people, you can easily see something of the chaos we'd have in trying to communicate if we didn't have some safeguards and guidelines. Fortunately, we can recommend a few: (1) define your terms carefully; (2) be concrete and specific; (3) be accurate; (4) use commonly understood terms—not jargon; and (5) compare the strange or unknown with the familiar.

Define your terms

   As the General Semanticists advocate, we should always try to "put some recognizable territory under the word maps" we use. This is another way of saying "Call your shots" or "Define your terms." If the meaning of the word *democracy* can be "interpreted" in so many possible ways, obviously your definition and your listener's definition had better be the same—or pretty close to it. At the very least, you have the obligation to let him or her know—with some exactitude—the definition *you* are using. You can do this in a variety of ways—by *examples,* by *classifying* (putting the term in a class or subclass), and/or by *stipulat-*

ing what the term is or is not or what it means or doesn't mean to you.

For example, in a speech before a college audience, Philip Hilts, author of *Behavior Mod,*[2] a book exploring how behavior modification is being used and misused, argued that all other branches of psychology are not truly scientific. In order to make his point, however, he first established what he meant by "science," classifying and contrasting its two "streams" and giving a historical definition of the term:

> About the year 1620, with [Galileo] the great move toward science first began. He brought together two streams which were kind of small at the time: two streams of science, two methods. One was *reason.* People used to sit down and think things out. They thought they could discover the world that way. . . . It didn't occur to them to use experiments. . . . You got some broad theories from this; you got some inclusive theories; but you could never tell whether they were right or wrong.

> The second stream was *experiment.* There were people who did experiments, but they were small experiments. They were not testing anything; they were experimenting for the sake of it. . . . What Galileo did—and this is really not a true anecdote, but it's one which is famous in science and does explain something—Galileo went up to the tower of Pisa one day with two stones, one very large and one very small. There were two competing theories at the time. One was that they [the stones] would hit the ground at the same time, and the other was that they wouldn't—the big one would arrive first.

> . . . [But] what Galileo said was: "I don't care. It doesn't matter what side I'm on. I'm going to test it. Because I don't care, I can be on either side, whichever comes out right." So that was the beginning. He brought together reason and experiment. And that was the beginning of the scientific revolution.[3]

Notice that Hilts, even in defining a term, includes a small story about Galileo. He recognizes the importance of telling stories—in this case, not only to create interest, but to clarify his meaning as well.

1 Small-Group Speaking
Defining a Term

Give a two-minute speech defining a term you think your group doesn't know. Choose a word you've learned in another course or on your job, or a "pet word" you use with your family or good friends. Don't merely supply a synonym for the term, however. Use as many different methods of defining terms as you can: exemplify, classify, stipulate, compare and/or contrast, etc. Extend your definition, perhaps by tracing the term's origins or history if you can, by citing an example or two of its use, or—best of all—by telling a little story to illustrate the term you're defining and a way to use it.

Be concrete and specific

Not only do definitions increase your listener's understanding, but so does choosing the most concrete, specific language, especially when your listeners aren't familiar with your subject.

Suppose, for example, a Martian has landed on Earth in a field of grass, and sees several large, four-legged creatures chomping the vegetation in great quantities and uttering an occasional "moo." Puzzled, he approaches our old friend, fearless Art Schmutz, who is leaning on a nearby fence.

"Say, mister, excuse me. I'm new in the neighborhood and was wondering if you could tell me what those odd creatures are."

"Oh, sure, green fella," Art replies. "Always happy to contribute to universal understanding. Those are animals."

Art's answer is, of course, too abstract; so the Martian asks for more specific information.

"But what kind of animals are they, sir?"

"Well, you've got three eyes. Can't you see they're mammals?"

This answer tells the Martian more than the first, but still not enough; so the Martian presses on.

"Sir, I hate to be rude, but what kind of mammals are they?"

"Oh," Art drawls, deciding to stop playing games, "they're cows. There aren't many, though. You can count all six of them on the fingers of your hand."

If Art wishes to become more specific, more concrete, he can add that they are three-year-old Guernseys, weigh about 1000 pounds each, and are named Bessie, Elsie, Susie, Trudy, Belinda, and Esmiralda. The more concrete Art's language, the better the Martian will understand.

2 Small-Group Speaking
Explaining a Task Concretely and Specifically

In a job, a hobby, or in school, you've probably learned and performed a particular task many times: operating a forklift or a telephone switchboard, running a teletype machine or a day-camp program, harvesting wheat, carving a model ship, tuning your car, setting up an experiment in chemistry class. Choose any one of these tasks, or a similar one, and to the members of your small group give a five-minute explanation or description of how you typically perform this task. Don't be abstract; be concrete and down to earth in your choice of words—realistic and practical. Illustrate your explanation/description with brief stories or incidents from your experience—the time the forklift broke down, the morning your boss almost fired you, the crucial moment when the test-tube stand col-

". . . Always happy to contribute to universal understanding, fella'. Those are animals."

lapsed. Take special care to make your language clear, vivid, and specific. Help your listeners experience the task as you supply them with graphic and particularized details, possible bits of dialogue, and even a metaphor or two. Try in every way to ensure that they will *understand* and *feel* what performing the specific task is like.

Be accurate

Accurate word choice, like concreteness, is also crucial to direction-giving or information-sharing. A ³⁄₈″ bolt is too large for a ³⁄₁₆″ nut, so you have to specify the exact size. *Pasting* is different from *gluing* (try pasting two pieces of wood together). A *ball* is different from a *circle; a holler* different from a *scream,* a *castle* from a *palace,* a *joke* from a *quip,* an *argument* from a *spat.* Especially in theoretical explanations, language should be precise. A *democracy* differs from a *republic, fiction* from a *lie,* a *prejudice* from a *bias,* a *native* from a *savage.* Such distinctions may seem petty, but are often necessary.

Use commonly understood words

Slang or specialized vocabularies can cause misunderstandings, too. "My Chinaman has enough clout to get me inside to see the man on five" makes sense to a Chicago Democratic precinct captain, who knows that *Chinaman* is an influential person, *clout* is influence, and the *man on five* is the fellow on the fifth floor of city hall—the mayor. But would a New Yorker understand? One hip dude may say to another, "Those are stone bad scouts"; for both know that *stone* means very, *bad* means good, and *scouts* mean shoes (they lead the way). But how many other people would get the message? Similarly, "contusion of the left femoral muscle" makes sense to a doctor, "catatonic schizophrenia" to a psychiatrist, a " ¾ T-coupling" to a plumber; but none may elicit more than a "huh?" from *you.*

Therefore, your word choice depends on your audience. Slang and technical vocabularies are perfectly appropriate for audiences who understand them. But for those who don't, you'll communicate more clearly and successfully if you choose words and terms that are frequently used and commonly understood by most people. In such circumstances, carefully restrict your use of slang and jargon terms, or avoid them altogether. If you must use strange or technical language or slang terms, clearly define what you mean by them.

Of course, as you strive to be concrete, specific, and accurate, and to avoid slang and technical words, you may feel frustrated by a poor or inadequate vocabulary. A part of the solution to this frustrating problem—one thing that you can do to help eliminate the problem—is to plan carefully what you're going to say. The other part of the solution involves working to improve and enlarge your vocabulary. Each time you encounter an unfamiliar word in your reading, conversations, classes—anywhere—write it down and look it up in a dictionary as soon as possible. Perhaps even carry a small notebook for your new words and definitions. By keeping them in writing, you can review them occasionally and learn to use them in conversations and elsewhere whenever they seem appropriate.

Compare the known with the unknown

You learn about the unknown through comparing or contrasting it with the *familiar*. The more foreign an idea is to your experience, the more you must translate it into one you've lived with for a while. Do you understand *radar*? Compare it to bouncing a ball off a wall. If you know the speed of the ball and the time it takes to hit the wall and return, you can compute the distance between you and the wall. Radar works on the same principle, except that radio waves, traveling at about 186,000 miles per second, replace the ball.

Do you understand an *atomic reaction*? Compare it to throwing one Ping-Pong ball into a large pile of them. As the first ball hits two or three others, they in turn hit still others until eventually all of the balls are bouncing and moving around. Each ball in the first pile might then hit another pile, causing a similar knocking and bouncing of balls until thousands or even millions of piles are set in motion. That's an atomic reaction, except that the piles of balls are nuclei of atoms; and the first ball you throw is a single electron fired from an electron gun.

In each of these examples, we've explained, described, and analyzed an unfamiliar concept (radar waves and atomic reaction) in terms of an everyday, easily understood happening, namely, the movement of a ball. *Comparisons*—or *analogies* as they're sometimes called—can simplify the most complicated ideas. Albert Einstein, the story goes, was once asked to explain his theory of relativity. "Well," he said, "time is relative. If you're sitting on a park bench with a pretty girl for an hour, it seems like a minute. If, on the other hand, you sit on a hot stove for a minute, it seems like an hour." Thus by using a comparison with a touch of humor, Einstein effectively clarified and simply illustrated a small part of his theory—how time *seems* to slow down in relation to the circumstances. Einstein's analogy, like most analogies, both instructs and surprises since, to make its point, it establishes a familiarity or relationship between similar and dissimilar ideas or subjects. It teaches something in a pleasing, painless way.

The following analogy from a student's speech entertainingly explains why people need health insurance:

> Having health insurance is like taking an umbrella with you on a day that is only slightly cloudy. Something uncomfortable might happen in either event [rain or sunshine], but you are taking some protection along to make you feel better while it is happening.

Jerry Baker, the plant expert and author of many books on gardening, spoke before a group of homeowners and compared caring for their lawn with caring for their hair. He personalized his examples and wasn't afraid to joke:

First of all, to have a good head of hair the first thing you have to do is remove dandruff. If it gets in there, you get it out. How do you get it out? You scratch it out. Well, let's scratch out the dandruff from our lawns. . . . Lawn dandruff is grass clippings that were left from last fall. . . . Once that's done [removed], once we've removed dandruff from our head, what do we do? We shampoo, naturally. . . . O.K., what do you use? You use any biodegradable, phosphate-free liquid dish soap, as long as it doesn't have any hand creams in it, and as long as it's green—and that's Palmolive.[4]

3 Small-Group Speaking

Explaining by Using Comparison

As in Small-Group Exercise 2 occurring earlier in this chapter, choose as your subject a task or activity you've done many times. Or select an idea or theory the members of your group may not be familiar with (for example, why the earth's continents are slowly shifting positions). If you're stumped for a subject, simply play around for a while with a comparison like "Marriage is like an automobile wreck," or "School is like the ancient trial by fire," or "Your first date is like a visit to the doctor's office." Here are a few other subjects you might choose to explain through analogy: a car, studying, training a dog or cat, a summer job, parents. Actually, for this exercise you must make *two* choices: a subject and an analogy or comparison you will use to develop it.

Then, in a five-minute speech to the other members of your group, use the analogy or comparison to explain and clarify the task, activity, idea, or theory you've chosen as your subject.

You'll probably need to plan this speech more carefully and fully than your previous speeches. Devising a comparison or an analogy that can extend over an entire speech isn't easy. Usually the first comparison that occurs to you would occur to anyone—it won't be very original. So *experiment*. Fool around with the idea a bit in your mind. Then work out carefully all the various points of similarity between the two things you are comparing. If you find enough, use them to determine the plan or structure of your speech. If you can't find enough similarities to carry you through a five-minute talk, discard your analogy—and/or your subject—and start over.

In summary, you'll achieve *clarity*—one of your most important goals of speaking—only through careful attention to language. Words, your principal tools in speaking, are often too abstract, ambiguous, and obscure. So be specific and concrete, define some terms, avoid some others. Illustrate by telling stories, explain through comparisons. Ensure that the information you give is the same that your audience receives.

Reference Notes

[1]S. I. Hayakawa, *Language in Thought and Action* (New York: Harcourt Brace Jovanovich, Inc., 1964), pp. 30–32.

[2]Philip Hilts, *Behavior Mod* (New York: Harper Magazine Press, 1974).

[3]Philip Hilts, "Behavior Modification: Its Uses and Implications," speech delivered at Wilbur Wright College, Chicago, Illinois, March 5, 1975.

[4]Jerry Baker, "Never Swear at a Gladiola and Other Plant Talk," speech delivered at Wilbur Wright College, Chicago, Illinois, April 17, 1974.

6 Adding Interest and Clarity with Your Voice

If you were asked to describe your best friend's face, would you respond like this:

> "Um . . . umm . . . it's kinda round. Uh . . . and she has kinda . . . um . . . long, blond hair, y' know. Kinda . . . um . . . straight. Umm . . . and she has . . . mmm . . . brown eyes. And . . . uh . . . her nose is sorta small, y' know?"

Perhaps you would provide a clearer and more smoothly flowing description, but many people would probably say something that sounds very much like our example. They would fill all their pauses with vague or meaningless sounds and string all of their statements together with "and's," "but's," "so's," and "y' know's."

Speak the speech,
I pray you,
as I pronounced it to you,
trippingly on the tongue
—Shakespeare, Hamlet

RECOGNIZING PAUSE-FILLERS, VOCAL LAZINESS, AND OTHER CRUTCHES

What creates such pointless mumbo jumbo? We've . . . um . . . got an idea, sorta. People are leaning on verbal crutches. As they stop the normal flow of their speaking to search for words (describing someone's face from memory isn't easy), they often fill the silences with vocalized "noises" to shorten or close the gaps. All of us are confronted with this problem from time to time. The greater your difficulty in expressing yourself—the harder it is to find the "right" word or phrase—the more frequent and prolonged your pauses and fillers. But, generally, when your words feel most comfortable, when your voice sounds most alive, your speech flows more smoothly and you stumble far less. You're involved in your subject and not leaning on crutches. The message, then, clearly is: try to be involved.

1

Discovering for Yourself

Becoming Aware of Pause-Fillers, Vocal Laziness, and Other Crutches

Try being an eavesdropper—a "*sound* sleuth"—today. Listen for all the "um's," "uh's," "y' know's," "kinda's," "doin's," "goin's," "and's," "but's," and "so's" in a conversation between you and another person. Perhaps even try counting these kinds of verbal/vocal crutches. Record your findings in your journal.

As you carry on your sleuthing, however, keep certain cautions in mind: Don't laugh aloud; the person you're talking with may get angry. Remember to listen to the *ideas* amidst all the vocalized garbage; otherwise you may not hear the talker ask you a question. Finally—as a result of this kind of zeroing in on all of the things that can and do go wrong in forming and articulating speech—don't become paranoid or hypersensitive about your *own* vocal goofs and foul-ups and be afraid to open your mouth.

At times, of course, you will have to search for words, but you can do something to eliminate the "um's" and "ah's." When you feel yourself about to say one, pause and take a breath. For a while, you'll sound as if you have emphysema, but stick with it. Gradually you will find less and less need to fill the pauses and gaps in your speech, and your words will come more easily and smoothly.

Our sample description of a friend's face also shows vocal *laziness:* "sorta," "kinda," "y' know." Forming each consonant or vowel in a word or series of words requires a complex movement of many muscles, tissues, and bones. Notice the difference between saying "doin' " and "doing." The final *g* in the latter requires some movement in the back of the mouth—an extra effort—so many people just skip it. "Why strain yourself?" they seem to be asking. "Why bother to 'tune' your

"No, she didn't break anything . . . She's just leaning on her verbal crutches."

vocal mechanism and make it work a little more carefully or precisely when you can mumble and mutter along and hope that your audience will somehow manage to figure out what you're trying to say?" The unfortunate fact, however, is that very often they *don't* figure it out. Your obvious indifference to vocal precision and your dependence on pause-fillers and other verbal/vocal crutches make your line of thought difficult to follow. Rather quickly your hearers tend to equate sloppy speaking with sloppy thinking, and lose interest in you and in what you're trying to say.

2 Discovering for Yourself — Working in Pairs
Putting the "g's" and "ing's" in Your Words

To ensure that you don't drop the "g" in -ING words, read the following list to a friend. Try to pronounce each syllable distinctly, but try also to say the words rapidly. Did your friend have any difficulty understanding you?

sittings	longing	singer
walking	looking	coming
breaking	dancing	talking
thinking	bringing	tongue
settings	hangar	springing
handing	going	seeing
bracing	clinging	reading
joining	meringue	hang[1]

Basically, the "y' know's" and other forms of vocal laziness are as unconsciously habitual as the "um's" and "uh's." But you say them when you can't expand upon or adequately explain your ideas. You can't find the right word or the right details, so almost reflexively you slip in a "y' know?" as if to ask your listeners if they understand you. There's a two-part "remedy" for this. The first part is to be *detailed,* as we've suggested earlier; the other part is to pause and take a breath when you feel a "y' know" coming on. Use this pause to think about what you've just said and what you want to say next. At first, this may give your speaking a slow, even choppy, effect. But as you practice and form a new habit of saying what you mean — *really* mean — you will gradually pick up momentum, and your words will flow more easily and probably more smoothly than before.

The "and's," "but's," and "so's," with which many of us generously sprinkle our speech, are in a slightly different category. These terms are perfectly acceptable and even necessary means of joining words, phrases, and ideas into understandable patterns and relation-ships. But too often we use them merely to fill a pause or string together thoughts which would be more effective if they were separate. At such times, they are forms of vocal—and mental—laziness you should avoid.

DEVELOPING A SOUND VOCAL BASE

You may think that for everyday conversations, leaning on verbal crutches and limping uncertainly along will take you to your communi-cative goals. You may delude yourself into supposing that if you be-come accustomed to and ignore other people's "uh's," "um's," and similar vocal/verbal garbage, they will do likewise for you. Or maybe you hold to a double standard, feeling that in public speaking your listeners' expectations are different and that you should avoid verbal garbage because it will annoy people, but that in person-to-person communica-tion being as careless and slipshod as you wish is perfectly acceptable. Or, again, you may rationalize your "and-uh-y' know" habits by think-ing: "I sound more 'friendly' and 'informal' that way." If so, you're kidding yourself on all counts.

Regardless of the speaking situation and the number of persons involved, if you persist in using pause-fillers and are content to limp along on the entire collection of verbal crutches, canes, and walking sticks, you're almost sure to find the road rocky and unsatisfying. You may—if you're lucky—reach your communicative goal *eventually,* but more often than not the route will be roundabout and frustratingly slow. In both formal and informal circumstances—friendly conversations, in-terviews, small-group interchange, platform speeches, oral reading, announcements over a public-address system—listeners are entitled to expect clear articulation and oral expression uncluttered with "uh's," "um's," "kinda," "y' know's," and similar junk sounds. If they don't demand vocal care and clarity, they at least *appreciate* it. They know that few, if any, speakers can be interesting, clear, and—at one and the same time—verbal stumblebums.

3 Discovering for Yourself—Working in Pairs

Practicing to Overcome Vocal Laziness

Your sloppy articulation will be most apparent when you say similar-sounding words. For this exercise, your small group will be divided into pairs. From List One (below), read aloud to your partner a pair of words; then your partner (whose book should be closed as you read) will repeat the words as he or she heard them. If either of you is unable to distinguish between a pair of words, say them again. When you finish List One, stop, close your book, and switch roles with your partner for List Two.

List One		List Two	
tug	dug	ate	aide
mut	mud	written	ridden
eight	aid	town	down
matter	madder	height	hide
tame	dame	light	lied
bet	bed	heated it	heeded it
bat	bad	tip	dip
atom only	Adam only	sight	side
ties	dies	ought	awed
kit	kid	it is	id is[2]

Developing a solid base of good vocal skills and habits obviously requires regular exercises, which means *continual practice.* But don't be discouraged. As you throw away your crutches in everyday speech, Tiny Tim, your chances of succeeding in the social, scholastic, or business world — or any other world — should improve. The better you speak, the more intelligent you sound. The more intelligent you sound, the better impression you make. The better impression you make, the more likely that people will respect your ideas and abilities. Don't feel you will be — or need be — putting on airs. You'll still be yourself; you'll just speak a bit better.

In fact, what you'll really be is more *adaptable.* You've already taken some long strides toward adaptability. You already speak differently to each audience you face. So in casual conversations — if it suits the situation — you can drop your formality and all the final "g's" you wish. "How ya doin?" may sound fine as a greeting to friends. Now set your goal at adapting your speech to a more formal style when the need arises. The important point is this: When you've trained yourself through careful practice to shape your speech sounds clearly and to maintain a relatively steady and uncluttered flow of words and ideas, you'll be skilled enough and flexible enough to speak appropriately in *any* situation.

Discovering for Yourself — Working in Pairs
Continuing Your Efforts to Overcome Vocal Laziness

When you run together the sounds of your words, clarity can suffer. Have a friend listen as you read aloud the following list of words. Can your friend understand the meaning of each pair of words you read? If not, slow down and pause slightly after each word:

so lame — sole aim
fine Dan — find Ann

are made — arm aid
may cry — make rye

school zone — school's own	have ice — have vice
how sad — house ad	seem eager — seem meager
oh, thunder — oath under	one ear — one near
may drum — made rum	deep plot — deep lot
play nice — plain ice	gray zebras — graze zebras
low fin — loaf in	one sum — once some
so prim — soap rim	sue them — soothe them
gray train — great rain	dry very — drive very
your own — your roan	bar noise — barn noise
big roan — big groan	oh, no — own no
cash owed — cash showed	four thousand — fourth thousand
with ease — with these	pie plant — pipe plant
each ear — each cheer	see much — seem much
look lean — look clean	they do — they'd do
wants Ed — want said	I leave — I'll leave
both ought — both thought	par two — part two[3]

Like a good musician, you should practice to extend the range and potential of your prime communication instrument: your *voice.* Otherwise, vital or fascinating ideas can sound like a great song played off key. We're not saying you can be a disk jockey or television announcer tomorrow. Professionals practice good speaking habits over a period of months or years—and then *continue* to practice. But if you want to sound less like a creaking chair or a dripping faucet, begin tuning your vocal instrument. Start today. Don't procrastinate like those overweight hefties who say they are going to exercise class tomorrow or the day after or next month. Start working out *now.*

. . . AND PUTTING SOME *EXCITEMENT* INTO YOUR VOICE

Some speakers are just plain dull—boring, boring, boring. With them, nothing ever *happens:* no excitement, no change, no variety—nothing. They stand like a murmuring mushroom, mumbling along at the same rate, the same pitch, the same volume, and then fade from the consciousness of their listeners, unheeded and unnoticed. We're not urging you to shout, sing the musical scales, and lead cheers. Simply get *involved* in your subject, push aside your restraints, and let the real, OK you come out.

This alone—just for starters—will do wonders for your voice. This will help you achieve *vocal variety:* variety in the *pitch* of your voice, in your *rate* of speaking, and in levels of *loudness.* Very probably your voice already evidences considerable variety. With friends, you probably raise your voice or speak slowly to emphasize a point. You're loud when happy, quieter when pensive. You speak faster and at a higher pitch when excited. These are normal behaviors—and valuable ASSETS. *So now begin to carry them over into all speaking situations.* With your small in-class group, if you can't already speak naturally and animatedly, you can soon learn to do it. Try to project your voice—make your words carry; vary your "volume" and intensity, your pitch, your rate of speaking. Fight vocal monotony by *feeling* what you're saying. And don't worry about sounding too loud or too enthusiastic or strange at first. That's far, far better than sounding dull.

5 Small-Group Speaking
Working for Vocal Excitement and Variety

With the members of your group as an audience, talk for three minutes about a funny or scary or some other emotion-filled incident from your past. You're the focal figure in the episode, so "throw yourself" into it—get personally and immediately *involved.* Try to be yourself: alive, interesting. Vary your vocal delivery: your speaking rate, your pitch, your loudness-level. In accordance with your remembered feelings, speak rapidly at times—more slowly and deliberately at others. With your feelings given a fairly free rein, your vocal pitch should tend to range from high to low—and back again. Occasionally pause for emphasis. Be animated. *Talk* to people. Stress *feelings* as the incident unfolds. Make your listeners want to listen.

If possible, prior to the presentation, arrange for someone to tape-record your story as you tell it. But tell it to the members of your group; they are your audience. Speak to *them*—not to the microphone.

6 Discovering for Yourself
Listening to Your Voice

If the story—as you told it in Exercise 5—was tape-recorded, arrange to listen to a playback of it in private. If you haven't heard your voice before, you'll probably cringe at the sound of it. A tape recorder can't reproduce the sounds you hear *inside your head* where they resonate more. Nevertheless, the playing of the tape is almost sure to reveal a great deal about your voice—things you didn't notice while you were speaking. Try, first of all, to answer the question: *To what extent do I really sound involved in what I'm saying?* Then, as you play back the tape again, listen for variations in pitch, loudness, and rate of speaking; and try to note the effect that your emotional involvement seemed to have upon each of these voice variables.

To summarize what we've said in this chapter, the greatest musical score sounds awful if played off key with a poorly tuned instrument, with no sense of its rhythm, no variety in volume or in pitch. Your voice is your prime instrument, too. Use it well. Don't just speak words. Get involved. Vary your pitch, your volume, your pace. Don't lean on "um's" and "ah's" and all the other vocal/verbal crutches. Keep your instrument in tune, and practice eliminating the flat notes. And *continue to practice.*

Reference Notes

[1]Words for this exercise were taken from Merritt Jones and Mary Pettas, *Speech Improvement: A Practical Program* (Bradenton, Florida: Communication Research Institute, Inc., 1974), p. 122.

[2]Words for this exercise taken from Jones and Pettas, p. 74.

[3]Exercise adapted from pp. 102–103 in *Voice and Articulation Drillbook,* 2nd Edition by Grant Fairbanks. Copyright © by Grant Fairbanks. Reprinted by permission of Harper & Row, Publishers, Inc.

7 Increasing Interest and Understanding with Your Body

Your voice is your prime and certainly your most particularized communication instrument. But it is only one part of the orchestra. Every movement of your body contributes to the symphony. All your behavior communicates, and everything you do is behavior. You can shut your mouth, but you can't shut off the rest of you. Smile, stare, fold your arms, cross your legs, jerk your head, scratch your nose, bite your nails, hitch up your belt, saunter or swagger or swoon—with each of these behaviors you'll be sending off a message.

Consider the beginning of a male-female relationship. You see someone attractive across the room; you shift your body into first gear—stomach tight, back straight, hand arranging hair, slight smile, sidelong glance—and pause for results. (Positive response—glance returned.) Second gear: second glance, larger smile, attempt at eye contact. (Again, positive response—eye contact and smile reciprocated.) Third gear—and you're rolling across the room, not to begin, but to *continue* the conversation.

So clear and so clearly established over the years are these male-female nonverbal exchanges that one psychiatrist, Albert E. Scheflen, has diagrammed the entire process, from hand-holding through the marriage proposal. He calls it the "quasi-courtship" ritual.[1] Each step furthering the relationship is a subtle series of signals and countersignals to proceed, back off, or preserve *status quo.* If the male, for example, holds the female's hand, will she squeeze his: a signal to intertwine their fingers?

Nonverbal communication, or body language—your winks and waves, your finger and eye movements, your grins and grimaces, your posture, your dress, your scratching and fidgeting, your turns of the head or turns of the hips, your touching other people or keeping your distance—all provide the harmony or counterpoint to your voice.

In this chapter you'll be taking a look at yourself: at your gestures, your facial expressions, and what they communicate. Then you'll take a look at these same behaviors in others, at the messages *they* send back to you as you speak. Finally, you'll take a look at the context in which you look at each other—where you and the people you speak to stand or sit—and how it affects you both and the communication which takes place.

LOOKING AT YOURSELF IN ACTION

Like all languages handed from one generation to the next, but continually in flux, nonverbal communication both changes and remains the same. Even more than words, however, body language evades precise definitions. We might be able to find general agreement about the meanings of thousands of words. Not so with body language. Though many have tried,[2] no one has succeeded in cataloguing the meanings of the furrowed brows, tight lips, yawns, stares, and slumping walks that communicate ideas. Why? Partly because each person's behaviors are distinctive and individualized—the result of upbringing and experiences—and partly because virtually no behavior has meaning outside the context of the situation, its relationship to other movements, and the words it accompanies. A wink can be a sexual come-on or a friendly hello, an "I told you so," or a "He doesn't know what I know." A wave of the hand can be a greeting, a farewell, a "get lost," an emphatic gesture, or a swat at a fly. In fact, we can agree upon the precise significance of very little in the nonverbal realm.

Emblems: Gestures that can play a solo

However, in our culture a few gestures unambiguously communicate a certain message. Two researchers, Paul Ekman and Wallace V. Friesen, call these gestures *emblems.*[3] For example, a handshake, evolved from the practice of knights' grasping each other's sword hands in peace, is a friendly greeting. A nod means yes; a shake of the head means the opposite. Applause signals appreciation or respect. And, of course, there are numerous obscene gestures. You probably don't use these emblems often. Indeed some — like the obscene ones — you may not use at all. You rely on emblems heavily when you don't want to talk or can't easily be heard.

1

Discovering for Yourself

Looking for Emblems

In your journal, list as many emblems as you can. Then, in a class discussion, pool your list with your classmates', and prepare a master list. Now, again in your journal, classify the emblems from the master list into three categories: (1) those you use most frequently, (2) those you sometimes use, and (3) those you never use. Based on what you have recorded, how large is your repertoire of emblems?

Illustrators/Batons: Gestures that help to "harmonize" body and thought

Since emblems have somewhat limited use in communication, the great majority of body movements serve, in Ekman and Friesen's terms, as *illustrators.*[4] Out of the context of what you're saying, they can't convey meanings with any reliability; but in conjunction with your words, they emphasize, reinforce, and clarify ideas. The largest proportion of your illustrator gestures create *emphasis.* You may pump your arms or slam your fist into your palm to make a point, wave your hands in a circle as you speak rapidly, or snap your wrist downward with index finger extended as you say, "Yes, I agree." Ekman and Friesen call these idiosyncratic gestures *batons.* No two people twirl and wave the same collection.

EMBLEMS: Gestures that can "play a solo"

ILLUSTRATOR/BATONS: Gestures that "harmonize" body and thought . . . and, always, facial expressions that can supply the "mood music"

You also use illustrator gestures frequently to *reinforce* and *clarify* ideas. You can point to an object or person you're discussing. You can describe the size of the fish that got away by spreading your hands four feet apart, or indicate the height of the fellow you met yesterday by holding your hand two feet above your head. Descriptively, you can show the shape of a rectangle by sketching an imaginary picture in the air with your index finger, or suggest the shape of a spiral staircase by moving your hand downward in a circular motion. You can imitate movement by pointing two fingers downward and swinging them forward like the legs of a person walking. And, finally, you can show the direction of your thoughts by moving your hands circularly as you search for an idea, or extending your left hand palm up as you mention one side of an issue ("on the one hand"), then switching to your right as you mention the other.

The trouble is, it's not easy to practice any of these movements. They should be natural and spontaneous accompaniments to your efforts as a confident communicator. There are a few things you can do, however, to make use of all your communication instruments, to bring your voice and body into harmony. First, you can try to convince yourself prior to speaking that you won't allow nervousness or inhibitions to restrict your natural movements. Remember, you're OK. You can also make an effort to become more aware of these bodily behaviors. Notice the various ways in which you and others complement speech with nonverbal messages. Then, as you prepare the wording of the speeches you will present in class, think also of some of the bodily gestures and expressions which might enrich and enhance your words. If you have given thought to these matters before your speeches, you will find that gradually they will become a useful and natural part of your behavior.

2 Small-Group Activity
Testing How Body Movements Reinforce Clarity

Outside of class, draw some geometric figures on a sheet of paper. Here's an example:

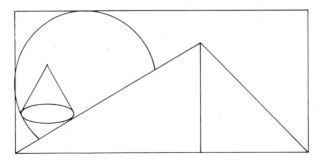

Then bring your drawing to class and give it to someone in your group, making sure that no one else sees it. After the person who has your drawing or diagram has had a chance to study it for a few minutes, he or she should attempt to describe orally (without using body or hand movements) the figures and their positioning. Meanwhile, another member of the group—following the first "describer's" instructions—should try to draw the figures on the chalkboard. No one may ask or respond to questions while the exercise is in progress. Afterwards, for the benefit of the group as a whole, compare the original sketch with the drawing on the chalkboard.

Now, using another student's sketch, let two other group members repeat the same procedure. This time, however, the one giving the instructions is allowed to use hand and body movements. Are the results any better? Draw some conclusions about the values or advantages of clarifying and reinforcing oral/verbal communication with nonverbal communication. Discuss some of the implications for using "visual" aids in small-group presentations and in public speaking.

As a speaker, you also communicate attitudes and feelings nonverbally. You can't mask nervousness or discomfort. However, with your classmates' help, you can also experiment with finding the position and posture that looks and feels best when you speak.

3 Whole-Class Speaking

Testing Whether You Seem Natural and Relaxed Before an Audience

Take a look at yourself as an audience sees you. With the videotape machine on, go to the front of the room and talk for a minute about whatever you choose. Don't worry about looking foolish. Everyone will look a bit foolish. This may be your first dive into public speaking. If you belly-flop, you'll just continue springing off the board until you get used to the water. Cicero probably felt uncomfortable for a while, too. We know that we did (and still do occasionally).

After everyone has had a turn to talk, replay the tape and discuss each person's posture and mannerisms. Which postures and mannerisms seemed to communicate the greatest sense of confidence and well-being? Offer each other suggestions for improvement and change. Then, if time allows, repeat the exercise and try to make some of the suggested improvements.

Your face supplies the "mood music"

After you check your physical appearance in the mirror before traveling to class, you may not see yourself again for several hours. But others see your face continually. Even before you speak—or even if you don't speak at all—your face is a beacon flashing information on your moods and thoughts, your health and physical condition. A friend's inquiry, "What's wrong?" may not be in response to an evil green disease creeping up your neck. It may be just concern over the bags under your eyes or the furrow in your brow. You may not be aware that your all-night study session has ravaged your face, but others will see it.

Silence more musical than any song.
—Christina Georgiana Rosetti,
"Rest"

Whenever you speak—*while* you're speaking—your face tells a story, too. If you don't feel excited or strongly about what you're saying, your face will betray your apathy. As you stand before your listeners, they will see you as a granite-faced sailor with a message to match—expressionless, emotionless, dead. So, in the parlance of the sea, "Look *alive!*" Your face may not launch a thousand ships, but what it has to say about you and your message and how you feel about both can help you stay afloat before an audience. Up anchor—set bravely, boldly out to sea. Let go a bit, forget about making a fool of yourself, and make somebody watch you instead. A lively, emotionally honest face—like a compass—charts the course of your ideas, your beliefs, your convictions, your feelings, and helps your listeners read the direction in which you and your message are heading. If you are saying something *vital* and *meaningful* to *you,* your face will be saying something vital and meaningful to your audience—and will say it with smiles, winks, grimaces, and grins. You won't have to force or fake these behaviors; they'll come spontaneously and naturally.

READING FEEDBACK

Speakers speak and listeners listen. But speakers also listen, and listeners speak, too—verbally after your presentation, and silently during it. If you watch and respond to their responses while you speak, you've gained valuable data for mid-course or mid-message adjustments. This is the positive side of the guess-and-look strategy we described in the very early pages of this book. The information which listeners convey about your message is generally called *feedback,* and reading feedback is like reading a weather report. Stormy responses warn you to change directions and follow alternate routes or shorten the journey. Sunny smiles and unclouded understanding tell you to roll right on through to the destination you mapped out originally.

Look for the signals. Are your hearers nodding their heads to agree with and encourage you, or nodding off to sleep? Are they smiling with enjoyment at your message, or smiling at a daydream? Are they leaning forward with interest or leaning on their elbows with boredom?

 Whole-Class Exercise

Role-Playing and Interpreting Nonverbal Feedback of Emotions

Your instructor will deal you three cards from a double deck. Each card represents an emotion:

ace	= anxiety	eight	= sexual love
two	= hatred	nine	= sadness
three	= mild dislike	ten	= happiness
four	= fear	jack	= indifference
five	= nervousness	queen	= boredom
six	= warmth	king	= frustration
seven	= love		

One member of the class — a volunteer — will place one card down on the instructor's desk and portray for the whole class the emotion the card represents. The portrayer may use no spoken words — only nonverbal attitudes, gestures, and other "silent" behaviors. If you think the emotion thus portrayed corresponds to a card you hold, place it face down on your desk. Your instructor will compare all of the face-down cards with the volunteer's card. If they match, your instructor will remove them, leaving those players who have "matched" successfully with only two cards. The instructor will give an additional card to those who "mismatched." Then the volunteer will leave the original card with the instructor and call on another person to portray an emotion. That person, like the first, will place one of his or her cards face down on the instructor's desk and attempt to portray the emotion designated by the card. The procedure, as outlined, continues until one of the players has no cards. That person is the winner.

In interpreting nonverbal feedback, of course, you won't find any sheet music with all the body-language notes already recorded, but you can begin to compose your own overture. Let's continue the investigation.

5 Whole-Class Exercise
Role-Playing and Interpreting Nonverbal Feedback of Ideas

Look at the twenty messages listed on page 94, and then add any others you think an audience might typically express nonverbally. Then join your classmates in forming a circle. Three or four of you will select a message from the list to role-play while the other members of the class observe. In presenting the message, use only nonverbal behaviors and cues—no spoken words. Immediately following the performance, the observers will discuss how effectively the role-players have communicated their message, the specific nonverbal behaviors which seemed to be most effective and those that were less so, and whether the message could have been construed to mean something other than the one the role-players intended. For example, suppose the role-players decide to convey "I don't understand." One person might shake his head; another might frown, rub her brow, scratch her head, etc. From these behaviors, can you "read" the right message, or might you just as easily interpret them to mean "I disagree completely," or "That's impossible"?

Repeat this procedure until all members of the class have had an opportunity to participate in the nonverbal communication of one of the messages on this list:

Feedback Message Suggestions

1. I can't hear clearly.
2. I disagree completely.
3. I don't understand.
4. Not this again—we heard it before.
5. This is really funny.
6. I don't believe one word of that.
7. That's impossible.
8. I know a better example than that.
9. I'm sleepy.
10. Now where are we?
11. I'd like to help out.
12. I want to hear more about this.
13. It's late, and class is almost over.
14. I'm distracted by something happening outside.
15. My chair isn't comfortable, and I have sat too long.
16. That's amazing.
17. I can't see what you are doing.
18. I have to prepare a lesson for my next class.
19. I am really curious about that.
20. I have a question.

In follow-up discussions with members of the class, consider the resemblances among the nonverbal behaviors in the role-played messages and also how the behaviors differed. Keep in mind, of course, that outside the context of reacting to a particular speech, these nonverbal messages can't be a completely accurate barometer. Nevertheless, you should become accustomed to looking for them.

6 Whole-Class Exercise
Watching and Interpreting Actual Feedback

At a time when your instructor is talking, one person will be videotaping the entire class, panning across the room. Try to be yourself and ignore the camera. Afterwards, replay the tape—complete with the instructor's voice on the sound track—and stop whenever you wish to note individual listener reactions. Speculate about what motivated each one. Is a particular response-behavior directly related to the instructor's message? Can it be accurately "read" by the speaker?

As you observe and attempt to interpret the taped behavior, remember that watching yourself probably causes as much pain as listening to yourself. Try not to be argumentative and defensive when others point to your nonverbal feedback behaviors. Refute or attempt to correct other people's interpretations only when you genuinely disagree, not merely to protect yourself from criticism or embarrassment. Don't forget that you're OK. Likewise, your instructor is OK and wants to know how people respond to his or her communicative efforts. Every good speaker does.

Give me where to stand,
and I will move the earth.
— Archimedes Pappus,
Collectio, Book VIII

ADJUSTING TO SPACE AS A NONVERBAL FACTOR IN SPEECH COMMUNICATION

Another aspect of nonverbal communication concerns the relative position (physical and psychological distance) between speaker and listeners. People depend on a combination of senses—especially sound and sight—to interpret messages. They can hear more clearly when they can see a speaker; and, as we've emphasized, they can certainly find a good many nonverbal message clues by looking at a speaker's face. The size of an audience and its position in relation to the speaker can change the whole "feel" and meaning of a speech for everyone involved. Winston Churchill preferred that the House of Commons' chambers seem claustrophobic, having fewer chairs than members. He reasoned that the overflow crowds would create an atmosphere of urgency in the sessions during World War II. Perhaps. But people standing on each other's bunions or blocking their view of the speaker can create some difficult communication circumstances, too.

Where do you stand—or sit?

In simplest terms, the best place to stand or sit is wherever you can feel closest to what's going on *communicatively*—the position or location where you can best hear the oral/verbal elements of a message and where you can most easily and clearly perceive the nonverbal elements. This is true, of course, whether you find yourself in the role of listener *or* speaker. (Actually, you're both—for much of the time.) This spatial or distance factor is of considerable importance in all types of communicative situations—person-to-person, small-group, or public— because the larger the number of speakers/listeners, the larger the space must be. In public settings, however, the space/distance factor is a primary concern. Attending formal lectures, we've seen speakers stand behind or lean on the lectern, walk freely across a stage, sit on a chair, or even on the edge of the stage. We've seen them stand in the middle of the stage or get as near to the audience as possible. In our culture, *public distance*—where personal intimacy diminishes—begins at approximately twenty-five feet and extends back as far as eyesight and sound can reach. The greater the distance, the more pronounced the loss of personal contact.

In small groups, public distance is less likely to be a problem, but where you stand or sit in relation to each other helps or hinders your interaction and affects your feelings about it. The better you can see each other, the more you can read each other's body language and feedback. The less isolated you feel physically, the greater your potential involvement.

7 Small-Group Speaking

Experimenting with Speaking and Listening Positions

Prepare a three-minute speech on any one of the following "wise sayings":

1. Life begins at forty.
2. Haste makes waste.
3. Too many cooks spoil the broth.
4. Children should be seen and not heard.
5. Charity begins at home.
6. One rotten apple spoils the whole barrel.
7. A woman's place is in the home.
8. A bird in the hand is worth two in the bush.
9. Into each life a little rain must fall.
10. You win some and you lose some.

Don't be deadly serious with your topic. Have some fun with it. Just prior to your speech, your audience—the members of your group—will decide under what conditions you should deliver it. They may specify one of the following:

a. You and the entire group standing face to face.

b. You and the entire group sitting on the floor face to face.

c. You standing before the other members of the group as they sit in two straight rows, double-file fashion, with one person behind another.

d. You standing before the other members of the group as they sit side by side.

e. You and the entire group sitting on the floor, with you in the center of a circle.

f. You in any of the above situations, but speaking to two groups or to the entire class.

Furthermore, the members of your group may decide to devise some other physical barriers, spatial/distance variations, or distractions, depending on how devilish they feel. They shouldn't, however, create a situation where speaking is impossible.

Repeat this exercise until everyone has spoken and each member of the group has experienced each physical arrangement, either as a speaker or listener. Afterward, discuss your observations and feelings with the other members of your group. Under what conditions as speaker or listener could you see most, feel most at ease, interact most easily, feel most like equals in the communication transaction? Which conditions seemed to create the most opportunities for internal or external distractions? Record your observations in your journal.

In summary, though your nonverbal communication and your verbal/oral communication may serve independently of or as a substitute for each other, more frequently you use them *in combination,* clarifying, amplifying, modifying, or otherwise influencing the message you send and receive. Probably, it is most useful to think of them—for all practical intents and purposes—as being inseparable, as mutually reinforcing, and as an indispensable aid in every situation where you communicate. Use *actions* as well as *words* to get your messages across. As we've seen, you can reinforce, emphasize, and clarify a remark with hand and body movements, with an animated face, and by maintaining a comfortable, natural posture and a seeable/hearable position in relation to your audience. Further, you can become more aware of and adjust to the nonverbal feedback your listeners send you, especially in physical circumstances that maximize potential interaction. So as you speak, get involved, and *orchestrate your body with your mind and voice.* Bring the entire orchestra together. Make sure all of the "instruments" are playing in harmony—and in tune.

Reference Notes

[1]Albert E. Scheflen, "Quasi-Courtship Behavior in Psychotherapy," *Psychiatry,* Vol. 28, 1965.

[2]See, for example, the following excellent works: Ray L. Birdwhistell, *Kinesics and Context* (Philadelphia: University of Pennsylvania Press, 1970); Edward Twitchell Hall, *The Silent Language* (New York: Doubleday, Inc., 1959); Erving Goffman, *Relations in Public: Microstudies of the Public Order* (New York: Basic Books, Inc., 1971); and Albert E. Scheflen, *Body Language and the Social Order: Communication as Behavior Control* (Englewood Cliffs, New Jersey: Prentice-Hall, Inc., 1972).

[3]Paul Ekman and Wallace V. Friesen, "Hand Movements," *The Journal of Communication,* Vol. 22 (December 1972), pp. 357–58.

[4]Ibid., pp. 358–61.

8 Making a Useful Point Through Anecdotes

Let's return to storytelling again. Originally, in Chapter 4, we opened this unit of the book by urging you to tell stories. We wanted you to start speaking from your own experience. We wanted to get you speaking extemporaneously, get you generating details, and get you concerned about being *entertaining* and *clear*—the first two goals of speaking. Now we want you to tell stories for an additional reason: The best stories also shape their details, concreteness, vivid language, and presentation around a *central idea* or *thesis.* In the stories we want you to tell now, everything should add up to a clearly identifiable *point* which teaches or reminds your listeners about some small or large truth. Whether in a short speech or a long one, this thesis or point helps make your story relevant, significant, and *useful to your listeners*—the third goal of speaking. The best stories—the kind we'd like you to begin working into your speeches now—can serve as more than entertaining decoration. *They can also serve as vehicles to introduce, illustrate, and/or develop your ideas.*

MAKING A POINT WITH YOUR STORY

The point of a story is not its subject. The subject is what the story is about: your emergency appendectomy, your experience as a three-year-old lost in a big department store, your parents' escape from the Nazis in 1941. The *point* or thesis of a story, on the other hand, is what the story means or can be interpreted to mean: *the central idea or thought that the story presents or demonstrates.* The point of a story about an emergency appendectomy might be that we are always terribly vulnerable to the physical demands of our bodies; the point of a story about being lost in a department store might be that to a small child the world is large, alien, and sometimes hostile; the point of a story about escaping from the Nazis in 1941 might be that even in a threatening and hostile world, good people will risk their lives and property to help others.

Shaping a story around a point can also be useful to you in selecting the details to include. In the story about your appendectomy, you could select details which contrast the ordinary with the extraordinary: the numbing details of a typical day against the sharp pain reminding you of your body's vulnerability. You'd include some details, omit others. You wouldn't necessarily describe the doctor's careful examination of your achy abdomen. Instead, you might focus on the incongruity of each moment: starting out for school and ending up in the hospital, expecting to see friends in the cafeteria and finding them later at your bedside, feeling the tearing pain in your side before the operation and the dull ache afterward.

Unfortunately, although a clearly identified thesis helps you choose the appropriate story with appropriate details, unless you state your thesis simply and succinctly, many listeners may hear only the details and miss the point, especially a more subtle point. As we said in Chapter 3, listeners at best retain only half of what you say. Therefore, you can aid their understanding by underlining your story's point or thesis in a concise, clearly worded sentence or two. This short announcement of the point is called your *thesis statement.* It can come either at the beginning, to alert listeners to the significance of what they'll hear; or at the end, to explain the significance of what they've just heard; or probably at both the beginning and at the end and maybe in the middle, too.[1] Each time you may want to restate it a bit differently because slight variations lend interest. The main thing is to repeat your thesis statement often enough so your listeners will be sure to understand it.

Using the anecdote to introduce a point

Frequently, as a speaker you can choose to make a point with an *anecdote,* an interesting narrative that can be amusing, serious, or even shocking. Quite often, you will find that the best anecdotes probably come from your own experience; but you can draw effective ones from the experiences of others, too. Let's examine several examples from *outside* a speaker's experience. In the first example, the story grabs and focuses the listeners' attention on the subject of the speech ("moral rules") and lays the groundwork for the thesis statement to follow. C. S. Lewis, the late British novelist, essayist, and philosopher who often lectured over the radio about religion and ethics, began one broadcast like this:

<table>
<tr><td>Anecdote to
introduce subject</td><td>There is a story about a schoolboy who was asked what he thought God was like. He replied that as far as he could make out, God was "The sort of person who is always snooping round to see if anyone is enjoying himself and then trying to stop it."[1]</td></tr>
</table>

Lewis then tied this anecdote to his real subject — morality — and went on to make his point by developing a comparison between human actions and a machine. His last two sentences establish his thesis:

<table>
<tr><td>Subject</td><td>And I am afraid that is the sort of idea the word Morality raises in a good many people's minds: something that interferes, something that stops you having a good time.</td></tr>
<tr><td>Point embodied in
thesis statement</td><td>*In reality, moral rules are directions for running the human machine. Every moral rule is there to prevent a breakdown, or a strain, or a friction, in the running of that machine.*[2] [Italics ours]</td></tr>
</table>

In a second example, Dr. Allen Hynek, former Chairperson of Northwestern University's Astronomy Department and consultant to the Air Force on Unidentified Flying Objects, spoke on the subject of U.F.O.'s. He introduced his point — the scientific community's inability to explain U.F.O.'s — with this anecdote, and then moved right to his thesis statement — the last two sentences:

<table>
<tr><td>Anecdote</td><td>It reminds me a little bit of the story of the little girl who was asked in an examination, "What are rabies and</td></tr>
</table>

what can be done about them?'' And she wrote, "Rabies are Jewish priests and nothing can be done about them.''

And most of my colleagues feel the same way about U.F.O.'s. They don't know what they are, but they're quite sure nothing can be done about them.[3] [*Italics ours*]

Using the anecdote to develop or illustrate a point

In each of the preceding examples, the anecdote—occurring either at the very beginning of the speech or very soon thereafter—served to introduce the speaker's subject, and the speaker then drew a relationship between the subject and the anecdote's point. Sometimes the connection between the anecdote and the point of the speech is so clear and immediately relevant that it can stand alone, requiring no explanation by the speaker. Such anecdotes, especially when you derive them from your own experience with the subject, can serve as powerful illustrations of your point.

For example, S. David Dinwoodie, who as a college student had spent a summer in the ghetto of East Harlem, New York, could speak firsthand about what he called "conditions that work to degrade and defeat its people to an extent that is hard to imagine.'' In a speech at Cornell University, he spoke on the subject of his experience in the ghetto. To illustrate his point—the lovelessness of the ghetto is a destructive social force—he described a visit to one home, a three-room apartment occupied by two mothers and eight children:

Anecdote

> I had been exchanging pleasantries with the mothers and playing and joking with the kids for about only ten minutes, when little Mary, a three-year-old with the kind of arresting beauty that makes you wish you were a poet, boosted herself up onto the sofa where I was sitting, crawled into my lap, planted her feet flat on my legs and stood up, bringing her face on a level with mine. She raised her arms and entwined her hands about the back of my neck, gazing into my eyes through long dark lashes with a look that I can describe only as rapt adoration. She stood like that for at least a minute and then, drawing her face close to mine, she kissed me on the cheek.[4]

Dinwoodie then described his reaction to this spontaneous display of affection, and this description led naturally into his *thesis statement* in the last two sentences:

> I was overwhelmed—of course—but as I realized only at the end of the summer, after living for two months with many kids who have no permanent fathers, the same thing would happen to any male who gave East Harlem

kids his attention and affection. *To Mary and the many
like her, East Harlem bequeaths a heritage of lovelessness. Such lovelessness is tragic because it warps lives;
and as intelligent, sensitive people we can no more ignore the social tragedy of East Harlem than we can ignore the social problems of polio and economic reces-
sion.*[5] [*Italics ours*]

We'll include one more example which, though long, is rich in
broad humor, vivid metaphors, precise description, and attention to
detail—and also makes a serious point. Dr. Daniel Fader, author and
Professor of English at the University of Michigan, spoke to an audience
of both teachers and college students on the subject of the problems of
teaching reading in inner-city schools. Dr. Fader, who has spent years
directing and evaluating such programs, argued the point that such
schools encourage students not to get involved in their education, and
even encourage them to hide what they already know.

To illustrate this point, he described in detail one of his visits to a
large urban junior-high school. In the back of the classroom for non-
college bound or "terminal" ninth-grade students, he sat watching a
student he would later come to know as Wentworth. Notice that Dr.
Fader presents a succession of incidents, really, each with an implied
point and each a part of the big story. Basically, his progression is
chronological, describing the events in the order in which they occurred. "Picture the scene," he said:

First incident: Setting
the scene

The seats are slightly skewed away from the teacher so that she can see only his [Wentworth's] left front.
From that view, he's apparently dead (this is the "terminal" program). But from the right rear which I can see,
which she cannot see because the rows are slightly
skewed away from her, he is reading—slowly—a car
magazine. He's got it next to him on the seat, and he is
slowly turning the pages. . . . He has read that magazine, or at least he has turned the pages slowly, for an
uninterrupted thirty minutes—when a dreadful thing
happens. Every one of you who has ever been in a classroom—which means every one of you—will know how
bad this is.

Second incident:
Continuation of the
scene setting

There are right-answer machines in the class.
They may look like kids, but they're really not kids. Underneath a thin covering of skin is a fair number of cogs
and wheels that the teacher oils and greases before a visitor comes. A shot of oil in one ear, turn the arms a cou-
ple of times, place them strategically around the class—
three of them—and then ask questions of them so that
the visitor will believe there are at least some kids in the

class who do some work. It is called the "right-answer machine syndrome" and it is universal throughout the Western world.

Third incident:
Beginning the action
One of the right-answer machines is sitting next to Wentworth. The teacher directs a question at that machine. . . . She means to look at the right-answer machine, but she really *looks* as though she's looking at Wentworth. Which wouldn't normally have mattered — as Wentworth told me later, he ain't looked up in no English class in nine years. Tragically, at just that point in his life, Wentworth decides to look through the window to see if the world is still there, if it's worth trying to survive the next fifteen minutes.

He couldn't believe it, he told me later. There she was, looking at him. *She* knew better than to look at him. She knew he didn't have no answers. But *she* didn't know she was looking at him; *she* thought she was looking at the kid next to him. Wentworth was sure he had been called upon. Which was purely amazing, since he couldn't remember *ever* having been called upon before in an English class. Wentworth knew there was a visitor somewhere behind him. All he wanted to do was to give some kind of answer because he's a decent kid. He doesn't want the class to fall to pieces. Next to him, the right-answer machine is trying to crank up, but you must remember that in a bottom ninth-grade English class the quality of right-answer machines leaves a lot to be desired. The kid was still trying to get something up when Wentworth answered.

To this day, *he* can't remember what he said. *I* can't remember what he said. *She* can't remember what he said. All we all knew was that it was wrong, and there was a visitor in the class. We shuddered collectively as a class. The right-answer machine, moved by our tremor, groaned and moaned and something came up and out. The class stumbled to its conclusion.

Explanation of the
next incident
If you have ever been a visitor or have ever been visited (and who has not?), you know that that was not the end of the incident. When such a thing has happened in your class, you *explain* to the visitor why it happened. There is *no way* for a visitor to get out of your class without being *explained* to. Your honor as a teacher rides upon that explanation.

. . . .

Fourth incident
. . . Remember, I was sitting on the door wall. She was sitting on the window wall. She was *at least* twenty years my senior — but I mean *at least*. THE BELL RANG.

104 *Making a Useful Point Through Anecdotes*

And the miracle of the Transubstantiation of the Mass was enacted in front of my eyes. Without moving a muscle, she was transubstantiated to the doorway. . . . Even as her cells were still regrouping, she was already talking: *"Doctor Fader!"* I was stuck. Her reformed mass blocked the doorway. There was *no way out.* "Doctor Fader (*Doctor* is used like a club in the schools), that boy," she said, pointing to his now empty seat, " . . . he's so frustrated. He's in the ninth grade and can't read a lick!"

I had just watched him, for 39.7 minutes out of 40, going slowly through a car magazine. I stepped out into the very wide hall of this old-fashioned school. . . . All the way across the hall, opposite the classroom door, Wentworth was standing with friends against the wall. Because he didn't know that I was looking at him, he didn't hide his eyes. And his eyes were *bright.* Can you have bright eyes, be in the ninth grade, go slowly through a car magazine written in the only language you've ever known, and not be able to read? You can't do it. It's not possible. It takes an act of concentrated genius, which is beyond most human beings even to approximate.

Fifth incident

I pursued Wentworth for three whole days: Wednesday, Thursday, and Friday. Everywhere he went, I went. He went to the ball field, I went to the ball field. He ate lunch, I ate lunch. He went to the john, I went to the john. Wherever he was, there I was, asking him the same question. I'm too big for a junior high school kid to belt out. Either you put your gang on me, or you got to talk to me. Finally he talked to his gang. Cleo, his gang leader, gave him permission to talk to me; I paid each kid a quarter—cost me a buck and a quarter—and I got the information.

Concluding incident, in which the point is implied

The information was very clear. "Sure," he said, "I can read." We were standing on Tenth Street, right across from the school. "Sure, I can read," he said. "I've been able to read ever since I can remember, but I ain't never gonna let *them* know about it." He was pointing at the school. "Cause iffen I do, I'm gonna have to read all that crap that they've got."[6]

1 Small-Group Speaking

Telling an Anecdote to Make a Point

Prepare a five-minute speech for your small group about an experience that taught you a lesson—a story with a point. You need not write out your entire speech word-for-word, but do *write out your point as a thesis state-*

ment, and decide when in your speech or how often you will say the thesis statement.

After you have given your speech, each member of your group will write down on a piece of paper a restatement of your point and give the paper to you. This will enable you to check whether your point was clear to everyone. After you have collected the slips of paper from your classmates, the instructor will call on three or four of them to state the point *orally.* In this oral interchange, you will learn how others heard and interpreted the point of the story and if they heard or interpreted it differently. Moreover, from this interchange you should receive some suggestions as to how you might improve the presentation of your point.

CREATING TENSION TO KEEP THE THOUGHT TRAIN RUNNING

Your own experiences in themselves, of course, won't guarantee that you have powerful or even interesting speech material. Every anecdote worth telling requires not only a careful choice of words and details, but also the element of *tension:* an opposition of moods, feelings, situations, or events within the story. In the examples of anecdotes we've cited, the speakers establish a pattern which presents the details in surprising or unexpected ways. These storytelling speakers create suspense; they create irony; they create sudden twists and turns of events or moods. Dinwoodie, for instance, jokes casually, then finds a three-year-old girl staring seriously and lovingly into his eyes. Fader sees Wentworth secretly reading a magazine in a class for non-readers; the teacher calls on a "right-answer machine," but Wentworth answers instead; Fader wants to follow Wentworth, but the teacher wants to follow Fader; Wentworth admits he can read; but, for purposes of "self-protection," he won't read. Good speakers thus create tension and, hence, interest.

As you look for and plan the telling of an anecdote, think in terms of the slightly offbeat, the unusual, the humorous—the story where the unexpected bounces off the expected and reverberates. Here's one story that exemplifies this offbeat quality. It deals with the caliber of criticism Chicago's WBBM-TV news reporter Walter Jacobson claims he encounters in his job. As he told it, he had just completed a commentary on the debate in the Illinois legislature over the Equal Rights Amendment:

Introductory
explanation
        I had been critical in my remarks of a member of the House of Representatives who had proclaimed in

debate that the Equal Rights Amendment was being supported by "bra-less, brainless broads" who have nothing better to do than bother the state legislators. I as much as said that the guy [the legislator] was a jerk. The first caller was a woman who insisted that I was a communist because I was being critical of an elected state official. She said the member of the House of Representatives was absolutely right. And further, she hollered at me over the telephone, the reason that some women are bra-less is that bras are too expensive. And the reason for that is that there's too much welfare, and *that* is a communist plot. She said the only way to afford a bra is buy one on sale, and by the time any decent person can get to a sale the only things left are the forty-eights anyway.[7]

Incident which illustrates point

Arrangement of unexpected details

Jacobson's pattern of ordering the incident's details holds the listeners in suspense because they can't predict the outcome. A woman complains about the communists when her real gripe is over the price of brassieres: the tension of opposing situations.

COUPLING ANECDOTES TO DEVELOP
A LONGER TRAIN OF THOUGHT

Anecdotes aren't just the stuff of *short* speeches. Each story can form a link in a long chain of ideas which together become a quite fully developed or "full-length" informative or persuasive speech. In such a speech, each individual story has its own point. And each of these points, when added to the others, contributes to the overall point and thought-impact of the message. For our final example, we'll cite a student's talk. His subject was his own experience with mental illness. His point was that "abnormal" behavior can seem quite normal if you understand the conditions which caused it. Throughout his speech, he told little stories from his own experience, each one making a point, then leading into the next story. He flavored his narrative with occasional metaphors and created tension by contrasting his own ideas about abnormal behavior with the usual or accepted ideas; he presented further contrast between his reactions and his mother's, between his former state of mind and his present. Although the student's speech lacks some of the precision and polish of the previous examples we quoted from professional or experienced communicators, it contains many virtues, and it is a good example of a speech drawn from several stories linked together to make an overall point.

TITLE: "Coping"

SPEAKER: Franklin E. Jones

SUBJECT: Mental Illness.

PRINCIPAL POINT: Behavior which departs from the usual standard of normalcy, if seen in light of the conditions which caused it, can be better understood and therefore will seem less abnormal.

Introduction	I'd like to say first that when I was in the army, I was a neuro-psychiatric aide in a mental hospital. I worked for two years at that. I'd like to talk about what
Point embodied in thesis statement	mental illness is, perhaps what you think it is. *Many people sort of think of it as a disease, as a creature, as a monster. . . . I'm saying that it's normal, even though it seems abnormal to us.* [*Italics ours*]
First anecdote (hypothetical)	For example, if somebody is locked in a room as a small child for, say, a year, six months, or five years, and they grow up and they have trouble coping in elevators, somebody can term that claustrophobia. We'd say, "Now, that's not normal. It's not normal for people to react that way." But it's perfectly normal for the person who was locked in the closet to grow up and say, "Wow, I'm afraid to be in close places." So we have a cause and an effect. I'm not saying it's that simple. I just gave that as an example.
Second anecdote (personal experience)	People react in different ways to different things. If you look at a rat, most people would go "Aaaaah! It's a rat." Or an insect—though my father, I remember, used to play with spiders. He was a strange guy. *(Laughs.)* I'd watch him; and when I was a little kid, I'd let spiders crawl on me. I was never frightened—until I picked up a black widow. It didn't bite me. But my mother reacted to the experience by screaming, and then cutting, slicing at it with a butcher knife. That stopped me from playing with spiders because I had discovered that there were bad spiders.
Summary of first two anecdotes	But, anyway, what's normal when you look at each other? There's a statistical example: what the majority react to. If fifty million people drink tea at three o'clock on Sunday and one person doesn't, then that person is
Restatement of point—thesis statement	not normal, in a sense. *But normal, as far as I am thinking about it, is relative to the person, and different for each person's reality.* [*Italics ours*]
Third anecdote (personal experience)	I was a mental patient, ironically, in a hospital two years ago. I had what's called a nervous breakdown. And

"He says he's coupling anecdotes to develop a longer train of thought."

I was hospitalized only for six weeks. But what led up to that was extreme depression. I was walking under water all the time. I was really down. And because, partly, I'd had a recent divorce, I'd been in court for three days in a trial over my children. I lost them. It was really a trauma. . . . But that caused me to be depressed. I drank a lot—I was drinking a lot of alcohol, smoking a lot of grass. I was anesthetizing myself, freezing myself. But I wasn't aware of it.

There is a kind of Spartan ethic in this country that people, especially males, have a kind of masculinity concept of themselves. And you have to be strong. You can't let yourself cry. You can't show emotion because that's not masculine. And this Spartan ethic puts a lot of guys in the hospital. Even myself—I don't go to a doctor when

I get sick. You know, I almost have to be down on my back before I admit that something is wrong with me. To be sick is to be weak. So, it causes a lot of guys to die in this country.

The drinking kind of numbs your emotions, you know. But it just deepened a kind of general depression. I had headaches for, like, eight months. I was really down. But I pretended nothing was wrong. And I'd go to classes. I'd read whole books, and I wouldn't know what they meant. But I'd go through the motions of reading them very carefully. And then I'd get to class, and I'd sit there and listen, but nothing was coming in. I was like a zombie.

I'd go to the locker, and I'd open the door, and I'd say, "Raise your right hand. Put your books up there." And I'd put my books up there, and "Now stand straight and walk," and I'd go through the motions like that until, finally, I went home one night and had this revelation: "I have got to go to the hospital." I thought, "This is absurd. I don't know where I am." And I went in the hospital, voluntarily. They gave me tranquilizers and time. And they alleviated the emotional problem. But for me, the reason was because I kept things inside of me. And I

Point of
third anecdote

learned through hospitalization and talking to the doctor that *one is not so weak that they have to be so strong,* that you can learn to show your emotions. But first you've got to know what they are. You've got to be honest with what you're feeling.

Fourth anecdote
(shows speaker's
personal application
of main point)

Recently I walked into my girl friend's house. And her ex-husband is sitting there drinking out of my cup. *(Laughs.)* I muttered, when I was in another room, alone, "Wow. He's drinking out of my cup." And normally, before, I would have kept that inside of me for weeks. Normally, I wouldn't have said anything. I just would have kept it in. And weeks, or months, or a year, or a year and a half later I would suddenly scream one night *(screams and gestures wildly):* "HE WAS DRINKING OUT OF MY CUP!" Instead, as soon as he left, I joked: "Hey, what's he drinking out of my cup for?" And it was really a gas. She said, "Frank!" [and we discussed it and argued about it]. But she didn't think in those terms. As a farmed-out kid, I never owned anything. Our sense of property was different for different reasons.

Establishment of the
major point—and
speaker's personal
adjustment to it.

And so I'm learning how to feel, what to feel. I write a lot. I run a lot. I get rid of my tensions. And when something happens to me, the day it happens I just try to tell it like it is.[8]

Linking a Series of Anecdotes to Make a Point

Prepare a speech—to be delivered to your small group—in which you link together several (at least three) stories or anecdotes from your own personal experience in order to make a point. Spend more time in preparing this speech than your previous speeches. Begin by reading what you've written in your Communication Journal, especially your Interests-Inventory, and making additional notes in your journal as ideas and stories occur to you. As you choose which stories to include, consider that each one should make a *point*—phrased in the form of a *thesis statement*—and collectively, they should *prove or illustrate or demonstrate the overall point of the speech.* If you find that you're having difficulty, refer to the example of the student speech we've just quoted; it may provide some guidance and direction to your efforts. Decide which story should come first, which second, and so on. The order in which the incidents originally or actually occurred need not be the order in which you tell them. Rather, you should choose the order which seems to be most effective for making your point. Within each story, try to pattern the situations, moods, and details to create *surprise, suspense, contrast,* and *tension.*

In this chapter, we've shown that telling stories or anecdotes is an easy, interesting, and frequently effective means of accomplishing the third goal of speaking: to make what you're saying *useful* to your listeners. We've said that your speech is most useful to others when it makes a *point,* when it embodies your central thought or idea, when it serves to introduce, illustrate, and develop your principal thesis. Of course, since the mere narration of a personal experience or episode will not guarantee that anybody will listen to it and "get the point," you must work to capture and hold your audience's *attention.* One very practical way of doing this—after you've chosen the anecdote or story you believe will best introduce, illustrate, and establish your thesis statement—is to carefully select those important *details* to contrast the feelings, moods, situations, and events of the story. Then you can present these details in a pattern calculated to create *tension* in your listeners—either through suspense, surprise, or irony. Anticipating your audience's expectations, you can work in touches of momentary mystery, sudden turns of events, unexpected twists or stresses.

In this chapter, too, we've shown you ways to construct a longer, more complex speech by *coupling* or *linking* a series of stories or anecdotes. One way, as we've seen, is to start off with a dramatic anecdote to demonstrate or foreshadow your principal point, and then move through a succession of other anecdotes each of which makes its own point and each of which, in turn, develops your big, overall point. Another way to achieve effective linkage, we've suggested, is simply to move from a story-with-a-point to another story-with-a-point until—in total impact—you arrive at the major point of your speech: a point which reveals or reminds your audience of some small or large "truth" about life.

In Part Two as a whole, as well as in this concluding chapter of it, we've continued to emphasize three major objectives of effective speaking: (1) speak *interestingly,* (2) speak *clearly,* and (3) speak *usefully.* Throughout, we've shown you how—with careful choosing and handling—your stories or anecdotes can help you to achieve all three of these objectives. We've emphasized, further, that the *language* you choose and use significantly contributes to or detracts from your messages. We've carefully considered the importance of your chief communicating instruments: your *voice* and *body,* stressing that together and independently they work to clarify, communicate, and reinforce your intended meanings while, at the same time, increasing listeners' interest in you and your ideas.

Before sailing ahead into Part Three, let's take a reading, as mariners say, on the direction we've been and will be moving next. We've charted that direction to carry you from the easy to the less easy, from the simpler to the more complex aspects of speechmaking. This seems to be the soundest course for developing speaking skills and confidence. The closing exercise in Part Two, for instance—the hooking together of several anecdotes to form a longer speech with a thesis—foreshadows how in future chapters you'll be adding *more materials* and *more structure.* In the chapters of Part Three we'll be exploring with you that process of adding to what you already know about speech communication and can do with it.

Reference Notes

[1] C. S. Lewis, "The Three Parts of Morality," *Mere Christianity* (New York: The Macmillan Company, 1953), p. 55.

[2] Ibid.

[3] Dr. J. Allen Hynek, "Flying Saucers," speech delivered at Wilbur Wright College, Chicago, Illinois, November 19, 1969.

[4] S. David Dinwoodie, "The Inner City—Our Shame," speech delivered at Cornell University at the final hearing for the Woodford Prize in Public Speaking in 1958, printed with the author's permission.

[5] Ibid.

[6] Daniel Fader, "Is Literacy Possible or Desirable in Inner City Schools?" speech delivered at Wilbur Wright College, Chicago, Illinois, October 3, 1973.

[7] Walter Jacobson, "A Free Press, Government, Elections and Politicians," speech delivered at Wilbur Wright College, Chicago, Illinois, September 27, 1972.

[8] Franklin E. Jones, "Coping," speech delivered at Wilbur Wright College, Chicago, Illinois, fall, 1975.

Part Three

Adding Material and Structure for an Audience

9 Finding a Subject for Your Speech

America believes in speakers and speeches. Virtually every banquet, graduation, convention, political rally, church function, state fair, ground-breaking, sales meeting, or club meeting features a speaker. At some future point—or even now—you may find yourself *required* to be that speaker. You may have to say a few words at a business meeting, dinner, wedding, or funeral solely because of your role within the group—as an officer in the organization, a parent of the bride, a relative of the deceased.

At other times you may *demand* to be a speaker: at a school board meeting, a city or village council meeting, a meeting of a block club, community organization, union, or religious group. People who think they'll never have occasion to make "public" speeches suddenly find themselves on a podium, behind a microphone, or at a committee meeting when their children's school faces an increase in class size, when the local government wants to build a sewage plant down the street, when their employer wants to deny them a cost-of-living wage, or when they simply decide to get involved in some organization.

I was gratified to be able to answer promptly, and I did. I said I didn't know.
— Mark Twain, Life on the Mississippi

At still other times you may find yourself being *asked* to speak before an audience because of your reputation in your field. A group with a shared interest—auto safety, ecology, losing weight, improving the playground of the local school—may request that you address them. Or because of your popularity and fame—local or national—a group may invite you to speak on any topic you wish.

In any case, you'll be speaking on subjects you know. As the father or mother of the bride, for example, you know your daughter reasonably well (although your daughter might argue the point). As an expert in your field—astrology, medicine, engineering, psychiatry, law-enforcement, city-management, estate-planning, politics, witchcraft— you'll have studied your subject, lived it, learned to breathe its air. Standing before your fellow union members or neighbors on the block, you'll know about the cost of living, or the cost of moving away from the sewage plant; and if you don't know, you'll take pains to find out. In all cases, you'll want to make the best presentation you can.

That best presentation means fleshing out a speech with more than personal anecdotes and stories. People who have gathered to learn from you how to protect their homes from burglaries, for instance, want *specific advice.* They want *clear explanations* of what to do to keep burglars out, how to do it, and why it will work. They may even want *proof* that it will work, especially if the procedure is costly or troublesome. Thus, while you can and should flavor and illustrate your point with anecdotes, you'll need more material and more structure. You'll need data, statistics, quotes from experts; you'll need explanations, demonstrations, charts, and diagrams; and you'll need to organize and structure everything clearly, usefully, interestingly.

In Part Three of this book, therefore, we'll try to help you explore the process of developing and delivering an effective informative speech to a full audience—your entire class. In this chapter, we'll offer some advice about choosing and limiting a subject; in the chapters immediately following, we'll suggest some methods and resources for researching your subject; we'll provide some guidelines for challenging the worth and effectiveness of the materials you find; we'll help you investigate the needs, interests, and backgrounds of your audience; we'll suggest some ways of shaping your materials interestingly and clearly for that audience; and we'll show you how to organize your materials and make that organization clear to your audience. Then, finally, we'll get you on your feet, rehearsing your speech before your small group, delivering it to your whole class, and adapting it to the specific circumstances of the occasion and to still other audiences. Let's look at your first task now: *choosing and limiting a subject.*

DECIDING WHAT TO SPEAK ABOUT

As you leave your immediate experience to search for subject matter and supporting material which will be clear, interesting, and useful to your audience, don't be intimidated. You should know your subject well, of course; yet you may not consider yourself an "expert" on anything. But you are.

Unlike Margaret Mead, you probably haven't lived with the Trobrianders. Unlike Iain and Oria Douglas-Hamilton, you probably can't pack your bags and head for Lake Manyara in Tanzania to study elephants. You probably can't call up the President of the United States or the manager of the Houston Astros. You may not have the answers to the abortion controversy, the capital punishment controversy, the food problem, the energy problem, the welfare problem, or any of the other problems occurring daily. But you do know a great deal about other subjects.

You have lived, looked at, and listened to life. Your trip to Hawaii may not give you the credentials of the late Governor Dole to discuss pineapples, but it certainly gives you more knowledge about the state than most of your classmates have. Your grandfather's stories about his childhood may have bored you when you were younger, but they may fascinate your classmates who haven't tasted ice cream on the Via Veneto or Watneys in an Irish pub, who haven't sat down to a bowl of borsht or stood to sing at a Polish wedding, who can't imagine the Soviet invasion of Hungary or the sharecropping days in the South. The hours of sweat and backaches you have spent tuning your car's engine may not make you Andy Granatelli, but you may know enough to explain how to adjust a carburetor or change spark plugs.

Even if you occupy most waking hours with stereo headphones wrapped over your ears, you are qualified to discuss why Jethro Tull makes the hairs on your legs curl while bubble-gum music rots your teeth and mind. Even, in fact, if your brain has turned to bubbles from the soap operas on television, you certainly can argue why commercials are the eighth deadly sin. In short, if you think, read, talk to people, look and listen; if you travel, try gourmet cooking, paint, play pool, collect miniature cars or beer cans; if you have any hobbies or interests, opinions or passions, you have potential material for effective speeches.

Preparing an "Interests-Inventory"

So don't begin checking the flight schedules for Kenya just yet; travel instead over your own experiences and thoughts. Spend your time exploring the subjects there; and you'll be most comfortable, convincing, and clear. The most vivid, lively, and useful topics for an audience are vivid, lively, and useful to you. You can't sell enthusiasm you don't have.

Here's how to start the journey. In your journal, list everything from your experiences and interests that might serve as a subject for a speech. Specifically, you might try to respond to these questions (though you aren't limited to them):

1. What do you talk about most?
2. What social issue bothers or angers you most? Which issues do you know the most about?
3. What school issues turn you on or off? What issue should be discussed more?
4. What books or magazines do you read and enjoy? List a few titles.
5. What discussions or lectures in your other classes have touched your mind or emotions lately?
6. What jobs have you worked at? Which have you liked most? Which least? What skills have you learned in them?
7. What do you plan to do after you leave school?
8. What are your hobbies? How do you occupy your spare time?
9. If you grew up in another country or region of the United States, how did its customs and life-style differ from what you've found here?
10. If you've traveled to other places, how were they different from here? Consider the customs as well as the sights.
11. What unusual experiences have your parents, relatives, or friends told you about?

GEARING UP FOR AN INFORMATIVE SPEECH

Any ideas you capture in this inventory of your interests can serve as the basis for either an informative or a persuasive speech, since in either case you should choose a subject you know about and care about. As you will see in Part Four, one of the main differences between informing and persuading concerns not your subject matter, but your intentions. If you merely want to add to your audience's knowledge, you are informing them. If you want to add to their knowledge in order to change their opinions or move them to action, you are persuading them.

Later on (perhaps when you've completed your study of Chapters 9–14), you probably will be making a rather fully developed, ten-to-fifteen minute informative speech to the entire class. If so, you should begin immediately to think about it and plan for it. The first step is to choose a subject—*now*. Why now? Consider the circumstances of a speech in the world outside the classroom. Typically, the featured speakers (often aided by their ghostwriters) have weeks, sometimes months, in which they can prepare. They know their subject well in most cases and can spend their time thinking about their ideas, capturing the good ones with occasional brief notes, reading about or otherwise researching the areas they know least well, organizing the material, and finally rehearsing their presentation several times. You, likewise, should give yourself plenty of time. But you will have no such luxury if you delay finding your area of expertise.

Choosing and narrowing topics

After you've completed your Interests-Inventory, proceed — as we emphasized before — to look it over for subjects you know most and care most about. If your ideas are vague or general at this point, you must focus and narrow them. So, take two or three items from your inventory and write each down at the top of a sheet of paper, leaving a column under each. Then, for each subject, list as many terms as you can think of. If you've written *music,* for example, you might list under it:

concerts	listening in my room
Mick Jagger	my band
guitars	rehearsals

You're stuck now? Nothing else to say? Then look at what you've just listed. Choose one term, like *guitar,* and begin a new list under it on a separate sheet of paper.

bass guitar	orange amps
rhythm guitar	finger picking
lead guitar	strumming
Gibson	bar chords
Yamaha	five years of lessons
electric guitar	Greg, Pete, and John — my partners
folk guitar	

You're narrowing your focus and starting to see a number of possibilities: comparing bass to lead guitar, finger picking to strumming, straight chords to bar chords, a Gibson guitar to a Yamaha or a Harmony, or discussing the role each performs in the band. Your list should grow as you think about your experiences with the guitar and band. How did you learn to play? What skills came most easily? What with most difficulty? How do you rehearse? Choose your material? Work out the harmony and different instrumental parts? What is a typical gig like? Your task now is not only thinking what to speak about, but also limiting yourself to a single thesis you can develop in, say, ten minutes.

RELAXED STUDENT PULLS CORD **1** STARTING MOWER WHICH ROTATES SHOE PULLEY **2** KICKING ANNOYED CAT **3** WHO ATTACKS TOY BIRD **4** PULLING STRING TO TRIGGER GUN **5** SHOOTING BULLET WHICH CHOOSES FROM TOPIC LIST **A** THESIS LIST **B** AND ENLARGES SUBJECT IN LIST **C**.

Arriving at a tentative thesis

Try next to develop a thesis for your speech. Naturally, you can't teach your audience *everything* about guitars in a short time, especially when learning fifty-five chords well required seven years of constant practice, constant study, constant blisters; and working out routines with your band took so much more time and practice. *Banging away at the guitar,* you might conclude, *is easy; but playing it professionally in a band is a long and complex process.* And—you might suddenly see—that's exactly your point, the thesis you'll pursue in your speech. You'll explain only the difficulties of playing in a band, shaping your ideas around that explanation, deciding which ones to include or discard and what else you need to know to develop your thesis fully. You can always change your thesis later, but better to start with a point in mind than none at all. And even if your thesis is still tentative, you should write it down so you can remember it. Keep in mind that you'll be thinking about and tinkering with it from time to time over a period of several weeks.

Some further examples of narrowing and focusing your subject for a speech

Similarly, if you choose to talk about your trip to Yellowstone National Park, you may write:

Old Faithful

geysers

camping out

getting there

the motels along the way

Yellowstone's history

And you can go through the same process of narrowing one of these subjects—an explanation of how geysers work, for example—then expanding on and arriving at a tentative thesis about it. You may even have some brochures and pamphlets from your visit to look at.

Or, if you've spent your life in an urban ghetto, you may write a list like this:

basketball in the park

street gangs

hanging out

drugs

shucking

"It's really quite elementary. In searching out subject matter, I must draw from inside and outside myself . . . and you, my dear, just happen to be on the outside."

Then narrow one of these, listing whatever specifics come to mind. What's involved in *shucking,* for example? What are the initiation rites when you join a gang? Who were the stars of your pick-up basketball games, and how did the games' rules compare to college or professional regulations?

Remember, though, that your purpose essentially is to inform. Don't pick something from your interests-inventory you want to argue about or convince your classmates of. Stick with a subject you can explain and clarify, not something you must defend, condemn, or condone.

To restate what we've been saying, then, as you prepare for your longer speeches to larger groups (your entire class, for instance), choose a subject close to you, on which you are an "expert." You'll have more to say and say it more informatively and confidently. Materials you know best will probably be clearer, more interesting, and more useful to your audience. But begin choosing now. Allow yourself time to find a topic you feel comfortable with or strongly about. Collect an inventory of ideas in your journal, select a few, then narrow and develop them by listing related terms underneath each. Having found the right subject, you'll find the rest of your preparation easier going.

10 Hunting Materials for Your Speech

DRAWING FROM OTHER PEOPLE—AND PRINTED PAGES

Let's say that you now have a subject in mind—like playing your guitar. With this and a tentative point—that merely learning to play is less demanding than learning to play in harmony with a band—you can begin preparing for your speech. The first step is to ask yourself how much you know about your subject and how much you need to know. The clearer your understanding, the clearer your explanation. The more interesting your information, the more interested your audience will be. The more informative your materials, the more likely your audience will be informed.

To be sure, your experiences, the little stories you tell your audience, may be the most memorable and exciting parts of your speech. But experience alone has its limitations.

We should be careful to get out of an experience only the wisdom that is in it—and stop there; lest we be like the cat that sits on a hot stove-lid. She will never sit down on a hot stove-lid again—and that is well; but also she will never sit down on a cold one anymore.
—Mark Twain, *Puddn'head Wilson's New Calendar,*

Other people's experiences provide you with more perspective. Several people's opinions are better than one person's stereotype; a piece of knowledge grounded in careful research is better than one based on rumor or speculation; and a single statistic, if reliable, can serve as a typical instance characteristic of and applicable to many different experiences. So extend your knowledge with interviews and reading.

HITTING THE STREETS: THE INTERVIEW

The ideas from your interests-inventory should provide you with the basic "boundaries" of your speech and many of its details. However, for additional material, you'll need to travel *outside* your mind and into the minds of others. Can your guitar teacher give you some tips on the chords you don't know? Can you discuss the newest guitar equipment with salespeople in reputable music stores? Can you compare your band's rehearsal routine with what members of other bands could tell you? If you can, great. You'll learn more personally and sound both well informed and authoritative. The testimony and information you cite from people whose qualifications and reputations your audience acknowledges or respects will strengthen your qualifications and credibility, too. Moreover, materials from an interview often provide powerful and fascinating anecdotes.

For example, Philip Hilts, whose speech on "Behavior Modification" we quoted from in Chapter 5, used an anecdote based on an interview to illustrate his point about the dangers of manipulating others, about the behaviorists' threat to personal liberties. Here's his report:

> The next fellow I want to tell you about is Doctor Roger McIntire of Maryland University. . . . I went in and sat in a tiny office with him. He was an all-American-looking guy with blond hair, good build. He was sitting back

". . . And now, sir, can you tell me what you think of the new travel tax?"

in his chair with his feet up. And the first thing he said to me was, "When we start licensing parents, behavior modification will be very important."

My jaw dropped, and I went on listening. He went on to explain it all quite rationally, saying, "There's no question that we will license parents. It's only a question of when." He said, "Many people have wanted to do something about child abuse, about horrible beatings some parents give to their children, about parents raising children to be violent and crooked —about these worst parents, somebody has always wanted to do something." He said, "The only reason we haven't is that we haven't had a basis for licensing them. We couldn't [do it like] drivers' tests. . . . Go in, take your parent-training test; and, if you pass it, become a parent."

. . . McIntire told me it might be twenty years, maybe thirty years, before it was here—licensing parents—and he gave me his own scenario. He said, "We're already close to having a contraceptive that you take once and is effective until you reverse it. Then you develop a pill which unlocks it." And he said, "What we might do is give that pill freely to anyone we wanted, especially twelve- and thirteen-year-olds in school. That way, they could take it and have no problems throughout their teen-age life; and then when they get married, they could unlock it and have children. It would save a lot of pain among women. . . . Then, what's going to happen is someday there's going to be a doctor who says, 'Here is a girl

obviously who should not have her contraceptive unlocked.' This girl—
she may be on welfare; she may be thirteen years old; she may be mentally defective—you don't know what. There's bound to be a good reason. . . . And then a debate would start. Well, who should be parents and
who shouldn't? And what they will bring up in debate is education. Certainly there must be a level of education you must have before having
children. And then behavior modification would come in. Then, this
would be the basis for licensing parents."

That was his scenario. I found it all pretty scary, although at the time I
knew very little about the mechanics of behaviorism. McIntire had a trait
which I found in some of the other behaviorists: missionary zeal, enthusiasm, not stopping to look back at history or ask larger questions. Other
behaviorists called it the "flying Jesus syndrome," which is—you swoop
in and save everyone.[1]

Hilts' interview-example serves far better to anchor his point than
merely saying, "Behaviorists may be threatening our liberties." At the
end, after telling the story, though, Hilts makes sure his audience understands its implications; and he wraps it all up with a clever metaphor
about the "flying Jesus syndrome." Your interviews can provide the
same kinds of vivid illustrations and much information for *your* speeches.

Planning for an interview

An interview, like a speech, requires careful preparation and
thought. First, you should decide exactly what you want to find out, perhaps writing your thoughts down in your journal. Next, you should consider who would be the best available sources of information and opinions. Consider the qualifications of the people you could interview; and
if you don't know their qualifications, consider which ones specifically
you should find out during the interview—how long the people have
dealt with the subject, what material they've written about it, etc. Then
arrange for the interview: call in advance, explain your purpose, and
specify how long the interview should take.

Just as carefully, you should prepare the questions about the
subject matter you want to discuss. Formulate your questions beforehand, either writing them down or keeping them clearly in mind. Some
closed questions should elicit short answers on names, dates, circumstances, and the like; others, though open-ended, should specifically
elicit the information or opinions you want to know. As you listen during
the interview, consider using mirror questions, limiting questions, and
probing questions to focus and clarify a response.

Finally, be well prepared to record your information efficiently
and accurately. If possible, tape-record or take notes on the interview. If
your note-taking distracts the person you're interviewing, make notes

immediately afterward. Have your questions ready so you don't waste time, and keep your own opinions to yourself. Don't argue with or antagonize the person you interview.

1 Person-to-Person and Small-Group Speaking
Practicing an Interview

Choose one of the topics from the following list or any other topic you wish; consider what experiences you've had with it; then interview another member of your group about his or her experiences with it:

car accidents	lying
hospitalization	a boss
registration for courses or apply-	the police
ing for college admission	cats
a first date	a bad storm

Prepare your questions in advance, and follow up with mirror, probing, and limiting questions when necessary. Take notes on the responses.

After the interview, give your group a three-minute speech comparing your experiences with the experiences of the person you interviewed.

HITTING THE BOOKS:
READING FOR ADDITIONAL MATERIAL

You may not be able or want to interview anyone for the longer informative speeches you plan to give. However, you can allow people to speak to you in another form: on *paper.* You can read their words in books, magazines, newspapers, pamphlets, bulletins, and even questionnaires you've asked them to fill in. Roger Ebert, the Pulitzer Prize-winning movie critic, has seen thousands of movies and talked to many of their stars and producers. Yet when speaking about eroticism in film and its problems with censorship, he bolstered his knowledge and—as a result—enlivened his speech to a college audience with this report on something he had read:

> The movies have traditionally not been protected by Constitutional guarantees. And, in fact, in looking into a book called *The Movies and Censorship* by a Professor Randall, I was interested to see that a mere two weeks—two weeks—after Edison invented his marvelous new invention called the Kinetoscope, a movie called "Dolarita and the Passion Dance" was busted at Atlantic City on grounds of immorality.[2]

Ebert approached this material confidently; he integrated it into his discussion just as he would any experience he had lived himself. And he discussed it in natural and colorful language he knew would please his young audience.

Each book, each magazine article, or newspaper article was written by one or more people to share their thoughts, experiences, or research. Think of printed material as the words of people communicating to you on paper. Don't be intimidated by the library. Reading about a topic you enjoy can be fun if you consider it as an adventure, or as holding a conversation with an equal. Don't forget that you've had experience with the subject, too; you needn't be "snowed" by someone's credentials or fame. From time to time, you may even challenge an "authority's" conclusions or evidence—a subject we'll discuss in the next chapter. Right now, you should feel that you can conduct a transaction with another person's printed words on an *Adult*-to-*Adult* level; don't let your *Parent* or not-OK *Child* send you messages saying, "I can't do research."

Don't confuse reading about your topic with the "research" you may have endured for that strange creature called the "term paper" in high school: lots of quotes, footnotes, note cards, no opinions, "keep the word 'I' out of it," and "make sure you have at least a three-level outline." Yes, you will be going to the library and reading other people's words, but you won't be tacking them together like a prefabricated housing project. You'll be using them to flesh out and buttress *your*

"He says he's come to hit the books."

ideas. You will make the words of others come alive in your ideas, with your organization, your angle, your style of delivery. You'll choose what to say, and you'll decide on the supporting material.

Using encyclopedias for an overview

A good place to start is an encyclopedia, which provides you with a general view of the landscape before you rush into the thickets of specific material. You'll learn what you should learn more about. The better encyclopedias, like the *Americana* or *Britannica,* at the end of each article also list other books or periodicals to read for further information.

There are specialized encyclopedias in virtually every field (social science, art, education, even baseball) as well. For a complete list of specialized encyclopedias, look through Constance Winchell's *Guide to Reference Books.*[3]

Using books for specifics

Next is your library's card catalog, classified in subject, author, and title listings. If you can find no books under subject headings like "Rock Bands," try different headings, perhaps "Music: popular," or the names of specific bands. If you still come up dry, ask the librarian for help; or try dipping into *Books in Print,* a reference which tells you the names, authors, and publishers of every book in print in English. It's divided into three separate sections: one arranged according to authors, another according to the titles, and still another according to the subject areas. With the information you gather there, you can call or visit other libraries.

Using periodicals for up-to-date data

For most subjects, however, books usually can't provide information as fresh and timely as magazines and newspapers. Books often take as long as two years to write and publish, so information in them is frequently out of date, especially in subjects like science, economics, and international affairs. Also, the older the copyright date (found on the page after the title page), the greater the chance for stale information. For example, a statistic on traffic deaths cited in a book published in 1970 would not accurately reflect the current number of fatalities, since population, the number of cars, the speed limits, and safety devices have all changed.

In *Statistical Abstract of the United States,* which appears annually, the U.S. government publishes the most up-to-date statistics on virtually every subject, from the number of bushels of wheat harvested to the number of ethnic minorities in the Air Force. Yearbooks and almanacs also regularly provide up-to-date statistics and information.

If you want to find material in magazines, consult *The Reader's Guide to Periodical Literature,* which indexes almost every popular magazine published in the United States. *The Reader's Guide* appears twice monthly (monthly in July and August), and at the end of the year is bound cumulatively into a single volume. Generally, it lists articles under subject headings, though it uses some author-and-title headings as well. On the front pages of each issue, you'll find a full list of the magazines indexed and *The Reader's Guide* key to their titles. Suppose you wanted more information on guitars. If you looked on page 484 of the March-1974-to-February-1975 edition, you'd find:

GUITAR
    Guitar repairs you can make. J. Aaron. il
      Mech Illus 70:106–7+ Mr '74
    Kaman plucking profits from guitars. W. H.
      Gregory. il Aviation W 101:51–3+
      Ag 5 '74
GUITAR, Electronic. See Musical instruments,
    Electronic
GUITAR preamplifiers. See Musical instru-
    ments, Electronic – Equipment[4]

So you can better understand what an entry contains, let's examine the first one:

    Guitar repairs you can make (title of article)
    J. Aaron (author of article)
    Il (illustrated)
    Mech Illus (title of magazine abbreviated;
          the full title is *Mechanics Illustrated*)
    70 (volume number of the magazine)
    106–7+ (article is printed on pages 106 and
          107 and continues on other pages)
    Mr '74 (date of magazine abbreviated; full
          date is March 1974)

Copy all this information; check to see if your library carries the magazine either in its magazine section or on microfilm; then you can turn directly to the page where the article begins.

But notice the last two entries under "GUITAR" – "GUITAR, Electronic," and "GUITAR, preamplifiers." Both tell you to see "MUSICAL INSTRUMENTS, Electronic." So, turning to page 742 in *The Reader's Guide,* you'd find:

Build a guitar preamp. G. Kay. il Radio-
    Electr 45:36 – 7 + Je '74
Build a guitar sound intensifier. K. Lang.
    il Pop Electr 6:45 – 6 Jl '74[5]

These are articles telling you how to build your own preamplifier and sound intensifier, valuable information if you decide your speech should include material about how the band assembles its own equipment.

The publisher of *The Reader's Guide* also compiles specialized indexes of magazines read by professionals in many fields. Each index follows the same format as *The Reader's Guide.*

If you want to discuss a subject for which newspaper coverage might be helpful, you can consult *The New York Times Index.* Starting in 1913, and in some libraries as far back as 1851, every article of every issue of the newspaper is listed according to subject headings. Many large libraries carry copies of the newspapers on microfilm, so you can read about an event as it was reported at or near the time it occurred.

Keeping track of what you find

No matter what material you actually read or discuss with others, you should hunt your materials in some systematic way and organize them for easy reference and recall. Otherwise, when you need them later in assembling your speech, you may have forgotten some of the material or where it came from, or you may not understand your notes, or you may spend a great deal of time recopying them later.

To avoid wrenching our teeth and patience, as authors hunting materials to support our ideas we've found several helpful procedures. If these don't work for you, substitute others; but follow some sort of *system.* Here's what we suggest:

1. Make notes of everything – sources, material to quote, material to restate in your own words, ideas for organization, ideas for an introduction, ideas about what will please the audience. If you find or are reminded of a particularly good story to illustrate a point, write it down. If you're struck with an expression you know will hit your listeners hard, write it down. If you unearth a statistic you think is a gem, write it down – along with its source. Trust your instincts, not your memories.

2. Ask a librarian for a list of all magazines and periodicals the library carries, indicating whether they are on microfilm or in original form. Ask the librarian where to locate things or for any help you need. Most librarians are glad to accommodate you.

3. Take far more notes than you need, especially if you aren't sure yet what point you will make in your speech. You may, for instance, suddenly discover a relationship between two ideas or facts; or, late in the planning stages of the speech, you may change your mind about the point. Then previously irrelevant material suddenly becomes central. If you can't remember where you read it, you're stuck.

4. As you do your research, write each note on a separate 3 × 5 card or small sheet of paper you can file and find easily when you need it. If you keep several notes on the same sheet of paper, you can't separate and shuffle them around as you prepare your speech.

5. Keep in one place a separate list of the titles, authors, issue numbers, dates of publication, and whatever else will make identifying sources easy. That way, you won't lose some of them, and it will save you the bother of including all the same information on each note. On your cards or pieces of paper, put only the author's name or the title and page number.

6. Never handcopy the material you want to quote. Instead, photocopy the pages on machines in the library, which usually reproduce two average-size book or magazine pages at a price ranging from 5¢ to 15¢. (Some libraries can even photocopy microfilm.) The writer's cramp and boredom saved by photocopying far outweigh the expense.

7. Try to limit your quotes to a few, and shorten those as much as you can without altering the author's intent and context. Speaking to an audience in your own words and benefiting from eye contact, feedback, and the spontaneity of the moment work better than boring listeners by reading someone else's words at length.

8. Try not to burden your listeners with anything more than the name of the person or magazine you quote or allude to. However, when you come to the speech occasion, bring along the complete list in case someone in the audience asks for more specific references.

All this, we repeat, isn't intended to push the "research" speech on you. Everything you use, whether from your own experience or from *Who's Who in America,* should support your point, your thesis statement, your ideas, and not be a dull collage of clippings. We'll have more to say in Chapters 13 and 14 about shaping your speech, but try now to play a few games with hunting up some facts.

2

Finding Information in Reference Books

Along with each of the other members of your group, answer one of the following questions by consulting reference books, starting with those mentioned earlier in this chapter. Tell where you found the information and what false paths you followed first. Then, working with your group, compile all the answers into one list to give your instructor. Of course, the members of your group can make up different questions if you don't like those that follow:

1. What was Hank Aaron's slugging average his first year in the major leagues?
2. When was the temple of the Roman god Mars dedicated? Where was it located?
3. Who wrote *The Federalist Papers?*
4. What were the names of the third group of men to walk on the moon?
5. What percentage of the United States' budget in 1970 was spent for defense?
6. Who won the Nobel Peace Prize in 1972?
7. What college football team won the national championship in 1958? Who won the Rose Bowl?
8. What was the name and year of Bob Hope's second motion picture?
9. What was the first year the College Level Examination Program (CLEP) was given?
10. Who wrote the play *The Quack Doctor?*
11. What percentage of land in the continental United States is owned by the Federal Government? How does that percentage compare with the percentage in 1955?
12. What was the exact date of Pablo Picasso's second marriage? What was his second wife's name?
13. *The Sound and the Fury* is a Pulitzer-Prize-winning novel by William Faulkner. Its title is a quotation from a play. Who wrote the play, and what is *its* title? What is the full quote from which Faulkner took his title?
14. Billie Sol Estes was a Texan who was involved in a criminal-political scandal in the 1950s. Give a brief description of Estes and the scandal.
15. What is Kirk Douglas' real name?

3

Finding Information in Periodicals

The answers to the following questions can be found in periodicals. Each member of your group will report on one of them, mentioning the sources he or she consulted. Begin your research by consulting *The Reader's Guide to Periodical Literature.*

1. President Nixon traveled to China in 1972. What cities did he visit? How long did he stay?
2. In 1974, Bianca Jagger, Mick Jagger's wife, was a popular figure. Tell a bit about her.
3. What happened at the Pentagon Papers trial in 1973? What were the issues? Who was involved? What was the result?
4. In 1973, Marlon Brando starred in a controversial motion picture you won't see on television. It was called *The Last Tango in Paris,* and some people called it pornographic. Tell about it.
5. Describe the 1976 United States space probe to Mars.
6. Dick Cavett had a popular talk show on television during the early 1970s. Tell about it.
7. Midwives became popular in the early 1970s, too. Describe the phenomenon. Who was using them, where, and where were the midwives learning their trade?
8. In 1972, the private schools in this country encountered financial difficulties. Discuss the issues—which are continuing, by the way.
9. Doctor William Shockley, a Nobel-Prize-winning professor at Stanford University, gave speeches across the nation in the mid-1970s. Briefly, what did he advocate? What did he win his Nobel Prize for? What were his qualifications to speak on his subject?
10. In 1975, South Vietnam fell to the Viet Cong and the North Vietnamese. When did it surrender? Tell a bit more about its fall.

The sum, then—and the point—of this chapter's advice is this: you can fill in the holes in your knowledge on a subject for a speech by interviewing and reading. For an *interview,* come prepared. Decide ahead of time what you need to know about the person you'll be talking with; decide in advance exactly what you want to find out and the specific questions you'll ask. Use mainly probing and mirror questions during the interview, and tape-record or take notes on the answers you get. When you want to get information for your speech by *reading* about your subject, begin with a general reference work like an encyclopedia, but also check the card catalog for indexes to books and magazines like *The Reader's Guide to Periodical Literature* and *The New York Times Index.* As you read for your speech materials, take careful—but brief—notes on things you want to remember; make photocopies of materials you feel you may need; then systematically file them so you can shuffle them around as you prepare your speech. And remember, above all: use material from *outside* your experience as confidently, comfortably, and gracefully as material from inside. Know it well and discuss it well—clearly, entertainingly, colorfully, and usefully.

Reference Notes

[1]Philip Hilts, "Behavior Modification: Its Uses and Implications," speech delivered at Wilbur Wright College, Chicago, Illinois, March 5, 1975.

[2]Roger Ebert, "The Americanization of the Skin Flick," speech delivered at Wilbur Wright College, Chicago, Illinois, April 3, 1974.

[3]Constance M. Winchell, *Guide to Reference Books* (Chicago: American Library Association, 1967).

[4]*Reader's Guide to Periodical Literature.* Copyright © 1974, 1975 by The H. W. Wilson Company. Material reproduced by permission of the publisher.

[5]Ibid.

IS THAT A FACT? AND WHO SAYS SO?

11 Challenging Your Materials

Don't worship the printed word. A word is not an infallible, fixed-forever thing. The only ones from God came on stone tablets, not paper. *People* write books and articles, people with biases and opinions, people who make judgments and errors in judgment. Although every writer—and speaker—shouldn't carelessly or unethically misrepresent the facts, distortions do occur, so be skeptical of what you read, hear, and say. Challenge other people's information, statistics, and testimony for accuracy, biases, truthfulness. Investigate the credentials of "experts" and the reputation of the journals the experts write in. Don't swallow everything whole. Taste it and chew it over carefully.

In the pages ahead, we'll provide you with an idea of what to look for. First, we'll define what we mean by a *fact.* Then we'll suggest some tests for the credibility of *statistics, testimony,* and *examples.* Finally, we'll suggest a way to investigate the reliability of printed sources by testing them for biases.

WHAT'S A FACT?

For you, something you witness or experience directly is a fact. You saw it clearly; you know it's true. But if you didn't see it, you must rely on another person's description or report. Therefore, only a small number of facts come from a reality you can be sure of. The rest come to you secondhand, as other people's *statements* about reality—other people's road maps, but not the actual terrain. Their words can be verified, but with difficulty. Each report of an event, each interpretation of its meaning, each piece of data or statistic about it must be judged against the reporter's ability to perceive clearly, to understand the perceptions, and to report accurately, honestly, and without prejudice.

Take a simple matter like the exact time. Your watch shows 4:30. Is that time a fact? Before you hasten to say yes, consider that the only fact is: your watch *shows* 4:30. It could be slow or fast, or stopped, or set to the wrong time. Moreover, you may only *think* you see 4:30. You could be farsighted or careless; your vision could be distorted by the light. The matter would be further complicated if you asked others the time. Their watches and vision could be inaccurate; they could be lying, joking, or simply rounding off 4:28 to 4:30. And, if they've gotten their time "fact" from *another* person, the problems of reliability become even more complicated. Was *that* person careless or truthful? Did the inquirers hear the time information correctly? These kinds of technicalities may seem trivial to you, but they can cause you to miss a plane. In a court of law, they can free or convict a murderer.

Moreover, statements of fact generally exclude opinions or judgments. Facts involve some sort of objectivity. They can be proven through some agreed-upon procedure. In writing their stories on Watergate for the *Washington Post,* for example, Carl Bernstein and Robert Woodward supposedly accepted only information which came from at least two firsthand (but sometimes never identified) sources.[1] In legal trials, hearsay—testimony based on what another person told the witness rather than firsthand information—is usually not admissible. In scientific investigations, any experiment must be repeated many times, under many conditions, until its results become recognized as fact.

1 Whole-Class Discussion
Separating Facts from Opinions and Judgments

In a class discussion, examine the following statements and identify which ones clearly are facts.[2] How do you know they are facts? How would you verify them? What assumptions underlie each statement? If you can, rephrase and qualify a statement so that it can be verified more easily.

1. The moon orbits the earth.
2. George Washington was our first President.
3. $3 + 3 = 6$.
4. Shakespeare wrote *King Lear.*
5. Atoms contain protons, electrons, and neutrons.
6. Each day contains twenty-four hours.
7. All people will die.
8. Elizabeth Taylor is beautiful.
9. The United States is the most powerful country in the world.
10. *He don't* is poor grammar.

CREDIBILITY TESTS: HOW TO TELL IF YOU'VE BEEN HAD

When you read or attempt to weigh any statement of "fact," keep in mind these questions:

1. Is the tension surrounding an event so great that a person involved might misperceive or distort what occurs? Nervousness, excitement, and anxiety easily distract people or lessen their awareness. For example, many eyewitnesses to the assassination of John F. Kennedy swear they heard two or four shots instead of the three established by the Warren Commission's Report. But the general confusion and fear for their own safety, as well as for the safety of the President, were their most likely concerns—not counting the number of shots.

2. Does the source have something to gain by presenting these facts? A study minimizing the risks of smoking funded by a cigarette company, for instance, may be suspect.

3. Is the material first-, second-, or third-hand information? The further the information is removed from the event, the more opportunity for errors and distortions.

4. Is the reporter emotionally committed to a position that might distort his or her perceptions? Remember that people tend to see what they want to see and may inadvertently ignore the rest. In the 1960s those "factual" reports from Vietnam predicting we'd soon see "the light at the end of the tunnel" weren't necessarily lies. But the military and consulate people gathering them wanted to win the war and naturally noticed the encouraging signs.

5. Would facts to the contrary jeopardize the reporter's position? When Lyndon Johnson wanted so much to hear that we were winning the war, would the Vietnamese consuls risk placing themselves on Johnson's bad side by telling him we were losing it? Much was at stake, and optimism was the "order of the day."

6. Are the documents the facts are based upon authentic? Are they censored? Did the reporter or observer have complete access to the documents?

7. How long after the event did the person discuss it? Memories fade with time, and with them the precise recollection of details. Each year, for example, your uncle's fish-that-got-away grows larger in his retelling.

8. Is the report consistent throughout? The greater the number of contradictions, the greater the possibility the report is a fabrication or the reporter is confused.[3]

2 Whole-Class Activity

Testing Eyewitness Reliability

Your instructor will select several people to rush into the classroom and stage an exciting event with plenty of action occurring everywhere. Afterward, write an eyewitness description of what happened, and read it aloud to the rest of your class. The various accounts should produce some lively discussion and reveal some interesting facts about the nature of facts.

Although your "eyewitness reports" on what happened in the above exercise probably varied a great deal, you and your classmates might also have reached accord on certain details, thus demonstrating that facts *can* be verified and—despite the imperfection of the verification process—remain ultimately our only basis for decision making. A jury, for instance, is instructed to find someone guilty beyond all *reasonable* doubt. The point is: don't be afraid to doubt.

Statistics: Playing the Numbers Game

As we've said in Chapter 10, a good statistic — because it summarizes *many* episodes or opinions — is a more reliable source to generalize from than a few experiences of your own. Unfortunately, statistics also carry a kind of magical power: People often accept them unquestioningly. You see and hear statistics everywhere. Baseball managers will say an injured player is performing at ninety-five percent efficiency, though how you would measure that is a mystery. Politicians claim the unemployment rate is over seven percent, seasonally adjusted. But is a youth who loses a part-time job counted in that statistic? Is a person who simply quits looking for a job and no longer draws unemployment benefits counted? In reality, statistics are merely numbers and are meaningless until interpreted. Fortunately, there are a number of "credibility tests" that we can apply. When you encounter statistics, when you find yourself or someone else using them to back up a point or a claim, consider these questions:

1. Who is doing the counting? In 1960 a man named Richard Nixon was running for President. When he landed at Milwaukee airport, the Republicans claimed 12,000 persons were there to greet him. The Milwaukee police, charged with security, estimated the crowd at 8,000. A reporter for *The Milwaukee Journal* enlarged a photograph of the crowd and counted 2,300.[4]

2. What label is attached to the numbers? Those were human beings at the Milwaukee airport. But the Republicans called them "supporters," and attached adjectives of "enthusiastic" and "eager." The supporters of Nixon's opponent, John Kennedy, might have labeled the crowd "curiosity-seekers." The police might have labeled some of them a potential "threat" to Mr. Nixon's safety. In reality, the crowd was probably a combination of all these labels and more. Some of the onlookers may have been merely waiting to board a plane for a business trip or vacation, or attempting to meet people returning from one. How you describe a number or a statistic — the labels you attach to it — greatly influences its significance.

3. What are the numbers being used for? The Republicans, of course, wanted to prove the booming support for Mr. Nixon. The reporter who counted the crowd from a photograph may have wished to discredit the Republicans.

4. Are the statistics complete? The pollsters — Gallup, Harris, *et al.* — have developed complex criteria for determining the accuracy of the responses they receive from a small segment of the entire population. Most of the time, especially in predicting the outcome of an election, these samples prove highly reliable. But by omitting a portion of the results from a poll, a person can greatly distort its significance. For example, a news summary of a poll might stress that only forty percent of people interviewed favored busing to achieve racial integration of the schools. You might assume, therefore, that sixty percent opposed it. Not so, however. Thirty-five percent opposed it. Twenty-five percent expressed no opinion. Seen in this light, more people apparently favored than opposed busing.

5. How large is the sample? The smaller the sampling, the greater the chance it is unrepresentative. Seventy-five percent seems a large majority; but with a sampling of only four people, it's hardly significant. How many doctors in those aspirin commercials did the study actually consult? "Three out of four doctors recommend . . ." (And were they horse doctors?)

6. Do the statistics prove their point? The statistics from a football game show that Boondock Beach rushed for more yards and completed more first downs. But Cracker Creek won 40-12. Insurance statistics show that there are few deaths in the over-ninety age bracket. But does this prove that if you live to be ninety, you have less chance of dying?

7. How recent are the statistics? The United States has boasted the highest per-capita income in the world since World War II. But in 1976, both Sweden and Switzerland surpassed the U.S. Check dates carefully, and be suspicious of any undated statistics.

3 **Discovering for Yourself**
Testing the Validity of a Statistical Sampling

Poll the entire class for opinions on a controversial issue: capital punishment, mercy killing, abortion, marijuana, whatever. How many people support or oppose it?

Then experiment with different samplings. Divide the class into smaller groups, first arbitrarily, later according to whatever criteria you choose: age, sex, race, religion, geographic origin, economic status, hair color, dress. Now poll the members of these various groups. Do you find the same results as when you polled the class as a whole? Do you see any correlations between your groupings and their opinions? Which seem valid, which ludicrous?

Testimony: Taking the "expert's" word for it

Everyone is entitled to an opinion, but some opinions are more convincing than others. You respect the words of experts — that is, recognized authorities on a subject — because you assume that experts know what they're talking about. As with all forms of evidence, however, don't be afraid to challenge the experts. On most issues, you can find an "expert" taking virtually any side. Capital punishment has provoked controversy — and expert testimony — ever since Socrates swallowed hemlock. In their book, *Evidence,* Robert P. and Dale R. Newman cite a number of interesting examples of how supposed experts, all having high-credibility credentials, can offer strongly contradictory testimony on the effectiveness of the death penalty as a deterrent to murder.[5] In 1930, Sir Alexander Patterson, Director of British Prisons, claimed: "We who are in daily contact with professional criminals can safely say that with them the dread of the gallows is a strong deterrent. They have tasted prison and lost their fear of it. They have misused their lives, but they are loath to lose them."[6] More recently, Richard Gerstein, State's Attorney of Dade County, Florida, stated: "It is clear that for normal human beings no other punishment deters so effectively from committing murder as the punishment of death."[7]

Impressed? Look at one more example from Newman and Newman. Thorsten Sellin, Professor of Sociology at the University of Pennsylvania, compared the statistics on the frequency of murder in states with and without the death penalty. Though thousands of professionals swore it was a deterrent, Sellin found no significant decrease in murders in areas that hanged or electrocuted their perpetrators than in those areas which had abolished capital punishment.[8]

Each expert, as you see, presented an opinion, but whose is more credible? Part of the answer lies in examining the *credentials* of each expert — each one's experience with and training in the subject. Another part lies in examining each expert's *reputation* and *motivation.* And the final part lies in examining the expert's evidence — challenging it as you would any fact or statistic. There are, fortunately, also some credibility tests you can apply to expert testimony — some questions to consider when you read or hear an expert's words:

1. What makes the person an expert? What is the nature of the person's training? How much and what kind of experience has the person had in the field? Note, for example, that Sir Alexander Patterson based his observations on firsthand experience, on daily personal contact with prisoners who claim that capital punishment deterred them. Notice that Thorsten Sellin based his conclusions on a statistical survey. Which type of experience is more valid?

2. Is the person an expert in the specific field he or she comments on? You've seen baseball and football stars on television lavishing praise on a coffee-maker or a cologne. Obviously, they aren't experts. But evaluating a person's expertise is often quite complicated. A Ph.D. in engineering may have published five books and seventeen articles, but has the person ever studied the properties of the flywheel or the rotary engine? A psychiatrist may testify at a trial that the accused is a manic-depressive, but has the psychiatrist examined enough manic-depressives to draw a valid conclusion?

3. What are the expert's biases? The job of the State's Attorney of Dade County is to *prosecute* criminals. He puts them in jail, and isn't necessarily responsible for doing research on what might deter them from a life of crime. After working to convict murderers, would a state's attorney very likely be sympathetic to lessening their punishment? Why did he struggle so hard to convict them? However, more important than the expert's role or occupation is his or her reputation for objectivity, fairness, and care in making generalizations.

4. How good is the expert's evidence? Is it merely impressions from experience or the result of a careful, systematic study? Thorsten Sellin conducted a statistical analysis of crimes within each state. But can states with unequal populations and living conditions be compared credibly for their frequency-of-murder rate? How many executions were actually being carried out and how many delayed indefinitely? Richard Gerstein supplied no evidence for his conclusions. His opinions may have been based on numerous conversations with murderers. However, from his statement, you can't know whether there were many, few, or none.

Examples: Making sure they add up to credibility

You'll find many examples used to illustrate or prove points. But an example, after all, is only a single instance. You should have some reason to infer that it represents many other instances. Before you *use* or *accept* an example as evidence or support for evidence, probe it — test its credibility — with these questions:

1. *Does the example seem typical?*
2. *Was it selected fairly, without bias?* The guidelines about objectivity and reliability we mentioned earlier apply here.
3. *Are the examples sufficient in quality and number to justify the conclusions?*

THE SOURCES OF *YOUR* SOURCES:
STOP, LOOK, AND LISTEN—FOR BIAS

As you must have discovered by this time, every anthology, book, newspaper, magazine, or other public commentary—whether written or spoken—has a *bias*, a *point of view*. These biases—or "slants" as they are sometimes called—are reflected in the material each such source includes or considers significant, or in the viewpoints of the writers who worked on it. In extreme cases, you can spot the bias easily. *Pravda*, Russia's official newspaper, is hardly the source to consult for material critical of the Soviet Union. But what about the newspapers, magazines, books, and journals you will consult? We can't provide you with an explicit answer to this question or a set of quick-and-easy guidelines to

". . . Yes, Comrade, you need not look any further. We will give you all the unbiased, undistorted truth on communism you will ever want."

follow, because viewpoints and biases and prejudices are highly individualized concerns. However, as you work your way through the following "investigation," you should try to formulate a few eye-openers
that could prompt you to take a clearer, colder, and harder look at the
sources of information you use when preparing your speeches.

4 Discovering for Yourself and Whole-Class Speaking
Investigating the Biases of a Magazine or Newspaper

Choose a popular magazine or newspaper (your own local newspaper,
if you prefer), and investigate its biases and viewpoints. Look at its edito-
rials, the kind of subject matter it covers, its stands on particular issues.
Nose through it for a while. Look at past issues if they are available. Ask
others (especially people who read it regularly) what *they* think. Among
the possibilities of printed publications you might consider:

Newsweek	*The Christian Science Monitor*
Time	*The Saturday Review*
New Times	*Business Week*
U.S. News and World Report	*Esquire*
The Nation	*Playboy*
Commentary	*Penthouse*
Harper's	*Cosmopolitan*
The New Republic	*Ms.*
The National Review	*The Atlantic Monthly*
The New Yorker	*Rolling Stone*
The New York Review of Books	*Psychology Today*
The New York Times	*Vogue*
The Wall Street Journal	*The Center Magazine*

Then, in a three-minute speech, report back to your class on what
you've found, citing "evidence" to support your observations.

In conclusion, as you search for material for your speeches, don't
be merely an information-gatherer. *Challenge* the information, too.
Remember that facts, like all statements about reality, can—on occasion—be lies, distortions, opinions, or judgments. So challenge their
credibility and their origins. Does the person making them have something to gain or lose? Are they consistent within themselves and with
other known facts? Are they from firsthand and recent information?
From authentic and uncensored documents? Challenge the *validity of
statistics.* Are they recent, representative, gathered objectively, interpreted fairly? Challenge the *credibility of experts' testimony.* Check
their credentials, their biases, their sources of information. Challenge

the *range and quality of examples.* Check the magazines and newspapers in which the material appears for their biases and points of view. In short, be alert to human failings, for human beings write what you read and ultimately—depending on how much you modify it—much of what you speak.

Reference Notes

[1]Carl Bernstein and Bob Woodward, *All the President's Men* (New York: Simon and Schuster, 1974).

[2]Adapted from Bernard F. Huppe and Jack Kaminsky, *Logic and Language* (New York: Alfred A. Knopf, Inc., 1957), p. 166.

[3]Adapted from *Evidence* by Newman and Newman. (Boston: Houghton Mifflin Company, 1969). Used by permission of the publisher.

[4]Herbert A. Jacobs, "To Count a Crowd," *Columbia Journalism Review* VI (Spring, 1967), p. 38. Cited in Newman and Newman, p. 217.

[5]Newman and Newman, pp. 28–29.

[6]Originally cited in Sir Ernest Gowers, *A Life for a Life?* (London: Chatto and Windus, 1956), p. 45. Also cited in Newman and Newman, p. 28.

[7]Originally from Richard M. Gerstein, "A Prosecutor Looks at Capital Punishment," *Journal of Criminal Law, Criminology and Police Science* LI (July–August, 1960), p. 254. Cited in Newman and Newman, p. 28.

[8]Originally from Thorsten Sellin, *The Death Penalty* (Philadelphia: The American Law Institute, 1959), p. 63. Cited in Newman and Newman, p. 29.

12 Relating Your Materials to Your Listeners

When, like a good detective, you are investigating material for your speech—interviewing friends, employers, instructors, experts of one sort or another; reading books, magazines, newspapers—all too easily you can forget the "jury" who will ultimately decide its success: your *audience*. You may establish an excellent case in the abstract, but lose the verdict in the presentation if you do not match your message to the minds of your listeners. As you continue your research, therefore, find the most appealing information, or find a way to make it appealing.

Of course, fresh material—and a lot of it—is the best defense against listener boredom. An audience challenged with new ideas, new facts, new problems to solve, and new questions to answer won't likely yawn and scratch and think about the football game they could be watching. Clearly explained material is just as important; for if your audience can't understand your information, they'll quickly lose patience with your subject and you. So, to make your materials interesting, useful, and clear for your listeners, you must try to see, think, and feel as they do. You must "get inside their heads."

You can begin deciding what will be clearest, most interesting, and most useful to your audience by leaving your own mind for a moment and entering theirs. That's what we'll explore in the pages ahead. We'll suggest that you consider your audience as a group of *individuals,* that you place yourself to the extent possible in *each* person's position, and that you ask yourself — and others — some questions, then see what the answers tell you.

We come now to lay
this man's case
in the hands of a jury
of our peers.
—Clarence Darrow,
in defense of Henry Sweet

GETTING INTO THE HEADS OF YOUR LISTENERS

Selecting and shaping materials around your listeners' interests, needs, and familiarity with your subject require that you know something about your listeners. You must travel outside your head and into theirs; you must anticipate their thinking and assumptions. In your small group, your classmates have asked you questions about and commented on your speeches when you've finished. You have spoken, heard responses, then responded to them. Unfortunately, in formal speeches, though you can read (imperfectly) your listeners' nonverbal messages and try to adapt to them, ordinarily your listeners won't interrupt you with questions and objections. You must, therefore, anticipate their reactions in advance.

To you, your speech may seem perfectly clear, your language exciting, your examples meaningful; but to a listener or an audience, any one or all of these things may be inappropriate, indecipherable, or offensive. We recall what to us was a particularly moving speech about a student's grandmother, now impoverished, deteriorating, and lonely after many productive years as the head of the family. In the follow-up

". . . Oh, he's just practicing getting into the heads of his listeners for a speech class!"

discussion, while the majority of the class praised the student speaker's presentation and agreed with her on the need for more social-security benefits, one student—a policeman, married, and still living with his Italian immigrant parents—refused to sympathize with the girl's grandmother. He asked, "Where was her family? And, besides that, why hadn't she saved money?" The other students argued that she was too poor to save, but he would have none of their arguments. "Anyone," he asserted, "who doesn't save ten percent of his salary is a fool."

On the basis of his experience, his parents' instruction, his values, he was correct. Everything he said was sensible and prudent. He could not understand why everyone else didn't agree. Despite the one student's objections, however, the girl's speech—on balance—was a success. She achieved the effect she wanted with most of her listeners. But suppose they had consisted almost entirely of people like the policeman. How could she succeed with them? To begin to answer this question, let's examine what audiences are, what they think, and how you can anticipate their thoughts.

WHAT IS AN AUDIENCE?

A group of people . . .

As the above example illustrated, you can't think of an audience as if they were one person. You can only assume, first, that an audience is a group of people together physically at the same time (provided you don't address them over television or radio); and, second, that they share some common interest, either in you or the subject matter of your speech (provided they are present willingly). Neither assumption, however, guarantees success. Though an audience's bodies are present, their minds and imaginations may wander as you speak; internal or external noises may distract them.

. . . With a common interest and differing assumptions

Similarly, though they may share common interests, they may share little else. Two male college students—one eighteen and the other forty-five, a father, and a homeowner—may both want to hear a speaker's advice on moneymaking in hopes of "getting ahead." For the eighteen-year-old, getting ahead may mean stereo equipment, a fast car, and a bachelor pad. For the older man, it may mean meeting his mortgage payments, coping with his rising tax bills, financing his children's education, and—if he has any money left over—buying a few luxury items. The younger student may know nothing about taxes and mortgages, plenty about the cost of school since he is working part time to pay for it, a great deal about conceiving children, but little about supporting them. The two students share a desire to make money, but they share few other interests.

. . . And differing experiences

In addition, their immediate experiences prior to the speech aren't the same. The eighteen-year-old may have struggled through an exam, fought with his girl friend, played an hour of basketball or half an hour with his guitar. The other may have just mowed his lawn, written a check for twice what he expected for gutter repair, come from the late shift at the factory or from playing with his youngest child.

MEETING YOUR LISTENERS' MINDS

Therefore, to speak effectively to both students' interests—to adjust your speech to their differing concerns—you've got to find some *common ground*. The task, despite what we've said, is not that difficult. The two students *do* share the same concern about the need for money; you can build on that. If you were wandering off to Ruanda for a speech, where the Hutus and the Tutsis are constantly at war no matter what you say, you might have problems. Or, if you were the major-league manager in Philip Roth's *The Great American Novel*[1] (a spoof on baseball) who travels to Africa with missionary zeal to teach Our National Pastime to cannibals, you might have problems, too. The manager-missionary's students, though magnificent athletes, soon become infuriated with the Rules and Regulations (almost a Holy Writ for the manager) and in an elaborate ceremony strap the manager to a stake at first base, boil and eat the baseballs and mitts, and perform obscene rites with the baseball bats. A case of failure to transcend cultural differences, one might say.

Your problems aren't nearly as severe. Use your imagination. Take into account what the majority of your listeners know and feel—it won't be that foreign to your experience—and you'll succeed with many of them, though certainly not all. Even a quick glance at the people in your audience before you speak will tell you some obvious things—their approximate age, their sex, their race, and (from their clothing and physical appearance) even roughly their socio-economic background. Though accomplished and experienced speakers can adapt to an audience on the spot, most speakers prefer not to make such quick adjustments. Nor are they, in fact, usually *able* to. Tying together a bundle of examples for a group of senior citizens when you expected a group of newlyweds isn't easy. You may become nervous, less assured, and possibly sputter and stutter. You cannot avoid occasional surprises, but you can minimize them with some prior and careful investigating of your listeners' backgrounds, experiences, values, and expectations.

A few questions to consider . . .

In a typical speaking situation outside the classroom, someone might ask you to address a group. You, in turn, can ask that person about the group members' basic interests and general background. Depending on your subject, you may want answers to any or all of the following questions:

1. How much does the audience know about your subject?
2. What are the audience's attitudes toward the subject?
3. What does the audience know about you?
4. What is the general age and age span of the audience?
5. Will the audience be mainly or exclusively male or female?
6. What is the audience's general level and type of education?
7. What, predominantly, are the occupations of the listeners?
8. What are their predominant ethnic backgrounds, religions, and races?
9. In general, what is the socio-economic level of the audience?
10. Do the listeners belong to certain organizations or have special interests or affiliations?

1 Discovering for Yourself

Analyzing Your Classmates as an Audience

Speaking before the entire class gives you an advantage: You already know your audience rather well. From the OK Seat, you've heard about their interests and their backgrounds. From your group, you've learned a number of further specifics about at least a part of your audience. To be safe, though, try consciously now to examine what you know about the class and to anticipate their needs and interests.

In your journal, answer at least questions 1 and 2 from the preceding list as they apply to your classmates and to the topic of the informative speech you are presently planning. Look over the other questions, too. Can you answer them with complete certainty? If not, what do you need to know about all your classmates, and which classmates do you know least about? Make some notes, and also prepare some specific questions you'd like to ask your classmates concerning their familiarity with the proposed subject matter for your forthcoming speech. How much do they know, for instance, about guitar terminology — about frets, the neck and bridge and kapo, about finger picking and strumming? What do they know about playing lead guitar or rhythm guitar?

. . . And what the answers will tell you

Information about ethnic background, for example, can supply you with hints about the audience's life-styles and values. The Italian policeman we mentioned earlier felt a stronger sense of family ties than, say, a sixth-generation WASP (White Anglo-Saxon Protestant) might feel. Most countries in Europe, Asia, Africa, and Latin America haven't yet adopted the American "nuclear family" unit of a husband and wife and two children living apart from grandparents and relatives. When you are aware of the background of the audience, then you can consider how your topic fits or can be made to fit their attitudes, beliefs, opinions, etc. — a subject we will explore in Chapter 17.

Similarly, a group comprised mostly of semiskilled laborers with high-school educations might consider a "good job" one with security and an annual salary of perhaps $15,000 to $20,000. For a group of executives, job security may be less important because they often leap from one to another and move about the world in the process. However, they may place less emphasis on the amount of money they make — perhaps as much as $200,000 — and more on the prestige, status, power, challenge, and responsibilities they would have in directing the entire midwest division of their company.

Both groups may be homeowners, too. But the laborer may pride himself in fixing his own plumbing, paneling his basement, or tilling his garden. He may consider a neighbor who can't or doesn't work around the house as foolish or incompetent. The executive, on the other hand, may feel social pressure to hire plumbers, carpenters, and gardeners. Mowing his lawn while his neighbor's landscaper observes may even embarrass him. He could make furniture or cabinets as "a hobby," to arouse the admiration of his colleagues, provided they know he does so for enjoyment and not out of necessity.

Level of education may also influence a listener's attitudes. For example, John Scanzoni, a sociologist, discovered after three thousand interviews with midwestern households that men with college degrees were more likely to share the responsibilities for raising children with their wives while allowing their wives to pursue their own careers. Less-educated men more often expected their wives to fulfill the traditional housewife roles.[2] Don't assume that higher education guarantees open-mindedness, however. "An intellectual," one wag observed, "is a person educated far beyond his intelligence." More seriously, no one can completely escape the insistent voices of an internal *Parent* or *Child,* and everyone retains some prejudices and contradictory attitudes.

We have noticed a correlation between the type of education a person receives and that person's values and attitudes, though there may be no cause-effect relationship. Doctors tend to be politically conservative, we suspect, not because they have studied medicine rather than literature, but because the values that led them into medicine also influence their politics. Similarly, in the colleges and universities we've been associated with, though most professors have Ph.D.'s, those in the social sciences and the humanities tend to be political liberals; those in the natural sciences, business, engineering, and mathematics tend toward conservatism.

In the few examples of audience analysis we've cited here, we admit to stereotyping, to drawing large generalizations. But in preparing a speech we often have to play our hunches and trust our experience. We're not wizards at predicting human behavior; and when we're actually speaking, we (and you) haven't time to conduct a private Gallup Poll. But, nevertheless, we need to know as much as possible about our audience's attitudes and to know about them as early as possible so we can appeal to or counter them. And the width and depth of our listeners' education can provide valuable clues.

Moreover, the type and level of an audience's education helps significantly to determine—in addition to attitudes—an audience's probable *familiarity with your subject.* This familiarity must, in turn, affect your *word choice* for the speech. A group of naval cadets tried the experiment in describing the geometric figure we included in Chapter 7. From each other's explicit directions they accurately reproduced the drawing because everyone was familiar with terminology for shapes, angles, volume, and distance. However, the man conducting the experiment, a Ph.D. in social sciences, couldn't comprehend their terminology.

As a speaker, of course, your word choice must be geared pretty closely to your listeners' comprehension level—a reflection of the nature and scope of their vocabulary for the specific subject in question. Words "outside" this vocabulary you will have to explain or define. A doctor, for example, speaking to non-scientists might need to define *metastasis* and *malignant lymphoma,* or substitute other words for them. As a psychologist speaking to non-psychologists, you might need to define *projection* through a synonym, like *empathy.* Or you could try to explain the term through an illustration, like puckering your lips as you watch someone bite a lemon, or holding your waist as someone belly-flops off the high board, or pushing your foot against the floorboard when you see the driver of the car about to apply the brakes. If a word, term, or concept requires elaborate explanation, a speaker may even need to supply a short history. For example, Philip Hilts' explanation of *the scientific method* (quoted in Chapter 5) traced the evolution of the method back to Galileo.

On the other hand, of course, a doctor needn't define common medical terms to other doctors; a psychologist can assume other psychologists know what *projection* means. You should be as careful not to speak "under" your audience's heads as "over." Telling them what they already know will bore them. Telling them less than they should know will confuse them. You must know, therefore, what they know. If you don't, you must take the time to find out.

Verifying Your Earlier Audience Analysis and Gathering More Information About Your Listeners

Meet with your small group, and explain briefly what you intend to discuss in a fully developed, ten-to-fifteen-minute informative speech you've been planning. See if they agree with your observations about the whole-class audience—the analysis you prepared in Exercise 1—and ask each group member the questions you prepared at that time. Your group may suggest other matters they'd like you to explain in your speech, as well as ways to enliven your explanations and relate your speech materials more effectively to your prospective audience.

If necessary, interview a few classmates outside your group, especially the people you know least about. Afterwards, jot down some notes on what you've learned.

To summarize, your speech cannot succeed unless your audience understands and accepts it. You can't wait until the moment of your speech to find out how your audience will react, so spend some thought and time *before* your speech deciding who is in your audience, what they know, and what they feel about your topic. Take into account their education, their ethnic background, their age, their sex, their occupation. Then consider how you can adapt your materials to their interests and knowledge.

Reference Notes

[1]Philip Roth, *The Great American Novel* (New York: Holt, Rinehart and Winston, Publishers, 1973).

[2]John H. Scanzoni, *Sex Roles, Life Styles, and Childbearing: Changing Patterns in Marriage and the Family* (New York: The Free Press, A Division of Macmillan Publishing Co., Inc., 1975), pp. 36, 43–44.

13 Organizing Your Speech Materials

ASSEMBLING THE PIECES AND SHOWING HOW THEY FIT

With materials in hand, a thesis in mind, and some thoughts about the nature of your audience included, you can begin the task of planning and organizing your speech. Planning means just what it implies, leaving virtually nothing to chance. For your speech to be *clear,* you must shape your materials around your thesis: discarding the irrelevant; deciding on the most logical organization for the rest; then planning to show your organization with a presummary at the speech's beginning, a summary at the end, and transitions to link ideas throughout.

All easily stated, not so easily accomplished. Coming to grips with your materials—shaping them coherently and forcefully for an audience—is a process of trial and retrial, thought and more thought, shuffling and reshuffling. No magic formula can eliminate the struggle since each thesis, each audience, and each piece of data presents a different problem. But if you approach the task systematically, you can at least lessen the pain. Therefore, we'll offer you some advice about such systematic planning. We'll discuss the process of discovering a useful and comfortable organization: first, by verifying your thesis; second, by grouping your materials to develop it. Then we'll discuss the process of making your organization clear, interesting, and useful for your audience: first, by planning an introduction; second, by planning internal summaries and transitions; and, third, by planning a conclusion.

Each is given a bag of tools,
A shapeless mass,
A book of rules;
And each must make,
Ere life is flown,
A stumbling block
Or a stepping-stone.
—R. L. Sharpe,
Stumbling Block or Stepping-Stone

ORGANIZING YOUR MATERIALS TO DEVELOP YOUR THESIS

How do you start and where?

After her speech on sexual behavior and values (Chapter 3, pages 49–50), Dr. Renshaw was cornered by a student whose teacher stressed the importance of outlining. The student asked Dr. Renshaw if she had outlined her speech. The doctor paused, taken aback. "Why, no," she replied, "I just decided what I wanted to say and wrote it out a few times."

Dr. Renshaw made the process *seem* simpler than it was, however. She must have considered her speech for a while because, as she noted, she "wrote it out a few times," assembling it in a few different ways and changing the language as well. Though she chose to talk from a manuscript, her preparation probably wouldn't have differed significantly if she had spoken extemporaneously—that is, from notes—while formulating the exact language as she delivered the speech. She still would have left herself room for discovery and change, to shift her materials around until she felt satisfied with their organization.

A listener could have outlined Dr. Renshaw's speech as she delivered it, for—like any good speech—it did have form; it did have structure; but they emerged only after she had molded and probed and polished it. She worked in soft clay instead of chiseling her ideas once and for all into granite.

Does Dr. Renshaw's example suggest that you not outline your materials? Yes . . . and no. These days, few speakers use a *formal* outline, with all the I. A., I. B. headings and subheadings. But speakers do experiment with different structures until they know what to say first, second, and so on, and until they know the relationship between one element and the next. Then they commit their final structure to memory or paper. They may write it down grocery-list style, place each idea on a separate note card arranged in sequence, or write out the entire speech. Some speakers do outline occasionally or always in the final stages of preparation, but the physical method of organizing isn't as important as the need to organize.

In fact, teachers from grade school through college stress outlining, not so students learn how to outline, but so they learn how to *organize their thoughts.* Too many students, nonetheless, as good *Producers* instead of *Thinkers,* may neatly outline the order of the items they plan to include in the speech, but they can't explain *why* they want to include them or *what relationship* they see among them. Anyone can learn to make a list. The hard part is learning what to put on the list and why to put it there. The neatest outline can disguise the sloppiest thinking. Outlines are fine, provided they help you see the relevance of materials and the relationships among them, but don't let the *process* of outlining—listing your thoughts—obscure the *purpose* of outlining: to help you organize your thoughts.

So, whether you outline or not, carefully examine your ideas. Why are you giving the speech? What is the thesis of your speech? How do your materials develop the thesis? Then organize. And be flexible. Shift your materials around. Try different groupings and sequences. Crystallize your ideas through experimentation; don't freeze them initially and be afraid to change them. Organizing your speech coldly, abstractly, without first feeling the heat of materials rubbing against each other often eliminates most sparks of inspiration.

On the other hand, don't feel you can generate a burning interest within your audience without planning. To be sure, you want to appear spontaneous and creative as you speak. But careful preparation doesn't necessarily destroy a speech's liveliness. The Romantic poets encouraged the notion that true creativity flows only from inspiration which "our meddling intellect" destroys. "We murder to dissect," wrote Wordsworth. Yet these poets carefully revised their works many times to achieve that "spontaneous" effect. In short, don't be too casual or too rigid. Instead, think through your ideas; know your material and how it develops those ideas; and—ultimately—rehearse it before you speak. You'll be more confident, less prone to error, and more free to adapt as the need arises. Organizing should neither inhibit your creativity nor overcome your common sense.

Even when the laws have been written down, they ought not always to remain unaltered.
—Aristotle, Politics, Book II

Using your thesis as a yardstick

Since everything in your speech—from your opening statement, throughout the body of your message, and on through your final remarks—should develop your point or thesis, your first step must be to write out that thesis carefully, thoughtfully. Unless you know your point, your audience certainly won't. Here's a typical example of a pointless speech:

> My speech today is going to be about the state where I was born, Louisiana. The state's name comes from the French King Louis XIV.
> The state was originally French territory. The French claimed it in 1682. It was the eighteenth state admitted to the Union, achieving statehood in 1812. Its government is a parish system, with the state divided into sixty-four individual parishes. The state's population is 3½ million. Many people in Louisiana today still speak French.

This speech dumps unrelated facts on its audience like scraps of deadwood in a pile, where they rattle hollowly without weight or impact. The speaker says he wants to talk "about . . . Louisiana," a giveaway that the speaker knows his *subject,* but not his *point.* Although the speaker may have outlined his speech under headings like "Louisiana's History," "Louisiana's Government," and "Characteristics of Louisiana's Population," the speaker probably never asked himself *why* he should include such headings or the facts under them. Had he decided first on a thesis—like "Louisiana, although part of the United States, is almost a foreign land"—he could have eliminated the irrelevant material and fashioned the rest to develop the thesis interestingly.

". . . Oh, that was Professor Higgins' idea . . . he had his students assemble it to demonstrate how the pieces fit together in a solid speech!"

1 Discovering for Yourself
Verifying Your Thesis

Write out your thesis in a sentence or two, and exchange your paper with another member of your group. Check each other's thesis statements carefully. If your partner has written, "I'm going to talk about guitars," work with him or her until the thesis makes a point, like "I'm going to show how easily you can learn a few guitar chords and strums."

Grouping your materials

With your thesis established, you can begin to structure your speech. Organizing your earlier speeches about your experiences required merely that you start at the beginning and trace the events through to the end. No real problems there, especially with materials so familiar to you. However, discussing ideas, data, and statistics from things you've read or gathered in interviews creates different and more difficult problems. Every article or chapter of a book follows its own organization and develops its own thesis. And most questions and answers in interviews follow no carefully determined pattern. Consequently, as you try to develop your own thesis and integrate your research into your own organization, you may feel the information is controlling you instead of your controlling it. Finding a comfortable structure requires reorganizing and juggling the material a bit.

If you can't fit the pieces into a pattern you like, perhaps this method will work for you. First, arrange all the material into groups or categories: the history of Louisiana, characteristics of its people, characteristics of its politics and political system, etc. Second (the step the speaker about Louisiana seems to have skipped), ask yourself whether each category *develops* your thesis, makes your speech go where you want it to go. If your thesis is that Louisiana is a "foreign land," why bother to mention the size of its population? Perhaps, though, its history explains its foreign quality. Finally, discard the irrelevant categories; decide if you need more facts for others; and try arranging the remaining categories into a sequence of some kind.

Perhaps you may want to put the list of categories away for a few days and return to it as more ideas occur to you. Ultimately, you may rearrange the categories, or form new ones, five or six times before you're satisfied.

SOME QUESTIONS TO AID YOUR PLANNING

Remember that people listen poorly—inattentively, with frequent errors in understanding. Therefore, the best organization maximizes their interest and minimizes their misunderstandings. Here are a few questions to ask yourself as you decide what or what not to include and what order to include it in:

1. *Does my audience share my assumptions and vocabulary?* After tuning motors for seven years, you hardly think about a motor's parts and operation. Your audience, on the other hand, may scratch their heads at the mere mention of a socket wrench or an engine block. To them, "points" may mean the tips of arrows, "plugs" the things you put into bathtub drains. Similarly, a speech about picking a profitable stock may be worthless to a group who knows nothing about dividends, the Dow-Jones average, brokerage fees, and capital gains. Early on, you should establish your assumptions and define your terms.

2. *Would a large framework help my audience fit in the specifics?* If you're describing how to tune a car, a general description of what a tune-up entails should clarify your specific instructions later.

3. Can I break my subject down into a number of smaller units and explain each separately? Audiences best understand and remember one idea at a time, so divide a complex subject into simpler units. Notice, for example, how we have listed and discussed each question in this section separately. With a car tune-up, you might also divide the process into separate steps. Or with another subject, you might first establish categories, and then discuss each one individually.

4. Does one thing in my speech cause another? If so, establish the relationship and decide whether to explain the cause or the effect first. You could, for example, first describe the results of a car out of tune — poor gas mileage, a bucking motion as you drive, or a sputtering sound in the engine — and then explain why they occur. Or, you could start with the causes — a dead spark plug providing no combustion in one cylinder, the cylinders not firing in sequence — and then discuss the effects. Either way has advantages.

5. Does one thing in my speech seem to precede another logically? In a tune-up, before you can adjust the timing, you must change the plugs and points. In playing a guitar, before you learn to strum, you must learn a few chords.

6. Once I've fitted everything together, what links one idea to the next? Consider whether you are moving from first to last, cause to effect, largest to smallest, most serious to least important.

2 Discovering for Yourself
Practicing Forming and Arranging Categories

Look at the following list of information about *hypnotism.*[1] Assume that you are an amateur hypnotist and could add a number of personal examples and anecdotes to the list. Then decide upon a thesis like: "Though hypnotism is used in a number of ways, no one understands exactly how it works"; or "Hypnotism can be both beneficial and dangerous"; or another thesis of your own choosing. Write the thesis down, and underneath it group the items of information into categories, adding your own "personal" information to the list. Then arrange the categories in the order you would discuss them in a speech. Decide what information you would exclude, and decide *why* you would discuss each category in the *order* you choose. You need not write out each item; if you wish, simply use the numbers representing the item, as shown below:

1. Your personal experiences with hypnotism, how you learned it, what you've used it for.

2. *Bridey Murphy,* the identity in an "earlier" life discovered in a person under hypnosis.
3. The inability to feel pain under hypnosis.
4. Becoming hypnotized by looking at a fixed object or a trinket suspended from a chain.
5. Early superstitions and beliefs about hypnosis.
6. The first person to study hypnosis scientifically.
7. Hypnosis caused by drugs.
8. Bill Faul, ex-pitcher for the Chicago Cubs, who practiced self-hypnosis before each game.
9. Great muscular strength and the ability to make the body rigid under hypnosis.
10. Self-hypnosis.
11. Hallucinations under hypnosis.
12. Who is most susceptible to hypnosis?
13. Blisters and rashes appearing under hypnosis.
14. What various people will do under hypnosis.
15. Can someone be forced to do something against his or her will under hypnosis?
16. Suggestions carried out after the subject leaves a hypnotic trance.
17. Hypnosis in medicine.
18. Recalling or reenacting your childhood under hypnosis.
19. Hypnosis used for entertainment.
20. Legality of hypnosis.
21. Hypnosis as an anesthetic in dentistry.
22. Hypnotists without the proper qualifications.
23. Sigmund Freud, the first to use hypnosis in psychoanalysis.
24. Hypnotism and meditation.
25. Hypnosis as an aid in psychological treatment.

Compare and discuss your list with those of other members of your group, then hand your list to your instructor. You should discover a variety of organizations and categories for the same information.

---

3 Discovering for Yourself

Organizing Your Own Speech

Using the materials for your own speech, group them as you did in Exercise 2 with the materials on hypnotism. First establish categories, then decide on the order you'd present them. Discuss your organization with one or two others in your group who can offer you suggestions.

MAKING YOUR ORGANIZATION CLEAR, INTERESTING, AND USEFUL TO YOUR AUDIENCE

After determining the point you want your speech to make, and coming to grips with your materials to be sure they all develop that point, you should know the direction in which you want your speech to travel. The question is, however: Will your *audience* know?

There's an old cliché about making a speech: "Tell your audience what you're going to say, say it, then tell them what you've said." Old, but still valid. The more structure you build into your speech, and the more you make that structure apparent to your listeners, the greater the possibility they will understand—or not misunderstand—your arguments. Although shaping your materials in some logical way clarifies things for you, showing your listeners that shape will clarify things for them. Though you've traveled over your ideas many times and know the route, your audience hasn't. So plan to share your itinerary with them near the beginning. Plan to put up signposts throughout the body of your speech which summarize main ideas and introduce new ones along the way. And plan to review the route when you finally arrive at the end of your journey. In short, plan a beginning, an ending, and some links in between which show your structure.

Plan for more than clarity, however. First and last impressions are important. If you communicate insecurity or confusion or indifference as you start, your audience may start to lose interest or patience or their confidence in you. If you end with a shrug and a "That's all I have to say," your audience may say, "It wasn't much." So, in addition to planning the body of the speech, plan a beginning that makes your listeners want to listen to your speech, and an ending that makes them want to remember it. Let's examine such beginnings and endings, and the summaries and transitions that you'll use in threading ideas and materials together throughout your speech.

Planning your beginning

Though your introduction is the first thing you say, as you can see, it's often one of the last things you prepare. It develops from a careful consideration of your thesis and your speech's main points, and consequently should state your thesis and preview those main points. Just as importantly, however, it should open the lines of communication between you and your audience.

Observing the opening rituals. Every communication situation requires some opening ritual, a phenomenon called "verbal stroking" in the vocabulary of Transactional Analysis. In its simplest form, beginning a conversation, you exchange a "Hello. How are you?" with a "Fine, thanks. And you?"—a trade of two strokes apiece. Though neither of you is really inquiring about the other's health (you may, in fact, discuss your cold and lumbago *after* the stroking ends), to remove the trade of strokes would make you feel uncomfortable. Try greeting a friend with "Can you loan me five bucks?" and watch the reaction.

Most public speeches require some observation of rituals as well. At a formal occasion—a graduation, a commencement, a political nominating convention—you usually open your remarks like this: "President Sigfoos, Chancellor Swing, Reverend Alworthy, honored guests, ladies and gentlemen, I take great pleasure in addressing you this evening on such an august occasion. To follow the inspirational words of Mr. Tonguebender is a difficult task. I hope my remarks can equal his." At informal occasions you may begin with, "Thanks for that nice greeting, folks. I enjoyed this excellent dinner, but now I'd like to share a few thoughts with you."

Curiously, speech classes don't often witness this kind of verbal stroking at a speech's beginning, probably because as student speakers you tend to consider your speeches "assignments" and not real attempts at communication. Obviously, you can't pretend you're speaking at San Francisco's Cow Palace, but you can attempt a few sentences of preliminary verbal stroking. You can start by commenting on the relationship between your speech and the previous one: "John made an excellent point about saving money by setting up a student used-book exchange. I think it's a good idea. And I want to suggest another way to save money, too, by tuning your car yourself." Or, if you're the first to speak to the class, you can simply say, "I want to begin today's speeches with one on a subject of great importance to me and, I think, to you." Either way, you'll both open up the communication lines and give yourself a moment to adjust to facing an audience.

Deciding on an angle. After your audience has begun listening, you must supply them with a reason to keep listening. Once, after an abstract and rambling speech on "Suicide Prevention," we overheard one person grumble to another as they made for the door: "I had no idea suicide could be so dull." Although the speech dealt with death, the audience's initial interest in it was alive. Yet the speaker killed that interest, too. He hadn't related the subject to his listeners, shown them why they ought to listen, then kept them listening through presenting them with strong, vivid materials.

Any speech, no matter how well organized, can be boring if the speaker forgets about the concerns of the audience while focusing on the subject. Although you intend primarily to provide information in

"Leave it to Art Schmutz to come up with a new angle to hook his listeners' attention every time!"

your speech, ultimately you must also provide an explanation of the *current or potential usefulness of your material to your audience.* You must make them want to hear you out. You've chosen material exciting to you, which you want your audience to know and remember—perhaps, the recessive genetic traits of the wingless, hairless *drosophila melanogaster.* But who but a biologist cares about a fruit fly's sex life?

If your subject, therefore, won't grab your audience's attention, you must create a grabber which, in addition to being a hook, provides a sustaining link between your subject and your audience. Newspaper and television reporters call this their *angle.* They don't write or talk about a large, destructive fire in random fashion. They look for an aspect of the event with the most human interest, something which strongly affects them, and that they know will strongly affect their audience.

"Raging Fire Kills Mother of Three" a headline might read, with the story focusing on a twenty-eight-year-old woman perishing in a flaming room while her children escape to safety. The reporter naturally felt the human tragedy of the fire, not the dollar damage to the building, and knew the paper's readers would feel the same.

It's easy to find an angle when you are dealing with life and death matters. But how to play a guitar, tune a car, or make a successful marriage, however, doesn't generally bring an audience to the edge of their seats. So make your subject relevant. Think first about why it interests you and, therefore, why it should interest them. Explain what's in it for them. Is it joy? wealth? security? comfort? love? convenience? alleviation of pain? Whatever your subject, you must reach your audience where they live or, like the "Suicide Prevention" speaker, perish from lack of attention.

Here, for example, is a possible angle for your speech about playing the guitar:

> Three years ago, I got fed up with the plastic culture: all the artificial fabrics, the canned food, and the canned music. So I decided I'd start making my own things, including my own entertainment. I started learning to play the guitar—not so much to be the center of attention at a party, but so I could feel the satisfaction of doing something creative. Now I've reached the point where I write my own songs. You don't have to be so ambitious, but the knowledge of a few simple chords and strums is all you need to play a number of popular tunes.

Here's an angle for a speech on tuning a car:

> I began tuning my car for three reasons. I like working with my hands; I like to save money; and I don't trust mechanics. A car tune-up is a simple job that only takes a few hours, a job that you know has been done right because you did it. And with the savings—as much as fifty dollars each time—you quickly recoup the sixty or seventy dollars you pay out initially for the basic equipment.

And here's an angle for a speech about making a successful marriage:

> The reason I chose this topic is that I think it's so valuable for everyone—for married couples to examine their own relationship and check for danger signs to correct, and for single people who think they'll get married sooner or later. With one out of three marriages today ending in divorce—and the cost in dollars, unhappiness, and harm to the children so great—we all ought to be sensitive to making marriages work.

Notice that in the first two examples, the speaker begins with what attracted him or her to the subject, then implies or shows why it should interest the audience. In the third example, about making a marriage successful, the speaker says that everyone should be interested, since the subject touches everyone. The speaker doesn't mention personal motivations for choosing the subject because those motivations are universal. In all three examples, however, notice that the angle isn't forced or fanciful. It seems natural, valid, real. It grows from the needs and interests of the audience. Your angle should, too.

4 Small-Group Speaking
Formulating an Angle for Your Speech

Plan an angle for your speech, then explain your plan to the members of your small group, and get their reactions to it. Do they think it will touch the needs and interests of the entire class? Can they offer suggestions on what might better touch those needs and interests? After you've decided on your angle, make some notes so you don't forget it.

Strengthening your introduction. If you feel your introduction lacks sufficient strength to attract and hold your audience, you can choose from any of these standard devices, all of which should lead into your angle. One popular way to open a speech is with a question — like, "Do you share my rage about getting ripped off for auto repairs?" To be effective, though, your question should sound neither contrived, condescending, nor insulting to your audience's intelligence. It must sound authentic. Asking "Did you ever think about what marsupials eat?" is silly unless you are speaking to kangaroos. Asking "Did you know there is a worldwide food shortage?" is insulting because anyone who reads the papers or watches the news knows that. Better to skip the question than ask a phony one.

A second possibility is to begin your speech with an anecdote, like the ones you told earlier in the term. Here's a short one a Vietnam veteran might share to illustrate his feelings about combat, while inviting his audience to experience those feelings, too:

Reading about the war won't tell you what it was like. You can't know what it's like until you've walked through a rice paddy and seen your best buddy's legs blown off by a land mine. After that, killing the enemy isn't scary; killing isn't disgusting. It's easy—especially if you call him a "gook" and he looks different from you and speaks a funny language. Somehow he seems less human, kind of like a pest or a snake. You want to step on his head before he strikes at you.

Additionally, you can begin your speech with a dramatic statement: "In ten years, we're going to be abandoning our cars and freezing in our homes. That's how serious the energy crisis is." And, finally, you can select among these possible openers: a joke, a quotation, an important fact from your research, or several such facts presented in rapid succession. But as you select from these devices, remember that a joke must be funny, a quote or a fact must be interesting, and anything you say must be short. Don't lose your audience with the very device you've chosen to gain their attention.

Announcing your destination and describing your route. The next step in your introduction is, of course, to state your *thesis* in a sentence or two so your listeners will know where you'll be taking them. But to help them follow your journey, you may want to draw them a general road map. In other words, you may want to include a brief *presummary* which outlines your arguments or points in the order you'll discuss them. Such presummaries aren't always necessary if you clearly label each argument or point you discuss within the body of your speech. Nevertheless, a presummary provides your audience with one more aid to understanding, so we'd recommend including it, especially in longer speeches. Here's an example. Dr. Milton Rakove, a political scientist, spoke to a college audience about the reasons that Mayor Richard J. Daley's Chicago Democratic political organization, or the "Machine," has thrived for two decades. Since his argument was long and complex, he made his thesis (which we've italicized) and his presummary explicit:

> What I'm going to talk about tonight is *why I think this "machine" has lasted as long as it has in Chicago.* It's a fascinating machine. All the other big city machines in this country have gone to hell; they all disappeared. [Newspaper writer] Mike Royko said in a column about eight years ago that one of the reasons the other machines went down is because they got into bad habits—and they reformed. But this one has never reformed. . . .
>
> I think that's an oversimplification of why the machine has lasted so long. And I think it's lasted as long as it has and done as well as it has primarily for five reasons: one, its ability to adapt to a changing city; two, the concept of its demand for efficiency within the machine; three, the demand for loyalty that the machine makes of its members; four, the fact of the almost single-minded concentration that the machine has on political power; and, five, you can't talk about this machine, of course, except within the context of the role that Mayor Daley has played. So let me take those five things and talk about them briefly.[2]

Note that Dr. Rakove not only mentioned all the points he would examine; he *enumerated* them as well. Throughout the speech, as he moved from point to point, he repeated the key terms and his numbering of them: "Let me start with adaptability," he said. Then later, "Secondly, I want to discuss the concept of efficiency," and so on.

"Now then, Miss Jones . . . simply announce your destination, describe your route, and follow the signposts along the way."

Some speakers choose a looser kind of presummary, without the enumeration. They simply mention in a few sentences what they'll discuss, leaving the more explicit signposting for the body of the speech. Whichever method you choose, you will make the journey through your speech easier for your audience.

Planning for your signposts along the way

As we've already suggested, short statements which indicate *transitions*—that is, which show the relationship between one idea and the next—are a further aid to clarity within the body of your speech. They serve as signposts—"Leaving Idea Number One and entering Idea Number Two"—to guide your audience. Occasionally, in a longer speech, as you move from one major section to the next, you may wish to review where you've been before entering new territory. An audience has so much on their minds, so many noises in their brains and lives, that they may have missed parts of what you've said, especially at the end of each of your major ideas. You can do them a favor by restating or bringing together your ideas in a section summary or an *internal summary,* then moving on to the next section.

Such summaries can be planned; but you must know the direction your speech is going and perceive the major breaks, the points at which your audience would appreciate a refresher. For example, Philip Hilts used the following one in the speech we first quoted in Chapter 5. More than half an hour after he'd begun, after having related ten or more anecdotes and introduced a number of ideas, he summarized his main points (which we've italicized) before advancing into new territory. The words "The problem is" begin the transition.

> There is now no doubt as far as I am concerned that *behavior modification* is here permanently. . . . *I think the science of it is very clear and straightforward. I think the science of it is right.* The problem is: What about the horror stories? What about the abuses? How do you put the two together—science that works and technology that is horrible, and sometimes good?[3]

Hilts then entered the next section of his speech, discussing a way to resolve—through political action—the problem of the "horror stories" and "abuses."

However, in shorter speeches where such internal summaries may be unnecessary, you can still indicate the relationship between ideas with a single sentence. It can be a statement ("In addition to learning the guitar chords, you must also learn a few strums."), or a question followed by your answer ("What can be done about the energy crisis? Here are a few suggestions."). The important point is, whenever possible, give your listeners the guidance to stay on course.

Planning your ending

Since the last words in your speech will also be the last words in your audience's minds, a strong ending is crucial. You should plan your conclusion to accomplish two goals: (1) to *remind* your audience of what you've just said, and (2) to *show them the importance* of what you've just said. You'll be summarizing your speech and wrapping it up with a powerful statement, which can take the form of a quotation or anecdote embodying your main idea, or a return to the beginning of your speech. Your ending also can carry your main ideas forward, suggesting the positive results of their application, or warning of the consequences if they're not carried out. In any case, your ending should be bold, forceful, vivid.

Here's a conclusion of a student's speech to his classmates in which he had explained the disadvantages of buying a new car and the advantages of buying a used car. Notice how he summarizes most of his arguments and then ends on a firm, positive note:

So—to sum it all up—most of us can't really afford a new car. You could if you went out and borrowed, but then you are stuck with monthly payments. Monthly payments can cost a lot of money. Car insurance itself can be another thousand dollars. This is really quite a lot of money. And, to be paying for the car for three or four years, I think, is just ridiculous for anyone going to school. When we get older and are making more money, then we can afford a new car. But right now, while we're in school, let's buy a used car we can fix up inexpensively, a car which fits both our basic needs and our budget.[4]

5 Discovering for Yourself
Planning a Structure for Your Audience

Plan the whole structure of your speech: the introduction, the body, the conclusion, and the internal summaries and transitions. Decide what you'll say and where you'll say it. And prepare it in any way that feels most comfortable—with note cards, with an outline, with a list of ideas, with some sentences written out. Look over your structure a number of times and make any necessary changes.

Since we're dealing with summaries, let's summarize our advice in this chapter. An effective speech requires careful planning. You must plan your organization, first verifying your thesis, then shaping your materials to develop it while discarding those you find irrelevant, and—finally—deciding on the order you'll use to present your materials and the relationships among them. You must plan how to begin, how to sustain momentum through the body of the message, and how to close your speech—all for maximum clarity and interest. You must plan internal summaries and transitions to serve as signposts along the way. You must plan until you've left virtually nothing to chance. Then your ideas will be clear to yourself *and* your audience.

Reference Notes

[1]Many of the items in this list were adapted from Jacqueline Berke, *Twenty Questions for the Writer: A Rhetoric with Readings* (New York: Harcourt Brace Jovanovich, Inc., 1972), pp. 403–404.

[2]Dr. Milton L. Rakove, "Chicago: The City That Works?" speech delivered at Wilbur Wright College, Chicago, Illinois, February 26, 1976.

[3]Philip Hilts, "Behavior Modification: Its Uses and Implications," speech delivered at Wilbur Wright College, Chicago, Illinois, March 5, 1975.

[4]Mark C. Puchalski, "The Used Car," speech delivered at Wilbur Wright College, Chicago, Illinois, spring, 1976.

14 Humanizing, Vitalizing, and Visualizing Your Speech

A powerful beginning to your speech, as we've emphasized, should grab your audience's interest. But only clear, fresh, lively material in the *body* of your speech can hold it. Perhaps you've already found plenty of sparkling stuff. But, if not, think of ways to shine up dull facts and statistics. Even empty facts on a technical subject can take on substance if *humanized*. You can humanize your facts by making them vivid and alive in the eyes, ears, and minds of your listeners. For this, you have several practical means at your command: using *anecdotes as examples,* interpreting your *statistics,* utilizing *visual and auditory aids,* and *involving your audience physically* in your speech. In this chapter, we'll look first at each of these methods of enlivening your materials. Then, as a final wrap-up (and possibly also as a reminder before you present the fully developed informative speeches we anticipate you'll be giving), we'll conclude by tieing together all our observations about effective speechmaking, and by supplying you with the full text of a student's speech to illustrate them.

We must view with profound respect the infinite capacity of the human mind to resist the introduction of useful knowledge.
—Thomas Raynesford Lounsbury

HUMANIZING YOUR MATERIALS

Your audience may know little about your subject, but they do know a great deal about life. Cement the relationship between your listeners and your ideas with examples and illustrations you've derived from experience, with explanations of statistics which reduce large numbers to human terms, with things which your audience can visualize or hear or even hold in their hands. Reduce the abstract to the concrete, the particular; give ideas *human life;* make them real and understandable.

Remember the speech about Louisiana in the preceding chapter? It was full of facts and figures, but it lacked the soft stuff of life to cling to them. It needed a "for instance," a story, a comparison, a detailed example. The speaker was born in Louisiana, but didn't relate his experiences there to his listeners' experiences in the urban North. What makes Louisiana "foreign"? He could have contrasted his impressions of the French architecture of New Orleans to the cold sterility of the steel-and-glass highrises of the northern cities. He could have compared his memories of Louisiana's tree-lined streets and grassy plazas to the botanical gardens found only in the northern cities' parks. The speaker also could have considered his audience's knowledge of his terminology: What is a "parish government," and how does it compare with government of most other states? He could have considered his own experiences and his audience's, and attempted to relate the two.

. . . Through illustrative anecdotes

Here's a passage from a student's speech that does relate the two. The speaker discussed helping others survive drug trips — physically and emotionally. Rather than warning about the dangers of drugs or making abstract moral pronouncements which his audience had heard many times before, he assumed that some people would use and abuse narcotics anyway — an assumption he knew his audience shared. So he offered them practical advice on how to guide someone down from a drug "high"; and, avoiding generalities, he used as an illustration his own experience with a friend who had taken LSD. Not only did his example establish his point dramatically, but it established his credentials to give advice:

> I had a friend who had taken some "orange sunshine," which is acid [LSD]. We were in a very large room; there were a lot of people there, but yet he focused on the side of the room. And up on the wall was a small socket where the doorbell went, and he said, "I can see myself going through the socket." He actually projected himself through the socket.[1]

Then the speaker offered advice on how to deal with someone in this condition:

> At this stage, this is where you want to be really careful about what you say. You want to maintain a positive attitude toward the person who is "tripping," because it's also at this point that anything negative said to the person can really set him off. . . . You must remember to tell him that, as he's going through this trip, he's not alone — you're there to help him.[2]

Throughout the speech, the student referred to his own experience. He made his subject real by talking about real human beings.

. . . Through vitalizing your statistics

Statistics can supply either authority or tedium to your talk. They can broaden experiences, extend observations, and make them applicable to an entire population; or they can shrink your audience's attention to zero. Too many figures can overwhelm anyone except, perhaps, the baseball zealot who memorizes daily the top ten batting averages in both leagues. Too large a figure becomes too abstract, too far removed from reality, and thus loses its impact. In general, people respond best to smaller numbers closer to home.

You must, therefore, try to relate abstract numbers to the common experiences of your listeners. For example, large numbers can be broken down dramatically. If you divide the U.S. population into the total number of tons of garbage accumulated, you learn that every American throws away 125 pounds daily. However, in addition to everyone's milk cartons, candy wrappers, pencil shavings, old tires, and torn socks, the total includes industrial and municipal wastes as well. Nevertheless, the figure — even if somewhat distorted — is astounding.

Dr. J. Allen Hynek, whose speech on unidentified flying objects we quoted in Chapter 8, knew that large distances in space would be meaningless to a general audience. So he looked for illustrations in smaller objects familiar to his audience.

> You realize that if I, like our old schoolteacher used to do, if I put an apple here to represent the sun, and just *one foot* away I put a grain of sand to represent the earth, then on that scale, the very nearest of the 100 billion other stars in our galaxy would be fifty miles away. . . . The very nearest star to us — other than the sun, of course — is four and a half light years. Now, a light year — the distance light travels in a year — would be equivalent to taking a string and winding it around the earth 236 million times. That would be almost one light year.[3]

And in this final example, he described the distance of a star trillions of miles away in terms of the Stone Age on earth:

> Light travels pretty fast: 186,000 miles per second. Well, this photograph, the light that made this photograph which was made just a few years ago, left those galaxies when dinosaurs were roaming the earth. You're really looking at fossil light.[4]

1 Small-Group Speaking
Making Figures More Dramatic or Understandable

Try taking any figure from the *Statistical Abstract of the United States,* or from any other source, and breaking it down for your group into something smaller and more meaningful. You could show the distance to the moon in terms of the number of years and/or generations it would take to walk there. Or you could figure out the number of years required to drive there by car, as well as the number of tires you would wear out in the process if the road to the moon were paved. You could show that the population of blacks in the United States — twenty-two million, a mere twelve percent of the entire country — equals the population of twelve of the nation's largest cities (these figures came right from a dictionary: New York, Chicago, Los Angeles, Detroit, Philadelphia, Houston, Baltimore, Washington, St. Louis, San Francisco, Seattle, and Milwaukee.

If, in the process of breaking the number down into smaller units, you somehow distort it (as we did when we ignored industrial waste in our example about garbage), mention and explain the distortion. Astounding your audience is fine; lying to them is not.

What I can't see
I never will believe in.
—Samuel John Stone,
Soliloquy of a
Rationalistic Chicken

. . . Through using visual and auditory aids

You discovered in earlier chapters that words have their limitations. Since your audience sees as well as hears, however, you can let them visualize your explanation in a model, a chart, a diagram, or—if possible—by looking at the real thing. Large drawings of where to place their fingers on the guitar neck for each chord, followed by an actual demonstration of the chord, will teach your listeners far more easily than will abstract oral instructions. *You* learned to play by handling a real guitar and seeing how it works. Your audience is entitled to similar advantages. Unfortunately, though, a sizeable audience can't see the guitar neck up close, which is why you should enlarge it through drawings. A visual aid is no aid if not visual.

To overcome the problem, some student speakers have passed pictures around among their listeners. One, for example, wanted to use some photographs to dramatize a speech about cruelty to animals—a good idea. But as the scenes of mutilated and slaughtered creatures circulated through the room, the audience gasped and chattered among themselves—at all the wrong moments. No one paid any attention to the speech. While a speech is in progress, stones, cards, jewelry, and other bric-a-brac can only move from listener to listener at the speaker's peril.

The best visual aids, generally, are easily seen, easily comprehended devices you have prepared in advance. Drawing or writing on the chalkboard while speaking forces you to lose eye contact; and sometimes, at the very moment you need chalk and erasers, they disappear. Therefore, use the chalkboard only for drawing quick sketches or writing short phrases. Otherwise, bring a sketch or chart with you; elevate or display it at the appropriate moment; and, to avoid distracting the audience, put it down or remove it when you're through. In fact, deciding *prior* to your speech where you want to display it, and even practicing putting it up, can save you the anguish of watching it fall four times with a large crash in the middle of your speech.

Your visual aids needn't be elaborate or elegant. Graphs and diagrams don't require a Van Gogh touch; just a few heavy lines and bright colors and a large piece of cardboard will suffice. You can draw *line graphs, bar graphs,* and *pie-sliced graphs* to represent statistics. Or your library's visual-aid department may carry maps, diagrams, and pictures you can copy or check out overnight. Your bookstore may even carry inexpensive posters.

Slides, overhead projectors, short films, and recordings can serve ably, too. A photograph of a car motor's plugs, points, and condenser shown on a large screen, or a film illustrating their installation, is the next best thing to being there. A phonograph record or clear tape recording played on good equipment also makes a fine substitute for the real thing. But set your equipment up in advance, and be sure it works.

"She's got so many visual and auditory aids I forgot what her speech was about!"

Nothing irritates an audience faster than fuzzy pictures, scratchy recordings, or your fumbling with a balky machine. Plan a procedure for dousing the lights and flipping the switches quickly; or, better yet, enlist a few helpers beforehand to let you proceed without pausing. However, if despite your preparation, an apparatus breaks down or throws a tantrum, play it cool, adjust, joke about it, even do without it. Dr. Domeena Renshaw, whom we mentioned earlier in the book, was plagued with a wheezing sound system during the first few minutes of her speech. She handled it well—in fact, even turned it to her advantage:

> I'm getting quite a lot of echo in the microphone. Are you getting that, too? You are? [*She twists the microphone support to bring it closer to her.*] Let's see if that's a little better. Can you hear now? No? [*A person comes onstage, adjusts the microphone, making a loud noise as he accidentally bumps it.*] Oooh. [*She hits the lectern near the microphone several times with her pointer.*] If it won't behave, destroy it. Is that the idea? [*Laughter.*] That was terrifying.[5]

Specific visual and auditory aids and how to use them. No matter what device you employ as a visual aid, make sure it is integral to your speech and not merely a gimmick. A multicolored chart complete with tassels and spangles won't replace a clear explanation and a strong vocal/bodily delivery. Visual and auditory devices are only *aids* to clarity—not substitutes for substance. They add another dimension to your words and gestures, lessening the probability that your audience might misunderstand. But if such aids detract from or distort your speech, better leave them out.

In general, therefore, consider any of the following aids, but note our warnings about each:

1. *Graphs* are helpful to illustrate or dramatize the relationship between or a trend among figures. Only those figures absolutely central to your thesis require graphs, however.
2. *Slides and movies* are helpful to show what can't easily be explained, or as a reference as you explain. But each requires shutting off the lights and your listeners' view of you as the speaker. Don't talk in the dark throughout your speech, especially not during your introduction and conclusion.
3. *Maps* are helpful to show a route or a locale, but they must clearly indicate what you want to show.
4. *Charts* are helpful as a reference while you explain the steps in a procedure or the levels of an organization, but the procedure or organization should be central to your thesis.
5. *Models* or the actual objects are especially helpful in visualizing the object in three dimensions and demonstrating to listeners how it

works. The model or object must be large enough for all to see and portable enough to bring to the setting or occasion of the speech.

6. *Recordings* are helpful to reproduce sounds you cannot otherwise create, but be cautious about using recordings for mood music. Your audience should listen to *you,* not hum along with your background music.

. . . Through involving your audience physically

Sometimes an audience can in fact learn by doing, by becoming involved physically, as well as mentally, with the process and progress of a speech. A bit of clay or construction paper in their hands as you talk can make your speech a lot of fun. But the circumstances must be right. At one college lecture, a representative from the Argonne National Laboratory discussed the scarcity of current and future energy sources. To demonstrate his point, he gathered the small audience around four consoles of a machine called an Energy/Environment Simulator. Each group, playing the leaders of four large imaginary countries, manipulated the controls to conserve fuel, satisfy their country's energy needs, and prevent choking its inhabitants on the guck spewed into the air and water. Fortunately, since the subject was in the public interest and didn't fall under the category of entertainment, it drew a crowd small enough for all to participate.

NOW . . . SIZING UP YOUR SPEAKING SKILLS

As you've moved through successive chapters of this book and of this part in particular, we hope you've gradually formed a more positive image of yourself as a maker and giver of speeches. We hope that by this time most of our ideas and guidance about the speech behaviors that pay off and those that don't have crystallized in your thinking. So why not take a rest stop for a moment before climbing further, and ask yourself: "Just how good are my speechmaking skills?" and "How am I stacking up as a potentially good public speaker?"

You'll find, we think, a good many of the answers in this list of what we call the *traits of the effective speaker.* The list isn't sacred. It's not a list to memorize. It's a summary and a reminder of all our previous advice. It's a *profile* of the confident, effective speaker. Think about it. Measure yourself against it. Try it on for size . . . and see:

1. You *know yourself.* You feel confident in yourself. You are in command, fully prepared to speak, aware that you'll be a bit nervous, but not intimidated by the prospect.

". . . As the sign says, Mr. Schmutz — try again!"

2. You *know your subject.* You speak from experience about things meaningful and useful to you. And you broaden your knowledge through research.

3. You *know your listeners.* You respect and like them. You take an "I'm OK—you're OK" attitude and continually consider your audience's interests and knowledge of the subject. You choose an angle to make your subject useful to your audience, and you look for additional ways throughout your speech to relate your materials to your audience. You choose language you know your listeners will understand.

4. You are *surprising, original,* and *lively.* You create tension through contrasts, through rubbing the familiar against the unfamiliar, through drawing an unexpected but apt comparison, through flavoring your speech with occasional metaphors. You may create suspense or irony; you may make your listeners laugh; you always make them think.

5. You are *accurate, precise, detailed.* You draw vivid verbal pictures through careful word choice grounded in the concrete; you avoid the abstract.

6. You *employ the full range of your voice.* You vary your pitch, your speed of delivery, your volume. You avoid monotony and keep your presentation forceful.

7. You also *employ your body* well. Your gestures grow naturally from meanings and feelings. You gesture for emphasis; you smile, or frown, or grimace to reinforce what you say.

8. You *structure your remarks* to make them clear and easily remembered. You introduce one idea at a time. You show the relationship between ideas. You repeat and summarize whenever necessary.

9. You *enliven your materials* through illustrative anecdotes, interpretations of statistics, visual and auditory aids, and through involving your audience physically in your speech.

10. Finally, you are *adaptable.* You can read and interpret audience feedback and adjust your message to it.

This chapter has served a dual purpose: first, to provide additional advice about and practice in enlivening and humanizing your speech through illustrative anecdotes, interpretations of statistics, visual and auditory aids, and involving your audience in your presentation; second, to summarize and illustrate much of our previous advice, explanation, and description of what makes speaking effective. If you've mastered the skills and developed the traits we've described, not only will you be able to deliver meaningful, appealing, and even exceptional speeches to your entire class, but you'll also speak well and confidently any time, anywhere.

Reference Notes

[1]Reginald K. Little, "The Drug Counselor," speech delivered at Wilbur Wright College, Chicago, Illinois, spring, 1976.

[2]Ibid.

[3]Dr. J. Allen Hynek, "Flying Saucers," speech delivered at Wilbur Wright College, Chicago, Illinois, November 19, 1969.

[4]Ibid.

[5]Dr. Domeena Renshaw, "Sexual Behavior and Values," speech delivered at Wilbur Wright College, Chicago, Illinois, March 12, 1975.

15 Rehearsing, Delivering, and Adapting Your Speech

It's time to finish your silent planning and speak up. Throughout this part of the book, we've suggested how you might develop an effective speech of any kind and, in particular, a speech *to inform:* a speech which transmits fresh information to others, and does it clearly, interestingly, usefully. We assume now that you've planned, prepared, and polished such a speech for delivery to an audience—of your classmates, possibly. We trust you've developed a good speech. But the only way to see if it works for you and your listeners is to *speak* it. That means, first, rehearsing in private; second, rehearsing before an audience; and finally—with speech fully prepared—delivering it and adapting it to the requirements of the moment.

TRYING OUT YOUR SPEECH

In Chapter 1, we said that continual self-revelation leads to greater self-awareness. Through discussion, you discover your thoughts, emotions, and past experiences concealed in the Unknown and the Blind Areas of a Johari Window. We suspect that a similar process occurs in all acts of communication. Each time you talk or write, if you aren't discovering your ideas, you're examining or verifying them.

An advantage itinerant preachers have over those who are stationary, the latter cannot well improve their delivery of a sermon by so many rehearsals.
—Benjamin Franklin, Autobiography

We've heard people say they understand something, but can't explain it. They can't get the words out. Perhaps, but we're not convinced they *do* understand. A practical test of understanding comes through language, which is one reason why you take examinations. Studying for them is like a rehearsal. You read the material, put it down, think through and assimilate what you've read, and then try to restate it in your own words. If you can, you know it and probably will be able to say it again. If you can't, you don't, and won't.

This chapter, like a speech, evolved from constant discussion, thought, and revision. As its authors we met, talked things over, and asked questions: What should we say? How should we begin? As we talked, we discovered what we thought, what we knew, and what we didn't. Our hazy language — paralleling our foggy thoughts — gave way eventually to clearer ideas and words. Then we wrote them out, examined them, and wrote them again — and again. Comparably, at this point in its evolvement, your *speech* should be subjected to similar practice run-throughs, scrutiny, reevaluation, more practice, and more scrutiny. That's what happens in the real world.

For speeches by men and women in public life, rehearsals often are elaborate and meticulous. The President's major television address-

". . . Gee, maybe I oughta' change my speech!"

es may be the product of a half dozen or even a dozen speech writers, as many revisions, several practice readings under careful observations by advisors and coaches, and—eventually, perhaps—the preparation of an unobtrusive "cue-card" apparatus or Teleprompter which allows the President to read the speech while looking into the TV camera.

Since at this time you aren't running for election or reelection, you won't be using ghost-writers, and doubtless can't afford the expense of such preparation and professional aid, you'll have to settle for something a trifle less ambitious. Begin by rehearsing your speech once or twice in private. This should serve to refine your thoughts and formulate the approximate language you want to use. Then rehearse your speech before real people who can supply applause and criticism and advice. Make your mistakes beforehand, when they don't count, so you can correct them.

No two presentations of the same speech can be exactly alike, of course, especially when it's not written out. You'll change the wording, at least slightly, each time. But several run-throughs will minimize the number of false steps in the big parade past the judge's stand. You can also overdo practicing and become stale; but use your own judgment and common sense. As you gain experience, you'll need fewer rehearsals; but right now, include the extra try. Maybe even two or three.

1 Small-Group Speaking
Rehearsing Your Speech

In previous exercises, you have tested your speech's topic and organization with your group in several ways. Now, having practiced the phrasing and delivery of it in private, you are ready to try the entire speech—thesis, introduction, examples, conclusion, personal anecdotes, and all—before a small "practice" audience. Your instructor will divide your group into subgroups of three people so that rehearsals won't occupy too much time. Perhaps you haven't ironed out all the wrinkles or made every major fold yet, but give as close an approximation of the final speech as you can. Either before or after your practice delivery, tell your group where you are having problems, and let your rehearsal audience help you resolve them.

As you hear each other's speeches, your job is to listen—carefully. Since none of the speeches is polished yet, you'll need to help by pointing out the rough spots. Here's a procedure: After you hear a speech, take a minute or two to jot down its main ideas. Then compare them with the *speaker's* ideas. What point did the speech make? What did it accomplish? Once the speaker hears a statement of what you understand to be the major points, and similar statements from the other persons in the audience, you can discuss any hang-ups and confusions, ascertain possible causes, and consider remedies, adjustments, etc.

Practice run-throughs and small-group rehearsals should enable you as a speaker to examine the specific strengths and weaknesses of your speech. What explanations weren't clear? What examples and supporting material were misleading or irrelevant? What must be lengthened, shortened, emphasized, de-emphasized?

To collect still more accurate answers to such questions, as a speaker you can prepare a multiple-choice or true-false quiz for your group. Their answers may give you even more specific information about what your listeners understood or didn't, what held their interest or didn't, what was useful or wasn't. You can attribute some misunderstandings to inattention or poor listening habits; but even so, you must decide how to induce your audience to listen more carefully. As we've said before, poor listening may indicate that your listeners don't value your message highly. Or they can't figure out its organization or logic. So you and the others might also explore how to enliven your speech and make it more relevant to their needs and values. But, as critics of each other, remember to give positive suggestions for improvement. Don't dwell on the failures.

DELIVERING YOUR SPEECH TO AN AUDIENCE AND ADAPTING TO THE UNFORESEEN

As you finally deliver your speech, you should sail through confidently and easily. But you must be prepared to make occasional midcourse adjustments if you detect crosswinds or turbulent waters. You simply cannot *rehearse* throwing an improvised verbal lifeline to some of your listeners who, you sense, may be drowning in confusion or boredom. Yet if you delay the rescue attempt or fail to get them back on board quickly, they may have drifted too far away for salvation. You can see the signs: their gaze, like their spirits, begins to descend — or float aimlessly out the window to some faraway object. They stifle tremendous yawns and shuffle their feet nervously. Their attention has died.

For an improvised rescue operation, however, the secret as always is to *be yourself,* to allow your personal resources and the thoroughness of your preparation to pull you through. Many effective and experienced speakers who occasionally find their listeners beginning to drift away can count as their best strokes: a sense of *humor, vocal flexibility,* the ability either to *take advantage of or ignore the unforeseen,* and skill at *restatement.*

Maintaining a sense of humor to sustain or revive interest

One useful stroke for pulling an audience's mental focus back to you and your subject is the spontaneous joke. You can bail out with a quip or a bit of clowning, provided you don't overdo it. You've probably watched Johnny Carson make a career out of saving his monologues with ad libs, funny faces, and a little "soft shoe." Granted, his team of comedy writers probably supplies him with some of these "spontaneous" remarks; but basically his wit comes from his own sense of wellbeing. He thinks he and his audience are OK. He trusts his abilities and rapport with his audience. He knows the listeners want to enjoy themselves. If they boo him, it's out of a sense of having fun.

". . . When it comes to delivering a speech and adapting to the unforeseen, Art Schmutz is the coolest!"

Your audience, too, is probably pulling for you. At the very least they're indifferent—not antagonistic. Relaxed and confident, you can joke with them during the dull spots. But if you don't feel comfortable with quip-making, avoid it. With more experience, you may develop that skill, but right now you can rely on your other resources.

Making vocal adjustments to recapture your audience

A monotonous delivery—uninflected, unvaried, tedious—won't necessarily drown your audience in boredom; it will torture them like a slowly dripping faucet. Listen to yourself and watch your audience. If they're going under for the third time or sinking into a comatose state, apply a little mouth-to-ear resuscitation: Raise your voice, speed it up or slow it down, adjust. *Vocal flexibility* is crucial here. Of course, if you have been consistently practicing the voice exercises we've recommended, varied and emphatic delivery should be second nature to you now.

Trying to handle—or ignore—the unexpected distraction

Sometimes everything that can possibly go wrong, *does.* This you have to count on, prepare for, and be ever alert to. As you make your most important statement, a screaming ambulance outside the window shouts you down. As you draw your most serious point, someone sneezes and draws giggles. As you explain an important issue, your tongue sticks on a difficult pronunciation. In any of these situations, you have two choices: (1) ignore the problem, or (2) try to resolve it—often by capitalizing on it and turning it to your advantage. No rule works for every instance. Sometimes you can stop and joke about the distraction before continuing. You could say: "That ambulance just proves my point about the growing need for better health care." "It's nothing to sneeze at." Or "I wonder if a tongue transplant would help." At other times, your judgment will tell you merely to pause until the distraction ends and you can continue your speech. Again, just be *flexible.* Though your adjustments interrupt the flow of your speech, remember that in most cases you have been interrupted anyway.

Restating your point if your listeners aren't getting it

Depending on the size of the group and the formality of the occasion, you can—and should—stop to ask someone who seems puzzled if what you're saying makes sense. In addition to using humor and vocal variation and developing a knack for predicting and controlling the unforeseen, you can also hold—or regain—your audience's attention by *restating* an idea or point. In fact, restatement is a valuable mid-speech adjustment you should practice and utilize fully. Your audience's knitted brows and quizzical looks tell you that your point is still a secret to everyone but you. So you try again, stating things differently. Restatements work best within these guidelines:

1. *Try not to repeat the same terms.* Your audience didn't understand them the first time. Saying them louder, as the American tourist tries with the waiter who doesn't understand English, won't help either. Couch the same thing in clearer and—possibly—more vivid terms.

2. *Simplify your language* and avoid technical terms and jargon.
3. *Think of an example or an analogy.* Your chances of making yourself clear are best with the concrete and the familiar.

ADAPTING TO QUESTIONS DURING THE SPEECH OR IMMEDIATELY AFTERWARD

Question-and-answer sessions follow many speeches. Quite often they are an intended and planned-for part of the speech occasion. The questions your audience tosses at you may be just as hard and hot to handle as those that might be voiced *during* your speech. But knowting"—in which you speak partly determine your listeners' perception program gives you a chance to do some direct planning. This, plus the fact that your hearers—aware they can get in their shots later—may decide to hold their fire until they have heard you out, affords you an added advantage. For the listeners, these sessions can either increase their understanding or their frustration. Since increased understanding is the goal of all good communication, we remind you of our advice about answering questions in Chapter 3: (1) *Make sure you understand the question;* (2) *keep your answer direct and brief;* and (3) *try to interpret what a questioner means on more than one level.*

By the way, a handy practice is to hold back some of the material you might have used in the body of your speech for the question-and-answer period. That way, should you need a story or a specific instance or statistic to illustrate a point, you have one available. Also after your speech, you may be asked for the sources of your information, so keep them accessible for quick reference. You needn't load up your speech itself with too many of them.

ADAPTING TO DIFFERENCES IN THE OCCASION

As you saw in Chapter 7, the *physical* circumstances—the "setting"—in which you speak partly determine your listeners' perception of your message, and your perceptions of their feedback. For public speeches, of course, the setting is just as important. Will you stand or sit, be close to or far from your audience? Will the audience be large or small? Will you be indoors or out, in an auditorium or a gymnasium? You know the physical arrangement of your classroom and have prepared your speeches with that arrangement in mind. But in the real world outside the classroom, sometimes you must quickly adjust to an unexpected arrangement. You may have been told that you are to speak at a dinner, which you discover—as you arrive—is really a picnic. Instead of addressing people dressed in suits and evening gowns and seated at tables, you must speak to people casually attired and sprawled out on blankets and towels. You'd probably have to make your delivery as casual, and raise the volume of your voice to carry in the open air.

Even in the classroom, an occasional surprise can occur. The heating unit can be banging like a kettle drum; the air-conditioning can quit on a 98° day; the maintenance people may have decided to remove all the chairs in the room to make repairs. You'd try to adjust to these circumstances, too—by making a joke, speaking louder, asking your classmates to move closer to you, speeding up your delivery to shorten the time they must stand or sweat or listen to the noises in the room.

Inside or outside the classroom, another aspect of the setting you must adjust to is the *length of the entire program* and *your position in the order or sequence of events in it.* These factors are part of the *psychological* setting and require your thoughtful attention: Are you the only speaker? The first among five or the last among ten? Will the audience be listening to speeches for thirty minutes, two hours, or four hours each day for a week-long conference? Often you can anticipate these matters, but not always. Therefore, while you improvise an adjustment, consider these guidelines:

As the first speaker on a program, you are establishing the precedents for those to follow. The audience has no one to compare you with, so you can set the rules. You can probably stand where you want, speak informally or formally, joke or be serious. More than likely, though, the audience isn't settled yet, ready to listen. So you may have to wait for them to quiet down, begin loudly to startle them a bit, or begin softly so they'll stop talking and listen—whatever you think will be most effective to gain their attention.

As the second or third speaker on the program, you will be compared to your predecessor. Are you better or worse, as clever or as articulate? We suggested in Chapter 13 that you should build a bridge between the last speaker's remarks and yours, and then cross over into territory the last speaker hasn't explored. But suppose the last speaker made virtually every point you were planning to. We saw an example of precisely that at a college graduation. After the salutatorian had finished her address, the valedictorian began his with these words:

> In the four years I have attended this school I've never met Mary Jo or seen her in the halls or talked to her. I wish I had, because I just discovered that we are giving the same speech. [*Laughter.*] Rather than repeating what she said, I'll just add a few more ideas of my own.

With this little introduction, he rescued his speech and his audience from boredom. Additionally, as he pointed out, he shortened his speech to avoid repeating the previous speaker's remarks.

As the last speaker on the program, you have special problems. No matter how apt, how funny, how inspirational your remarks, if the evening has been long, or hot, or the seats too hard, you cannot expect to retain your listeners' attention for more than a few minutes. You and they both are tired, a fact you can acknowledge without insulting any of the previous speakers. Your speech may reveal the secret of the universe, but you'll have to reveal it in one-eighth the time you wanted, or it will remain a secret. Be prepared to adapt to the unexpected in the only way you can prepare: decide to be cool, not to panic, and to be yourself.

2 Whole-Class Speaking
Delivering Your Speech

After the shouting has died away and the confetti and ticker tape have settled, the final performance determines whether or not you have succeeded. Now is that time. According to a schedule your instructor prepares in advance, deliver your fully developed, ten-to-fifteen-minute informative speech to the entire class. You may be a bit nervous—everyone is—but remember that you're experienced, and you know both your subject and audience well. Relax and be yourself. You can cope. You're OK.

3 Discovering for Yourself
Adapting Your Speech to a Hypothetical Audience

Speakers frequently must deliver the "same" speech to vastly different audiences and must, therefore, adjust their remarks to each group. Choose one of the following groups as your hypothetical audience. View this adaptation as a challenge, selecting the "audience" that is perhaps the one farthest from your own experience or least likely to relate to your speech. You needn't assume, however, that the group will be hostile to it. Then write out *one* example of how you would adapt your speech to their values and interests. Some possible audiences from which to choose:

retired plumbers, electricians, and carpenters	a police union
	Minnesota farmers
bank executives	California migrant workers
elementary teachers	Florida real-estate developers
Catholic mothers	New York artists
a convention of rabbis	Colorado commune members
high-school seniors	young affluent suburbanites
dentists	or . . .?

4 Whole-Class Speaking
Adapting Your Speech to Fit Time Limitations

As you know, occasionally a speaker must shorten a speech because of time limitations or danger to the listeners' mental health after they've suffered through eighteen consecutive dull presentations. For fun, you and several classmates can volunteer to demonstrate your cutting-and-trimming ability with your speeches. A few minutes before you are to speak, your instructor will tell you whether you have three, five, or ten minutes to present what is—basically, at least—your major informative speech. Then you're on your own. Perhaps you'll decide to limit your objectives, too. Can you expect your audience to learn as much as your full speech would teach them?

5 Whole-Class Speaking
Adapting Your Speech to a Non-Receptive Audience

If you're very brave, try volunteering for this ordeal. The members of the class will role-play a (slightly) unruly group. As you speak, they will attempt to distract you—nothing too outrageous, just the ordinary (or at least plausible) disruptions that might occur in a large lecture hall where people can freely come and go. See how well you survive.

With this chapter we conclude Part Three on effective speech-making and speech-giving skills in general and, in particular, as they apply to informative speaking. Through it you've learned and practiced how to choose a subject, find materials for it, organize them, and polish them—all with the goals of making a speech clear, useful, and interesting to a particular audience. We've stressed the importance of being prepared, of planning a clear organization, a strong beginning, ending, internal summaries, and transitions. We've emphasized further preparation through rehearsals in private and in small groups, and have considered how you would adapt your remarks to unexpected circumstances. As we leave this section and enter Part Four, on persuasive speaking, we must emphasize that every communicative behavior you've practiced up to this point applies equally well to speeches and speaking designed to influence and move your listeners: You must speak about what you know, look for additional materials, consider your audience, plan, organize, rehearse, and adapt. Communication of any type is made effective by essentially the same means.

195

16 What Persuasion Is — and Isn't

Some people are born salespersons. They could peddle suntan lotion to coal miners, heating oil to Arabs, Pogo sticks to kangaroos. The worst types — the pushy ones — need not believe in their products. They only figure out a gimmick, a way to pressure or entice you. "The secret," a famous huckster once proclaimed, "is to sell the sizzle, not the steak."

You may not — and should not — be such a salesperson. In fact, you may never wish to sell anything, let alone a cardboard shirt you know will fall apart with the first washing. Nevertheless, in a sense, you will be selling what you believe in throughout your life: You'll be selling *yourself* and *your ideas* through persuasion. You'll be persuading a potential employer of the worth of your credentials, abilities, and personality. You'll be persuading co-workers how best to run a new office or a new system. You'll be persuading your village or city government that your school needs a larger playground or that your neighborhood doesn't need a new high-rise building. Even in daily conversations you'll be selling your political views or your views on why firing a football coach will make your favorite team a championship contender.

Let every man be fully persuaded in his own mind.
—The Bible

To better prepare yourself as a persuader, then, here in Part Four you'll be examining the process of persuasion and applying some principles of persuasion to your own speeches. In this lead-off chapter you'll see a little of what persuasion is and is not, how it works—and how it doesn't. And you'll be taking a first step toward developing a major, full-length persuasive speech: choosing a subject. In Chapter 17 you'll see how audience attitudes, needs, and beliefs affect the listeners' reception of your propositions and arguments. In Chapter 18 you'll take a critical look at the uses—and some of the abuses—of emotional and rational appeals. And, finally, in Chapter 19, you'll confront your "strategy" options for organizing and structuring your persuasive speeches.

WHAT IS PERSUASION?

People make up their own minds, but persuasion is a speaker's attempt to influence the decision. When you persuade, you provide people with reasons for *changing their beliefs* or *acting upon beliefs they already hold.* In no case, however, is persuasion an attempt merely to reinforce people's beliefs and do nothing else. The fact that your listeners may be *interested* in your views doesn't mean—unfortunately—that they will be *persuaded.* You must know how persuasion "works," and then put it to work.

How persuasion "works"—and doesn't work

All of us apparently desire (and probably require) consistency in our internal worlds, the worlds of our minds. Psychologist Roger Brown states the issue this way:

It seems to be a general law of human thought that we expect people we like and respect to associate themselves with ideas we like and respect and to disassociate themselves or disagree with ideas from which we disassociate ourselves. These latter disapproved ideas we expect to find espoused by the wicked and the stupid—those we do not like or respect. The "goods" in the world in the way of persons, things, and ideas are supposed to clump together and oppose the "bads," who are expected to form their own clump. This is a consistency principle. It describes the way the world ought to go, and as long as things work this way nothing much happens to our attitudes. But when a new girl friend dislikes our favorite music or an admired professor ridicules our religious beliefs or an esteemed critic attacks a play in which we are appearing, the mind starts working.[1]

When, in fact, our mind "starts working" we begin to feel uncomfortable, a state which another psychologist, Leon Festinger, calls "cognitive dissonance." He says when one's "knowledge, opinion, or belief about the environment, about one's self, or about one's behavior" encounters *conflicting* knowledge, opinions, or beliefs, the person tries to

"It's Professor Kaufman's idea for demonstrating cognitive dissonance and balance theory to his students."

resolve the conflict.[2] In persuasion, you attempt to influence the person to resolve the conflict as you would like it resolved.

Influencing people to act can be difficult, however, especially when the action you propose involves discomfort or danger—physical or psychological. To cite an example, if you asked disgruntled classmates to sign a petition for eliminating required courses, you might create severe conflicts within those too afraid to risk identifying themselves publicly as "troublemakers" and face possible embarrassment, condemnation, or punishment. They might resolve their internal conflict by rejecting your request, unless you can convince them that the benefits in taking action outweigh the dangers.

The odds for succeeding decrease even more when you want to *change your listener's firmly held beliefs.* As a persuader you must first encourage or generate cognitive dissonance in your listeners' minds, either by increasing the internal conflict they already feel, or by creating a conflict among their "cognitions" (knowledge), attitudes, needs, and/or beliefs. Then you must offer a solution to the conflict: you must quiet the dissonance; you must restore balance. But people—you, we, and everyone else—hold many of their beliefs and attitudes tightly. Despite occasional dissonance, they aren't easily dislodged from them.

In fact, James Harvey Robinson, an eminent scientist, claims that in our tenacious desire to protect what we "know," "believe," and "feel," our most common mode of thinking is *rationalization,* an attempt to justify our actions afterwards or to defend our prejudices from attack. Most people spend much of their time supplying "good" reasons for what they do or think rather than the *real reasons.*[3]

What are *real* reasons? Fear, hatred, ignorance, bigotry, selfishness, impulsiveness, unthinking acceptance of what others tell or have told them—you can add other motivations to the list. Once we have committed ourselves publicly to a position—making our views known or acting upon them—few of us will admit or even recognize our real motivations. Instead, we may adopt any of the following methods of justifying our actions:

1. We seek evidence to justify and reasons to explain what we've already said or done.
2. We refuse to take responsibility for our actions.
3. We ignore the evidence that contradicts what we've said or done.
4. We reject the validity of contradictory evidence.
5. We reject the source of the contradictory evidence.[4]

A detailed example should illustrate the point. Since you were fourteen or fifteen (or eleven or six), you've found comfort and joy in sucking tobacco smoke into your lungs. Originally, you smoked to conform with the crowd, to rebel against authority, to be cool or sophisticated (all real reasons). But now, as a mature adult, you automatically slap the pack of cigarettes against your palm, pop one into your mouth, strike a match, and stoke the fires of pollution on numerous occasions, including immediately after mashing out the last butt. Not that you aren't aware of the dangers: You've read the warning from the Surgeon General twenty times a day. You've seen your Aunt Millie die from cancer. You hack and wheeze with premonitions of emphysema or tuberculosis or bronchitis. Let's face it, though: you're hooked—you're a nicotine junkie.

"Don't bother me with the facts. My mind's made up."

But you won't accept that conclusion. "Not so," you protest, "I can stop any time. I've done it four or five times in the past." We, from the outside, smile at your unconscious self-deception. And we smile more when we hear you preach about health foods, watch you jog every morning, pop your vitamins, and diet at lunch.

"OK," you grudgingly concede. "So I'm hooked. But who's this Surgeon General anyway? He hasn't got all the answers. Those tests don't mean anything. My grandfather smoked seven packs a day and died at ninety-three. I read about a study from Ypsilanti Community College where cockroaches breathed cigarette smoke for seventeen years with no ill effects. So who can trust these studies?"

"Congratulations," we smile. "You've learned to ignore and deny the evidence, and to search for other evidence—no matter how weak—to justify your own irrational behavior."

"We all have to go sometime," you continue. "I could die tomorrow in a car accident. A lion could escape from the zoo and maul me. The Russians could wipe us out with an H-bomb in twenty seconds. Why should I worry about smoking?"

We continue to smile. "Those are obviously trivial and false analogies, and completely inconsistent with real concerns for your health."

"Well, it can't happen to me," you reply. "That's too many years away to worry about. By the time I get cancer, they will have invented a cure for it. And, besides, what makes *you* so perfect that you can criticize others?"

"Ah, hah!" we think. Ultimately, you turn away from the issue and turn on the person confronting you with it. An old practice—the Romans killed messengers bringing news of battles lost.

So much for the example. In it, we—as persuaders—were trying to counteract your strategies to defend yourself. You felt the inner conflict—the dissonance we created—and wanted to alleviate it. But the immediate pleasures of satisfying your addiction outweighed the remote threats of future illness and death. Thus you "balanced your cognitions," as they say, by rationalization. Some people might resolve their inner conflict differently by giving up smoking—cold. Period. Others play games with themselves, "giving it up" for a few hours and telling people they are trying to stop. But most smokers keep right on smoking, smoking, coughing, dying.

As a smoker, you weren't persuaded—yet. On the basis of our example, therefore, you might well ask: Does persuasion really "work"? *Can* you influence people to alter or act on their beliefs? The answer is clearly yes. But don't expect too much too fast. Don't expect to alter or influence every belief of every person every time. No common behavioral rules govern everyone, though ofttimes people seem to think that *their* rules do. Don't be disappointed if your speech doesn't win converts on the first hearing. Minds change, attitudes shift, action comes— but sometimes only over a long period of time. Millions do stop smoking, but only after the health warnings and television advertisements, the public speeches and posters on buses, the warnings from doctors and mothers and friends and cousins . . . and the terror of waking up one morning unable to breathe . . . have finally begun to sink in. The cognitive dissonance must be great enough that people finally change their views or their actions to alleviate it.

> I come not, friends, to steal away your hearts;
> I am no orator, as Brutus is;
> But, as you know me all,
> a plain, blunt man.
> —Shakespeare,
> *Julius Caesar*

Don't, therefore, expect persuasive miracles. Shakespeare's Mark Antony very quickly converted a hostile mob to his cause with a brilliant speech—in a *play,* for *pretend.* But not in real life. You might, at a town-hall meeting, attempt to convince your fellow citizens to change government policy on welfare. To this end, you deliver a beautifully organized, well-documented, rational appeal; you tap into your audience's emotions; you cite the Bible, the Constitution, statistics from the U.S. Census Bureau. You bemoan the suffering of the poor who languish in unlit, unheated, unkempt shanties, eating beans and cornflakes, while the rich people—off for a vacation in Jamaica—board their private Lear Jet lavishly equipped with bar, quadrophonic sound, and videotapes of the last seven Super Bowl games. You exhort your audience to lobby for the changes you propose, to work for the candidates who support your program.

Half your audience applauds politely, a few enthusiastically. A few shout, "Right on, Brother!" But others shout, "Right *out*—out of here, you commie! you pervert! you subversive!" Some sit, silently considering your argument, perhaps finding they agree; and then go home, turn on the television, and fall asleep. In many instances, that's about the best you can hope for. But remember, we've never said persuasion is easy.

Aristotle's advice about persuasion

Persuasion, obviously, is often a difficult and complex operation requiring a delicate combination of skills. You must challenge your listeners' viewpoints, perhaps jolting them, shocking them, but not generating enough voltage to kill their interest in your argument or you. Aristotle, one of the first persuasion experts, understood the process very well and had a good many useful and interesting things to say about it and about the way it "works." He said that your listeners change their attitudes and beliefs in reaction to:

1. Your appeal to their *reason*
2. Your appeal to their *emotions*
3. Your *credibility* as a speaker: your image (for them) as a sincere, trustworthy, believable person.

Aristotle counseled, therefore, that you observe "all the available means of persuasion." This, in effect, means that *you must adapt and fit your persuasive appeals to your listeners.* You must use whatever evidence, reasoning, references, quotes from authorities, and emotional appeals you find appropriate. For your little brother or sister who already loves and trusts you, your smile and a "Take my word for it" may suffice as persuasion. But for skeptics and people firmly fixed in their negative beliefs about your argument, you'll need to be more resourceful. In brief, to follow Aristotle's common sense and well-tested advice, you'll choose a persuasive "strategy" (the subject of Chapter 18) that is loaded with a balance of both "reasonable" and "emotional" appeals. Then, having reinforced your proposal, claim, or arguments with solid facts and information, you'll structure it all in a way that will most effectively put your "strategy" into action as you deliver your speech (the focus of Chapter 19).

WHAT PERSUASION IS NOT

Persuasion, as we've noted, is influencing other people to change their minds or actions; but we must warn you about what it is not. First of all, *persuasion is NOT winning an argument.* For you to win, somebody must lose. And nobody enjoys losing. Thinking you can "beat" others, openly challenging them with a smug or superior attitude, won't persuade. It will only antagonize. People who are told, in effect, "You're a fool and an idiot—your ideas are nothing more than prejudices and clichés," won't thank you for pointing out the error in their ways. They may, instead, point out the door to you. Granted, people do rationalize; but you cannot trap them in their rationalizations and expect them to agree with you.

Second, *persuasion is NOT simply stating your views and letting the chips fall where they may.* Saying what's on your mind regardless of the consequences may make you feel good. But, unfortunately, because you must concern yourself with how *others* feel, clubbing them with blunt statements won't do. You needn't be dishonest, but you must think of the least painful way of telling the truth. And you can learn to be generous, too. Though, to persuade, you can't expose and belittle the *real* reasons for people's actions, you can't ignore these reasons either. You must give people the opportunity to save face. You can suggest to your listeners that if a person—hypothetically, of course—acted impulsively, you could understand and sympathize with such an action. You can further admit that you also have acted impulsively on occasion. Given the transactional nature of communication—and, in particular, persuasive communication—for your listeners to concede an error they must receive some concession in return. Make things easier for your listeners. Let them admit a mistake without feelings of guilt or embarrassment.

Persuasion, then, is based on diplomacy and not confrontation. It induces people to change their minds, but doesn't threaten their self-image. In fact, persuasion should avoid all kinds of direct threats. Our third warning is that *persuasion is NOT coercion,* an attempt to intimidate or threaten others to behave as you'd like. A man pointing a gun at your head or threatening you with loss of your job isn't a persuader. He's a thug or a bully. He's not concerned with influencing people. He's concerned with *power* and *force.* If you believe in a democracy, you must respect the freedom and intelligence of other people. Perhaps coercion is more "efficient"—as long as you can protect yourself from retaliation. But efficiency sometimes must give way to decency. Treat others as if they're OK, and they'll probably treat you the same.

Fourth—and finally—*persuasion is NOT manipulation,* a conscious attempt to *exploit* people's dilemmas, frustrations, emotions, or lack of information. Manipulators take advantage of people's ignorance about a subject by distorting or omitting evidence, or simply lying about it. Some manipulation plays upon people's fears or prejudices or hatreds. Advertising, for example, often exploits people's insecurities, desires for acceptance, and hang-ups. Billions of dollars are spent yearly convincing Americans of their bad breath, frizzy hair, saggy skin, foul feet, obnoxious armpits, insecure futures — and giving people sleepless nights worrying about it all.

1
Investigating Attempts at Manipulation

From the time the clock radio awakens you in the morning with news of a traffic jam on the expressway and suggests you take a different route to work, people are trying continuously to influence your actions and beliefs. List ten such attempts directed at you in the last week. For each of these persuasive attempts, indicate the idea or object you're being "sold": a deodorant, a candidate, giving a cash contribution, obeying a non-smoking regulation, etc. Also indicate the specific intended audience: those, in addition to you, who are being subjected to the attempted manipulation. Identify the medium through which you heard or saw it: television, radio, magazine, newspaper, or lecture. Finally, indicate the emotions, attitudes, or interests it attempted to appeal to: the desire to be accepted, for instance; the fear of rejection; the desire to be sexually attractive; or the desire to compete with your neighbors.

Then, in a four- or five-minute speech to your small group, briefly report your findings, and focus on the least effective and the most effective appeals. Try to explain the reasons for their success or failure.

At first glance, this kind of manipulation in advertising may seem relatively harmless. Few suffer loss of life as a result (although many suffer loss of income). Manipulation by politicians or others in powerful positions can be more dangerous. Of course, ultimately, people cannot be exploited unless they *choose* to be exploited. People must be ready to follow a Hitler or a Mussolini or a Napoleon or a Manson. People can freely choose to accept demagoguery; they can individually choose to join the crowd and be swept away emotionally. They can choose not to investigate the evidence on their own. They can choose to be mindless. But they can choose, too, to stop and say, "Wait a minute! This makes no sense!" The late J. A. C. Brown, a psychiatrist, sums up the matter thus:

There has never been a time since history began when it has not been possible, given complete power and lack of scruples, to induce the majority of people to confess to anything, profess or denounce any creed we might wish, and that by the simplest and crudest of methods; nor has there been, or is ever likely to be, a time when a stalwart minority will not prefer to resist to the end.[5]

GEARING UP FOR A PERSUASIVE SPEECH

You're beginning preparations, don't forget, for a rather fully developed persuasive speech which, quite possibly, you'll be presenting to a whole-class audience when you've concluded your study of Part Four. Ideally, therefore, this is the best time to take your first step in that direction: *choosing your subject.* As you begin your search for a suitable persuasive thesis, bear this in mind: It's easier (and morally preferable) to sell real enthusiasm, so choose a subject you have some rather strong convictions about.

Looking for persuasive topics . . . We know you'll be tempted to lecture on the burning issues of the day; you'll want to be a vocal warrior in this week's popular crusade. With strong convictions, ample knowledge, and fresh ideas, you could talk about abortion, or pot, or three-year renewable marriage certificates. But if you really know little about these subjects, better stick closer to home — to something you really *know* and feel strongly about. Look again at your Interests-Inventory for topics that make you bubble up or boil over. Examine the personal experiences that give you some "expertise" in an argument. Don't allude abstractly to starvation in Calcutta; tell about the two days or two weeks you went with little food.

. . . Inside yourself. "But I don't have any opinions," we hear you saying. Take another look. Are your parents divorced, or are you? What sufferings, mental or physical, has it caused? Ripe stuff here to feed an audience about reforming marriage or divorce laws, or child-custody laws. Or, perhaps you can even advocate establishing a local Clinic for the Love-Torn. . . . Have you moved often, as your parents changed or lost jobs? Do you like our mobile society? What would you change, and why? . . . Have you ever been robbed (or been a robber)? What caused the act? How would you argue that our society could prevent it? . . . Have you witnessed the death of a relative or friend from cancer or some other "incurable" disease? Should people be allowed to languish in pain for months or years instead of dying quickly? . . . Have you worked in a factory or on an assembly line? Do you wonder how others spend their lives there? Just how long do others stay? What cure

would you propose for the "blue-collar blues"? . . . Are you black, Spanish-surnamed, American Indian? Have you lived in segregation? How can society cure segregation's frustrations or pain? What could you propose and argue that people should do about this? . . . Have you seemingly suffered for centuries, rooting for a losing football, baseball, hockey, basketball, or soccer team? Why can't they win? What's wrong with the management or the organization, and how should they change? . . . Does something in your schooling, past or present, annoy or distress you? How would you change it? And how could you change it within the bureaucracy, the unions, and the political structure—each with vested interests?

These are just a few examples, and any one of these personal reactions or experiences can be narrowed to something more manageable through the same process we suggested in Part Three for preparing any type of speech: *Choose a topic and a thesis, throw your ideas randomly on paper, then categorize them.* Eventually, your ideas and feelings will clarify; and you'll think of several good examples to use from your own experiences and reading. Then you can expand upon them with research.

    . . . *Outside yourself.* Here again, you must hit the books and the streets in search of speech material. Knowing your subject thoroughly is critical to effective persuasion. If you expect to convince intelligent classmates, you can't bluff them. No matter how much they may like you, credibility has its limits. When you hit the books or the streets in search of evidence you ought to try, despite all your convictions, to keep your mind—as well as your eyes—open. If you've already declared war on the enemy and you're merely searching for additional ammunition, you could be firing at the wrong target and rejecting any possibility for making peace. Sure, you can find all sorts of facts, figures, and fibs to support your viewpoint while ignoring everything that doesn't. But we can't respect or accept your "research" if you do it that way.

True scientists and genuine intellectuals formulate a hypothesis, then test it, challenge it, study it. They jerk neither their right nor their left knee on each issue. If their research confirms their hypothesis, so be it. If not, they show the courage to change or abandon their hypothesis, or to suspend judgment until they've seen or found further evidence. Emulate them as you search for a subject.

Propaganda, the presentation of your side of an issue in its most favorable light, is perfectly legitimate *if* you've arrived at your conclusions fairly, without prejudice, and without distorting opposing evidence. But the propaganda of biased half-truths or perversions of reasoning and the propaganda of narrow-mindedness or careless thinking should never be condoned. (We'll have more to say about this when we talk about "Emotional Appeals" in Chapter 18.)

Look at all the evidence you can. If opposing arguments do not change your views, you at least become aware of and can defend against them, or meet them head-on. Better to know them in advance than to discover while you're speaking that you can't answer a "yes, but . . ." from your audience. To persuade effectively, you can't ignore the opposing views or objections to your arguments. Anticipate them beforehand — and prepare to answer them — through thorough research and careful thought.

In summary, persuasion is an attempt to influence people to change their beliefs, opinions, or knowledge about themselves or their environment; it is also an attempt to influence people to act on beliefs they already hold. Persuasion is not coercion — in which you force others to obey your will; nor is it manipulation — in which you exploit people's ignorance and emotions. Persuasion is a legitimate attempt to make the best case you can, directing your appeals to your listeners' reason and emotions and basing them upon your credibility as a speaker. It occurs when people experience and wish to resolve conflict among their attitudes, beliefs, or knowledge — a conflict described by Festinger as "cognitive dissonance." But persuasion cannot occur when you challenge your listeners' beliefs arrogantly and blindly; it is much more likely to occur when you allow your listeners a way to save face. Finally, your most effective persuasion will occur when you speak on a subject you feel strongly about. So choose a topic — a proposal or proposition — well rooted in your personal convictions. Then begin the process of searching for material that supports (or refutes) your position on it.

Reference Notes

[1] Roger Brown, *Social Psychology* (New York: The Free Press, a Division of the Macmillan Company, 1965), p. 551.

[2] Leon Festinger, *A Theory of Cognitive Dissonance* (Stanford: Stanford University Press, 1957), p. 3.

[3] James Harvey Robinson, "On Various Kinds of Thinking," *The Mind in the Making: The Relation of Intelligence to Social Reform* (New York: Harper & Row, Publishers, Inc., 1950), pp. 41–42.

[4] Drawn and adapted from Leon Festinger, *A Theory of Cognitive Dissonance* (Stanford: Stanford University Press, 1957).

[5] J. A. C. Brown, *Techniques of Persuasion: From Propaganda to Brainwashing* (Baltimore, Md.: Penguin Books Ltd., 1963), p. 285.

17 Audience Attitudes, Needs, and Beliefs

You're female, a college freshman; and it's Wednesday night. Playing on your mind is tomorrow morning's biology test; playing at the show is the latest Robert Redford movie, which your boyfriend has invited you to see. Temptation time. You'd love to see your boyfriend. You'd love to see Robert Redford. You hate studying biology, but your parents—or you—have paid out good money for your college education. You want, or believe you want, a degree so you can become a social worker or a psychologist, or maybe an accountant later—you're not sure yet. But you do hate biology. And you'd love to see your boyfriend, not to mention Robert Redford!

A classical case of attitudes, needs, and beliefs in conflict: Long range, you believe you want a degree to establish credentials for a job. Short range, you need to pass biology. You obviously appreciate the love and companionship your boyfriend offers. But which of these needs, attitudes, and beliefs outweigh the others?

As a human being, you act on reason some of the time, on impulse at others. You won't debate the issue for long, and certainly not consciously in the terms we've used here (though maybe you should). You'll decide to see the movie or not, to fail the exam or not; you'll decide to avoid the temporary pain of studying while (unconsciously) accepting the eventual pain of failing the course. Like other human beings, you will often consider the issues rationally, and then probably make a decision on the basis of emotion or feeling.

I agree with no man's opinions.
I have some of my own.
—Ivan Sergeyevich Turgeniev,
Fathers and Sons

Naturally, since we're all different, each one of us responds to a persuasive message within our own system of attitudes, needs, and beliefs. If you expect to influence your audience, then, you had better anticipate and deal with their responses to your argument and you. All good persuaders are amateur psychologists.

As we've emphasized in earlier chapters, your ability to understand your audience depends primarily on your willingness to put yourself in its moccasins. In Chapter 12, for example, we urged that you ask questions and also play your hunches about your audience's *knowledge* of your chosen subject. Now we're suggesting a similar procedure to determine your listeners' *feelings and attitudes* about your subject and you because this will help you greatly in deciding how *persuadable* your audience is. Look at and compare their attitudes and yours, their needs and yours, their beliefs and yours. If they differ (and they will), try to see where and, if at all possible, why. Then, on the basis of what you discover, you can start evolving a *strategy* for resolving the differences and achieving your persuasive purpose.

A positive audience

A neutral or indifferent audience

A negative or hostile audience

AUDIENCE FEELINGS AND ATTITUDES

Audiences, being people, are logical, emotional, confused, self-assured. Their conflicting *Parent* and *Child* "tapes" have, more or less, helped your audience survive up to now. So, for them, the advice they hear on the "tapes" makes sense. In addition to their rationalizations which protect their beliefs and sanity, they also try to discover whether you are friend, foe, or an in-between.

These feelings of suspicion or hostility or distrust or friendliness or indifference toward you and your thesis are your audience's *attitudes.* Over the years, people involved with persuasion have used three categories of attitudes to classify audiences:

The positive audience. They may know and like you, but they may be totally uninformed about your topic. Or they may like your viewpoint, but they don't know you. An audience may come to hear Ralph Nader speak because, to them, he is saving the world. They know nothing about the complex hydrocarbons he is discussing, but they trust his judgment. They are the best kind of audience.

The neutral or indifferent audience. They care little about you or your topic. You must turn them on to either, or to both. You must demonstrate the topic's relevance and importance to them. You must develop their trust in you as the speaker. Neither task is easy, but both are easier than encountering the crowd we're going to describe next.

The negative or hostile audience. These are the headhunters. "That commie-radical Ralph Nader? Trying to destroy the free-enterprise system with his consumer garbage?" They resent you, or your thesis, or having to attend the speech, or the world in general. Be prepared to duck a lot, and wear sneakers for quicker exits.

1 Discovering for Yourself
Anticipating the Reactions of Other Audiences to Your Thesis

Prepare a hypothetical list of specific audiences who would be: (1) most *receptive* to your thesis, (2) *indifferent* to it, (3) *suspicious* about it, or (4) *hostile* to it. Assume in all cases that the audience does not know you or know about you.

To illustrate how your list might work, take the argument we'll develop in Chapter 18—that required courses should be abolished. The list might look like this:

1. *Most receptive:* many of your classmates or students throughout the school.

2. *Indifferent:* people who have not gone to college and who hold low-paying, low-status jobs (they may not know what goes on in college, or suppose it hasn't any relevance for them).
3. *Suspicious:* business people who expect college graduates to possess certain skills.
4. *Hostile:* the administration and instructors in the college or university.

Then, as speculation about how you would *adapt* your speech to each audience on your list, write out a concise statement or explanation of one thing you would include in your persuasive speech: a piece of evidence, an emotional appeal, a refutation of a counter-argument, an assumption you hope to establish, etc.

Although the designations of "Positive," "Receptive," "Neutral," "Indifferent," "Negative," "Suspicious," "Hostile," etc., may serve as a useful starting point for analyzing your audience's feelings and—hence—their attitudes, we don't wish them to oversimplify a complex problem. Their weakness is that they are rooted in an assumption that all members of an audience tend to react *uniformly;* they don't differentiate between the individual listener's reaction to a speaker's thesis or proposal and that listener's reaction to the speaker personally. Such terms do not explain *why* the listener feels receptive or indifferent or antagonistic toward the speaker or the speaker's message—or both. To understand *individual* response, therefore, we must try to examine the motivations at work *beneath* and *behind* human attitudes. In particular, we need to look at the *needs* and at the *beliefs* which influence and move the individual.

AUDIENCE NEEDS AS FACTORS IN PERSUASION

The late Abraham H. Maslow, a psychologist, has provided a useful framework for examining people's needs and, by extension, their beliefs. From his studies, Maslow formulated a five-step "ladder" or five-level "hierarchy" of needs—the desires which motivate our actions and thoughts.[1] These levels or step-ups begin, at bottom, with those most important to physical survival and ascend, at their uppermost, to those needs most important to the individual's self-realization: goal-fulfillment and the emotional/intellectual stability that goes with it. These needs are, to use Maslow's term, "prepotent," that is, in responding to them, we must work our way up from the lowest to the highest—*in that order.* For example, the physiological-survival needs come first and take priority over all the others. If these first-step needs can be satisfied reasonably well, we will be "motivated" to try to satisfy the needs at the next level or step-up, and so on.

Maslow's ladder or hierarchy

In more specific terms, Maslow's system of human needs looks something like this:

SELF-ACTUALIZATION NEEDS
(to be all that we *can* be)

ESTEEM NEEDS
(worthiness, competence, recognition,
confidence, status, reputation)

BELONGING AND LOVE NEEDS
(affection and love from family; acceptance
by friends; approval by social groups)

SAFETY NEEDS
(protection; security; predictability; stability; orderliness;
freedom from turmoil, uncertainty, and fear)

PHYSIOLOGICAL-SURVIVAL NEEDS
(food and drink, air, rest, sleep, sex, relaxation,
health, and general well-being)

Although people must satisfy lower-level needs first and then concern themselves with ever higher levels, they may slip or step down to a lower level again when faced with a crisis, threat, imbalance, or dissonance. Maslow didn't intend his hierarchy as a set of inflexible categories, each with its attendant set of "rules." He noted frequent exceptions, so don't apply the levels of "prepotency" too rigidly to yourself or others. Use them, rather, as a guide through new "motivational territory," to use when you're trying to gauge people's persuadability and the needs possibly affecting it.

The physiological-survival needs. This first group includes the needs for food, water, warmth, shelter, for avoiding pain. Fill your belly first, then fill your mind and soul. Not enough speakers consider their listeners' physical discomfort when they address an audience near the end of a long evening filled with eating and sitting through many speeches. *Their* message, they think, is so important, their delivery so witty, that they can speak on and on and on. Nonsense. Wise speakers shorten their remarks in such circumstances. They know that many in their audience are listening not to them, but to the call of nature in one form or another.

These temporary need-deprivations, however, only create impatience in an audience. More permanent ones may create intolerance or indifference. Why should poor people, wondering daily about paying the bills and keeping alive, care about your argument for shipping more grain to feed the starving in Calcutta? They hold more selfish beliefs. "Let's take care of ourselves first," they'd say, "then we can worry about the rest of the world." Consider, therefore, whether your argument appeals to your audience's basic needs or, just as important, whether it threatens them.

Of soup and love,
the first is best.
—Spanish Proverb

The safety needs.   Just above the most basic-level needs are the *safety* needs, which Maslow identified as "security; stability; dependency; protection; freedom from fear, from anxiety, from chaos; need for structure, order, law, limits; strength in the protector; and so on."[2] Every child, like every animal, is both curious and conservative. You've seen puppies and kittens explore, then recoil at a sudden sound or movement. You've seen infants cry or run after they stumble over a rock, or onto something unknown.

But as infants grow up, they don't necessarily grow brave. They grow wiser and more careful and more subtle in expressing their dependency needs. They replace their parents with other figures— the president, their boss, the government, their psychiatrist, their doctor—and limit their explorations and tolerance for new experiences. When you enter a classroom, do you head for "your" seat? That's security. Each day, do you eat dinner at about the same hour? That's stability. Do you ask your instructor how long your papers should be, how wide the margins, typewritten or handwritten? That's structure. Do you believe in a strong military, an assured nuclear deterrent against the Russians or the Chinese or whoever is the enemy this week? That's safety—a need for strength in a protector.

The urgency of these safety needs increases as crime or unemployment rises, or when an emergency occurs. Cries go up for law and order; people long for the "good old days"; they ignore other concerns to save their or their loved ones' necks or jobs. Threatened with loss of income, honor, or life, people may sacrifice their beliefs in privacy, freedom, and individuality and endure indignities and humiliations. At all times and in all places, people yearn for security and will sacrifice much to maintain or regain it.

" . . . Oh, Professor Ivanovitch is just building a model of an individual's hierarchy of needs!"

How well your audience receives your argument will depend in no small part on how well you've satisfied their safety needs. Isolated from the problems of the cities on a quiet, tree-lined campus, they may share your anger at police brutality and CIA, FBI, and IRS spying. Outside school, in a neighborhood outraged by nightly rapes and burglaries, your audience may hoot you off the rostrum or speaker's platform. They may want sterner measures, not what they believe is your "empty rhetoric." Even in relatively safe neighborhoods, the daily reports of violent deaths and brutalities on the evening newscast may increase people's fears. Are you arguing for gun control? Fat chance. If you know your audience doesn't feel safe, advance arguments and proposals that will relieve their fears.

The need for love and belonging. All people need someone to love them, to be concerned about them, to listen to them—if only to hear them bluster about their independence. You may like to believe yourself an island; you may enjoy being alone; but you prefer to make the choice freely. Too often, you must suffer alone—in illness, in guilt, in child-birth, or in dying—when you'd like to seek the company and under-standing of others. Similarly, you need to identify yourself with a group: a family, an organization, a community, a country. Everyone needs roots, even if traveling continually. Everybody needs some place or some thing or some body to hold onto, physically or psychologically or both. Maslow counseled never to underestimate "the deep importance of the neighborhood, of one's territory, of one's clan, of one's own 'kind,' one's class, one's gang, one's familiar working colleagues."[3]

Evidence of the need to belong is everywhere. On campus, your normal ties are to the larger community of students and to smaller groups within that community: a fraternity or sorority, the kids in your dorm, the engineering club, the Jesus movement, or simply your circle of friends. You surround yourself with people like you, or people you'd like to be like. Of course, you also feel ties to your family, your old neigh-borhood, your religion, your ethnic group. These vary in intensity and importance, but the strongest ones will influence your beliefs, too.

Of course, we know that you were immune to the social pressures to smoke cigarettes in eighth grade, smoke marijuana in freshman year of high school, and drink beer as juniors and seniors. We know that *you* resisted the pressure to go to the high-school football games and sit with the "right" crowd, to cruise or hang out on Friday nights, and to wear Oshkosh overalls even though you knew they looked silly. But most people, not as strong as you are, cave in. Therefore, consider whom your audience breaks bread with, bends elbows with, or likes to identify with. You'll know better what they think, whom they hate or at least don't trust, where their prejudices lie, and where within this system they place you. If you're the enemy, or not their "kind," you'll want to consider how to dispel their suspicions and gain their acceptance.

The need for esteem. Fourth up the ladder in Maslow's hier-archy are the *esteem* needs, including the respect of others and your own sense of worth. Are you *somebody,* a success, famous, prosperous, looked up to? In their most trivial form, esteem needs set the rules for the keeping-up-with-the-Joneses game, though the stakes differ ac-cording to your value system. For one crowd, the winners own the fastest cars with the most STP decals and the fanciest spinner hubcaps. For another, winning means the best grades in school. For still another, win-ners get the job with the prestigious firm, then compete for the larger office and the larger staff, become a partner, and finally company president. For still another, the winners work in juvenile homes or an old people's home or join the clergy.

Don't assume, however, that self-esteem needs can only be satisfied by competing and winning. To really count and endure, self-esteem—as the word implies—must be generated *from within*. If, for the sake of winning, you compromise your beliefs and values, you may severely damage or even destroy it. Nor should you ever conclude that fame, respect of others, and the so-called benefits of "success" can guarantee total happiness or peace of mind. For real self-esteem, you must perform work you enjoy, feel suited for, feel competent in; you must believe that you're OK, that you've *earned* your money, your social standing, the acclaim of others. Again quoting Maslow: "The most stable and therefore most healthy self-esteem is based on *deserved* respect from others."[4]

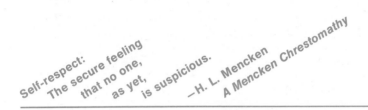

Self-respect:
The secure feeling
that no one,
as yet,
is suspicious.
—H. L. Mencken
A Mencken Chrestomathy

The esteem needs are the most fragile to handle in persuasion. Take an obvious case. Suppose you are arguing for increased welfare benefits before an audience of the genuinely impoverished. You urge them to organize, lobby, militate for change. They stand to gain from your suggestions—in their lower needs. But poor people may be just as proud as rich people. By your line of persuasion, you're suggesting that they beg for more handouts when they believe they should be accorded dignity.

As you travel into the upper-income brackets, you still must tread softly. There, the cracks in self-esteem may be concealed beneath expensive clothes and suburban walls, but they nonetheless exist. Remember, therefore, that when you are appealing to the esteem needs, for many affluent people, certain charities and certain social issues deliver bigger ego-payoffs than others. For example, your audience may feel the greatest self-esteem in helping the crippled or mentally retarded (the *deserving* poor).

The need for self-actualization.   At the top of Maslow's hierarchy sits the need for *self-actualization*, a need few people ever satisfy. Even deserved respect and healthy self-esteem cannot dispel some discomfort and restlessness if you aren't doing what you really want. If somewhere along the line you've compromised your ideals, sold your soul to the devil, or simply lost enjoyment in your work, you may believe you must move on, drop out, re-evaluate. Life can be better than this, you think, so you change jobs, or get a divorce, or rediscover religion. The true self-actualizing people do what they know is right, despite popular opinion, without recognition; they feel secure within themselves. They make personal sacrifices for others; they can be fully loving, fully giving, fully creative, fully human in its best sense.

With such a group as your audience, you need only state your case and supply your evidence. If your cause is just, they'll agree. Of course, we're describing a group of saints, so you'd better be more realistic. Yes, you'll meet a self-actualizing person occasionally and should strive to become one yourself. But unless you've a strong need for self-punishment, don't ascribe such holy virtues to others. Their lower needs (and yours) are usually too pressing. We don't believe, however, that you must become pessimistic or cynical. People are human and imperfect, but they aren't ogres. If not threatened, taunted, or challenged, they will listen and—occasionally—be convinced.

2 Discovering for Yourself
Examining Your Own Needs

You already know the intended audience for your impending persuasive speech—your classmates—and you know something about them. But now consciously consider their needs.

In some respects, you'll share the same ones because you, too, are a student and probably feel many of the same pressures for survival and achievement. Start by examining yourself, therefore. Write a page or two of self-analysis in your communication journal. Using Maslow's hierarchy as a guide, think about what needs you've most fully or least fully satisfied. Consider what groups, physically present or distant in time or space, you ally yourself with, identify with, aspire to in your need for belonging. Consider whose respect you value most, and how strongly you hold your self-esteem. These are tough questions, requiring honest answers.

Perhaps looking over your interests-and-attitudes inventory in your journal can supply you with some ideas for this entry. If not, consider the following questions:

1. *What does my choice of a college major tell me about myself—my needs, beliefs, and values?*
2. *Does my religion or ethnic background create strong needs in me—and in what specific respects?*
3. *In what particular ways does my economic or social background influence my needs and beliefs?*
4. *What do I spend my time thinking about most often, and how do these concerns or fantasies fit into my needs-structure?*

Now, again studying your communication journal and making appropriate notes in it, determine how the strategy you've chosen for your forthcoming persuasive speech fulfills or threatens the needs most important to you at this moment. Stated another way, suppose your proposal or proposition were to "come true," *what would be the consequences for you and others, and how would you react to these consequences?*

3 Discovering for Yourself
Comparing Your Audience's Needs to Your Own

How do your audience's needs match yours? Specifically, do they identify with the same groups, feel as comfortable (or uncomfortable) financially and physically as you, feel threatened or insecure in any way you've been able to notice? Do they hold themselves in high esteem? Are they strong enough to be self-actualizing? Rather than think of that great shapeless mass called your classmates, think about specific people in the class. What makes Roger slump in his chair with that tough-guy attitude? Why doesn't Julie ever shut up? What makes Chuck want to be an Air Force officer? Why does Patty so often smile and appear so gracious? Determine as best you can where most of the class members fit in Maslow's hierarchy, and record your observations in your journal; then also jot down what arguments to use or to avoid in making your persuasive speech.

How needs may affect audience response to a specific line of argument

Comparing your needs to your audience's needs (as you've just done for those of your classmates in Exercise 3) is no mere abstract, academic task. When you consider the primacy of certain needs, you can understand why people remain resistant to change on an issue. Take a familiar—and controversial—example: racial integration. Here are the typical beliefs *opposing* it, and the needs they stem from:

1. Crime will rise. *(safety and stability)*
2. Property values will decrease. *(economic survival and security)*
3. The schools will deteriorate. *(survival of your children later in life; also connected with the parents' and children's need for recognition and self-esteem)*
4. They simply aren't *my* kind. *(belonging)*
5. They'll take away my job. *(physical survival, security, and self-esteem)*

Now compare the arguments *for* integration and the needs they touch upon:

1. Integration is morally and legally right. *(self-actualization* and *esteem)*
2. Blacks have been discriminated against for three centuries, and now it is time to balance the scales. *(self-actualization* and *esteem)*
3. Integration is our only chance for survival as a nation. *(security* and *survival* and *belonging)*

Notice that many of the beliefs opposing integration stem from the lower and, therefore, more insistent needs—either wholly or in combination with some appeal to higher needs. The first two arguments for integration, on the other hand, appeal to the *higher* needs (the needs not found in many people). Only the last argument touches on the lower needs, but even then in terms of long-range, not short-range, benefits. Clearly, for most audiences (except for the self-actualizing ones) the *cons* would far outweigh the *pros.* To influence most audiences, therefore, a pro-integration statement would have to demonstrate that the principal arguments of the opposing position have no basis in fact.

Need-fulfillment thus shapes the feelings, attitudes, and—to an extent—the beliefs listeners hold about you and your presentation. The degree to which your thesis, ideas, proposals, and arguments prove persuasive hinges heavily on whether your hearers view you as a fulfiller-of-needs, an insider, an outsider, a protector, or a threat. As a speaker you dare not ignore the needs-systems of your listeners; you must deal with them promptly, positively, and honestly.

AUDIENCE BELIEFS AS FACTORS IN PERSUASION

No consideration of beliefs is possible without an understanding of *values.* In fact, values and beliefs are so closely allied, so interdependent, that they are difficult to separate. Your values result from your measurements of right and wrong, good and bad, big and little, high and low within your belief-system. If you believe in material success, for example, you may place highest value on objects that most visibly demonstrate that success, like a shiny new car. Similarly, if you believe in power, status, freedom to travel, or to be independent of others, you may also value that same car. The car, in effect, becomes a symbolic statement of who you are or want to be. A Cadillac symbolizes one kind of person, a Volkswagen another. The strength of your beliefs is a significant factor in determining your values.

One way to deal with beliefs, therefore, is to determine their relative strength within the individual listener and wherein they contradict each other. Since changing a belief results from cognitive dissonance — that is, some conflict with another belief or behavior — the stronger the conflicting belief you can unearth, the bigger the hole you can dig in a listener's or an audience's fixed position.

Rokeach's system of beliefs

Psychologist Milton Rokeach has provided a simple framework within which you can examine the strength of beliefs. He divides them, as you see in the target in the sketch below, into three categories: (1) *peripheral* beliefs, (2) *authority* beliefs, and (3) *primitive* or *core* beliefs; thus:[5]

The Peripheral Beliefs. Peripheral beliefs, represented by the outer segment of the target in the illustration, are those beliefs you hold least firmly and change most frequently. You feel attached to them, but — perhaps regretfully — you discard them. The Robert Redford movie we mentioned at the beginning of the chapter may fall in this category: You believe in or value it as escape entertainment, but next week a new

"Now, class . . . please note that the closer Ms. Baker's strategy comes to the Core Beliefs, the less persuasive she will be."

star may replace the old. Since your emotional commitment to these peripheral beliefs isn't total, you can sacrifice them when they conflict with stronger beliefs. If you believe in education—or the good job, the recognition, the self-esteem, and the opportunity to realize your potential it represents—you'll forego the Robert Redford movie. If you believe the momentary enjoyment is more important, to Robert Redford you will go.

The Authority Beliefs. Authority beliefs, those lying somewhat closer to the center of the target in the drawing, are those beliefs you value because you're impressed with the person or circumstances from which they originated. You respect or admire certain people or the positions they occupy; consequently, you trust their opinions or judgments. Suppose, for example, that after an auto accident, your doctor told you to wear a neck brace for your whiplash. The brace—in time—grew hot, uncomfortable, frayed, and filthy; and it looked just awful. But you wore it because you respected the doctor's advice.

Similarly, you respect the advice of others in other contexts. However, the people or positions you most revere, bow down to, and/or wish to emulate exercise the predominant influence in the circle of your authority values. These people, positions, or institutions consequently influence your other beliefs, especially your peripheral beliefs. Within your *authority beliefs,* what is said is secondary to who says it. So, when you already feel some doubt about an old belief, a new idea endorsed by a person you greatly respect may convince you to abandon the old for the new. Occasionally, it's true, the authority may lose credibility by backing a too-controversial issue. But, generally, the "right" person on your side of an issue can make your argument sound "right."

Discovering for Yourself and Small-Group Discussion

Testing the Effects of Authority Beliefs

Read the following opinions voiced by a woman discussing some typically controversial subjects:

On *premarital sex* (in response to a question as to how she would react if her daughter had an affair): "I wouldn't be surprised." If more people did, in fact, "I'm not sure that, perhaps, there wouldn't be less divorce."

On *marijuana:* "I'm sure my children have tried marijuana." Experimenting with it is "like your first beer or your first cigarette." If younger, she "probably" would have tried it herself, out of curiosity.

On *abortion:* The Supreme Court's decision legalizing it was "the best thing in the world . . . a great, great decision."

Discuss your reactions to these statements with the other members of your small group. Do you agree with these views? Would your parents agree? As your discussion proceeds, your instructor will tell you who made the statements on the controversial subjects—information found in the *Instructor's Manual* for this book. What is your opinion of the speaker? Does this new information *change* your reactions either to the statements or to the person who uttered them?

Following a further discussion by your group, your instructor will read you, again from the *Instructor's Manual*, a few statements made by members of the clergy in reacting to the statements in question. Discuss these comments, speculating on the beliefs which might have prompted them. Can you see any relationship between the credibility of a speaker and the ideas which he or she expresses? What is it?

The Core Beliefs. Some beliefs are so central to the core of your being, so strongly recorded on your mental "tapes," so closely allied with your sense of who you are and what the world is like, that to relinquish one might seem like losing an eye or even your heart. In Rokeach's system these beliefs are, in fact, the *primitive* or *core* beliefs. You abandon such a belief only after continual pressure, continual discomfort, continual evidence that it no longer serves you well.

Generally, you develop these beliefs in your strongest mental "tapes" from your childhood and carry them around the rest of your life. As a child, living in poverty, you may have become determined to be rich as an adult. Consequently, you worked hard and sacrificed your enjoyment to establish a successful business. Not only do you believe in the importance of accumulating money in large quantities, but you believe also in hard work and self-sacrifice.

Admiration: Our polite recognition of another man's resemblance to ourselves.
—Ambrose Bierce, The Devil's Dictionary

How these three sets of beliefs—peripheral, authority, and core—interact helps to determine the effectiveness of any persuasive appeal. Consider the example we just cited. You're the hard-working businessperson. How would you react to a proposal for a government-guaranteed minimum income, to be paid for by *your* tax dollars? But how would you react if the heads of the six largest U.S. corporations,

The Wall Street Journal, and conservative newspaper columnist William F. Buckley supported the proposal? The cognitive dissonance creating war between your authority beliefs and your core beliefs might destroy your peace of mind until you called a truce, held your nose, and followed your leaders. Obviously, we've loaded the dice with this example. But you can change your beliefs if someone creates enough dissonance, makes you feel uncomfortable enough.

5 Discovering for Yourself
Anticipating Your Audience's Reactions to Your Argument and You

You have a pretty good idea of your audience's needs by now, so you can contemplate their reactions to your argument and you. Consider:

1. What, if any, peripheral beliefs does your argument reinforce? If you find that you can reinforce a number of peripheral beliefs, then your chances of success in persuasion are good, but not assured.
2. What core beliefs does your argument reinforce? If it does reinforce core beliefs, consider carrying your argument further and appealing to your audience to take action on their beliefs.
3. Is your argument irrelevant to their beliefs? Then consider how to make it relevant, and strike at the core beliefs if you can.
4. What peripheral beliefs does it threaten? If you find some, consider what strong authorities and appeals to their core beliefs would reduce the threat.
5. What core beliefs does it threaten? If you find some, you've got problems. Consider what strong core beliefs you might bring into conflict with the ones your argument threatens. Also, consider quoting some authorities your audience respects.

Now ask a similar set of questions about *yourself* in your audience's authority-belief system:

1. How well does your audience know you? If not very well, spend some time at the beginning of your speech establishing your credentials; or allow the person introducing you to establish them.
2. How well are you respected? If the answer is "very well respected," then your chances of success are great. If the answer is "not well respected," again cite authorities your audience does respect.
3. Does your audience dislike you, or hold your views lightly? If your answer is yes, seriously consider whether you're selling yourself short. Without self-confidence, you may bumble and mumble and decrease the strength of your argument. But belief in yourself can make you believable, too. Remember that you're OK.

Gathering Additional Reactions to Your Argument

With your group, discuss the thesis you've chosen for your persuasive speech. Then have members of the group suggest at least two objections they think they or the class as a whole would raise against it.

Later, look at their objections carefully. Did they jump to any hasty or unwarranted conclusions or reveal any prejudices? How could you soften those prejudices—get people to look before they leap? Did your group's arguments disclose any needs or beliefs you hadn't considered? How, specifically, would you appeal to those needs and beliefs in ways that would strengthen your viewpoints and arguments? In your communication journal, make some notes about your findings and thoughts.

To sum up our examination of your audience's responses to your thesis and you, we've said that in terms of predominant attitudes you can classify audiences into *positive, neutral* or *indifferent,* and *negative* categories. We've urged you to investigate the *needs* and *beliefs* behind those attitudes. We've described Abraham Maslow's hierarchy of needs, which moves "upwardly" from the *survival* needs to the *safety* needs, to needs for *love* and *belonging,* to the need for *esteem,* and finally—at the top—to the need for *self-actualization.* We've also described Milton Rokeach's system of *peripheral, authority,* and *core* beliefs. Each of these systems, we've emphasized, can help you anticipate your audience's reactions and ways of dealing with them. As you can see, examining your audience's responses inevitably leads into a consideration of a *strategy* for your persuasive speech—the subject of the next chapter.

Reference Notes

[1] Based on Chapter 4 in *Motivation and Personality,* 2nd Edition by Abraham H. Maslow. Copyright 1954 by Harper & Row, Publishers, Inc. Copyright © 1970 by Abraham H. Maslow. By permission of the publishers.

[2] Ibid.

[3] Ibid.

[4] Ibid.

[5] Milton Rokeach, *The Three Christs of Ypsilanti: A Psychological Study* (New York: Alfred A. Knopf, 1964), pp. 19, 20, 24; and Milton Rokeach, "Images of the Consumer's Mind on and off Madison Avenue," in *Speech Communication,* ed. Howard Martin and Kenneth Anderson (Boston: Allyn & Bacon, Inc., 1968), pp. 256–262. In the first, Rokeach uses the terminology "primitive beliefs," "beliefs about authorities to rely on in relation to controversial matters," and "peripheral beliefs." In the second, he uses the terms "core," "authority," and "peripheral" in relation to *values.* Our terminology is thus a combination of the terms Rokeach employs.

18 Choosing a Persuasive Strategy

STRATEGY: THE "AVAILABLE MEANS OF PERSUASION"

You've chosen your subject and your thesis. You know your audience. Now, as you assemble and begin to structure your materials to make them clear and lively, you must also plan to make them persuasive. It's time to devise a *strategy*.

Although "strategy" sounds like a battle plan, it isn't evil. It's merely careful. A strategy is not purely *offensive* — in either sense of the word. It's defensive, too, a plan to counteract your audience's strategies for rejecting or ignoring your arguments. When your struggle to convince and their struggle to resist has ended, ideally no one should be injured or battle scarred. Your strategy — if you've chosen it wisely —

should peaceably resolve the conflicts between your beliefs, knowledge, and ideas and those of your listeners.

When you threaten people's beliefs, they can easily reject your information and arguments or—in some cases—lash out against you. Not to devise a careful strategy and thereby to invite rejection or attack is foolish and potentially dangerous. Unprepared, you'll go blindly into the battle and most likely lose it.

A good strategy, to cite Aristotle's terms again, involves enlisting *all the available means of persuasion.* It provides audiences with strong motivations, strong evidence, and a strong, believable presentation to maximize opportunities for people to *persuade themselves.* As a persuader, you'll give them the best information available and clear up misconceptions about it. You'll try to neutralize their prejudices, satisfy their needs, answer their questions, counter their objections. You'll be both reasonable and emotional, credible and likeable. And, as always, you'll be confident, in command, consciously and continuously aware of your task and your audience. In short, you'll enlist every ethical means at your disposal to be persuasive.

We'll try to help you by inspecting two of the most potent pieces of "artillery" in your persuasive arsenal: *emotion* and *reasoning.* We'll discuss what emotions to anticipate, how to appeal to emotions, and—in some instances—how to trigger or disarm emotional responses. And, as a precautionary measure, we'll attempt to gauge the dangerous "firepower" of a few dishonest emotional appeals. Then, turning to the process of *reasoning,* we'll single out some useful characteristics of "reasonable" or "logical" arguments, and finally wind up with an inspection of a reasoning-from-evidence-to-conclusion *model* that you can conveniently and convincingly fit your major persuasive arguments into.

EMOTION: THE FIRST BIG GUN
IN YOUR PERSUASIVE STRATEGY

No speech can avoid emotion. It's already present (as you saw in Chapter 17) at the very core of an audience's core beliefs. Emotion results naturally from the dissonance—the internal conflict—among knowledge, needs, or beliefs that causes changes in actions and attitudes. No matter how rational your argument, no matter how well documented, new ideas striking against old ones can send off sparks of insecurity, uncertainty, fear, resentment, anger, even hatred. Therefore, questioning whether to appeal to reason *or* emotion is irrelevant. The real questions are what emotions to anticipate arising in your audience, which to tap, and which to mute or channel in different directions.

One very important thing to remember when trying to anticipate audience emotions is that *nobody likes to be wrong.* If you attack people's attitudes, beliefs, and values with figurative elephant guns or cannons and mortars, they'll arm themselves to counterattack. Even as an animal will fight when cornered physically, so will humans fight when cornered psychologically. You must expect people to defend themselves emotionally and aim their cannonades at you, rather than your argument.

Instead of assaulting your audience emotionally, then, transact with them, as usual, through the "I'm OK—you're OK" position. Your strategy should be to explain to your listeners that their information—not they—is in error. If you respect them, addressing them as decent, reasonable people who would not hold a belief out of pettiness or bigotry, they will probably respond fairly and rationally. You're communicating that they're OK, so they'll act OK.

Using emotional appeals

Initially, in a persuasive-speech setting, emotions of audiences tend to run high. Sometimes, however, especially if your listeners are indifferent to or uninformed about the key issue, you will wish to *foster* an emotional reaction. Otherwise, you may be offering a solution to a problem that—for your audience at least—doesn't exist. You want them to know and to *care* about it—plenty. In such situations your strategy, for example, could be to begin with an appeal to their *pity.* Show slides of starving children with swollen bellies, shriveled legs, and open, pus-filled sores. Cite statistics: Most will eat nothing for three months; 400 will die this week, 1200 this month, 144,000 this year. Detail the example of one child, Muhamid Abutu, age eight months; grandmother a paralytic; father unable to work because so weakened by starvation and malaria; mother unable to nurse Muhamid because malnutrition has shriveled her breasts. Or, just as easily, you could appeal to your listeners' emotion of *hope,* or their sense of *joy,* predicting greater, happier days ahead, with fewer working hours, longer lives, and five chickens in every pot. In a persuasive strategy you can, in fact, appeal to virtually *any emotion,* provided you do not exaggerate the facts or distort the truth.

In selecting and using emotional appeals you must always, of course, exercise careful judgment, discretion, and tact. The more potent the emotion, the greater must be your skill in handling it. Appeals to fear, for instance, showing the unpleasant, threatening, painful, or horrifying consequences of a problem if your solution isn't adopted, require special caution. Fear can cause the greatest dissonance and foster the most unpredictable reactions because your listeners do mental somersaults to avoid the discomfort you've created. When using a fear strategy, therefore, you must first take care to shut off the easiest escape route for your audience: that your facts are wrong, that you're not telling the truth. Clearly establish—but don't exaggerate—the danger. Buttress the appeal with hard evidence and solid, factual speech materials. If you haven't done your homework thoroughly, you may end up back home, wondering why your audience hissed you off the stage.

Even with the strongest fear appeal and an airtight case, your audience may look for emotional breathing room outside of it. Cigarette smokers, as our example in Chapter 16 illustrated, already know the dangers of their addiction, but cannot or will not stop. Can a fear appeal be made to work with such people? If you show slides of lungs rotted and blackened, if you play tapes of victims' rasping cries and pleas

". . . And now, Professor, I'll use my 'big guns' to try and persuade you!"

to be allowed to die and not suffer further from cancer or emphysema, do you actually influence smokers to give up their addiction? Perhaps. Or, perhaps, you may get them so nervous they need a cigarette. More likely, however, they simply dismiss your arguments entirely—a conclusion Leon Festinger reached in his research on cognitive dissonance. He discovered that people blot out really unpleasant matters, ignoring them, or thinking them absurd, or becoming angry at the person creating the unpleasantness.[1]

If scrupulously researched, well intended, and constructively presented, however, a fear or "scare" appeal can work—maybe. Rather than threatening and berating them for their sins, suggest that cigarette smokers analyze which cigarettes are most important to them during the day. Is it the first one in the morning, perhaps? Or the one immediately after their meals? Ask them to note when they are most likely to smoke *unnecessary* cigarettes: with a cup of coffee, when talking on the telephone, while drinking, or at parties? Then offer your cigarette-smoking audience ways to avoid situations where they want the cigarettes, or advocate substitutes in those situations. Eventually, assure your listeners, they can eliminate the unnecessary cigarette, then the necessary cigarette, and finally stop altogether.

1 Discovering for Yourself—and in Your Group
Examining a Speech for Its Emotional Appeals

Read the following excerpt from a speech by Phyllis Schlafly, author, radio commentator, and a leader in the opposition to the Equal Rights Amendment. Identify the emotional appeals that you detect. Consider the appropriateness of her choice of words to generate the kind of emotional responses she seems to seek. Then, in your small group, compare your list of emotional appeals with those of other group members, and discuss the means and the degree of effectiveness with which the speaker has presented her persuasive appeals in this brief passage:

This is a grab for power at the federal level. This is what will take out of the hands of the state legislatures whole new areas of jurisdiction that the federal government hasn't yet gotten its meddling fingers into, including marriage, marriage-property laws, divorce, child custody, prison regulations, insurance rates, protective labor legislation, and any type of law that makes a difference between men and women. That's the reason we see so many federal payrollers going around the country at the taxpayers' expense, speaking and agitating, and talking, and debating on behalf of the Equal Rights Amendment. Time and again when I go out to speak and my friends have passed the hat to pay for my plane fare, I find my opponent is there on your taxpayers' money. They do this out of the White House; they do it out of the Department of Labor. They've been doing it for years: spending all their time working in behalf of the Equal Rights Amendment, distributing expensive government booklets paid for by the taxpayers to push the Equal Rights Amendment. I think they see a whole new area of jurisdiction that will come into their control, with more staff and more authority to run our lives.[2]

A final bit of advice: In weighing the use of any emotional appeal, consider the degree of your audience's *sophistication.* Several studies have shown that more intelligent and well-educated audiences are skeptical of emotional appeals. They are more likely to respect a speaker who seems objective and fair, and who gives the appearance of being a "reasoning" person.

Emotional appeals — communicating or conning?

Use emotion in persuasion, yes, but don't insult your audience by using *only* emotional appeals. Emotion, it should be apparent, can be a dangerous weapon. Too often, unthinking or unethical communicators exploit people's emotions to defend an indefensible position or proposal or "product." Such exploitation or manipulation works, for a while, with some things (like selling deodorant), until the emotions (and, perhaps, the deodorant) wear off. Then the audiences begin to smell something they don't like. Unethical speakers try bypassing the reasoning process and appealing directly and solely to their audience's emotions or prejudices. Or, worse yet, they distort or misrepresent evidence in order to strengthen their case. Sometimes such "cheating" is unintentional; but if you see it frequently in something you hear or read, you're probably being exploited by a second-rate mind or a first-rate hooligan. The British writer, George Orwell, in a much-anthologized essay, "Politics and the English Language," calls such attempts to distort issues or distract people from issues nothing less than "swindles and perversions."[3] Let's look briefly at a few of the more common ones:

The-Emperor's-New-Clothes-Ism.   Because an argument looks shabby dressed in its own clothing, the exploiter or manipulator dresses it up in the garb of something — or somebody — else. People generally regard the American flag, free enterprise, the Bible, our founding fathers, and Jesus rather highly. So, often, you'll find them or their "clothing" draped over the body of the most puny argument, padding it out to make it appear more muscular. A famous example occurred in 1896, when William Jennings Bryan was seeking the Democratic nomination for the presidency. A big issue, believe it or not, was whether gold or silver should back our currency. Bryan stood firmly behind the silver standard and delivered his resoundingly successful "Cross of Gold" address to the convention delegates. Among other arguments, he injected this emotional appeal:

> Having behind us the producing masses of this nation and the world, supported by the commercial interests, the laboring interests, and the toilers everywhere, we will answer their demand for a gold standard by saying to them: You shall not press down upon the brow of labor this crown of thorns, you shall not crucify mankind upon a cross of gold.[4]

Name-Calling, or So's-Your-Old-Man-Ism. If a persuader can't refute the reasoning of opponents, he or she may be tempted to call them derogatory names: agitators, troublemakers, un-Americans, fascists, totalitarians, socialists, communists, pigs, bleeding-heart liberals, fat-cat capitalists, wild-eyed reactionaries, mercenaries, long-hairs, short-hairs, hippies, perverts, freaks, bums, cowards, cretins, subversives, counter-revolutionaries. And never mind whether the names come close to fitting or not. People employing this tactic won't discuss the opponents' reasoning or analyze their case. We're not saying here that you should never call anything or anybody a name. Nothing is wrong with calling something "communist-inspired and financed" IF you can *prove* the allegation, and if it is *pertinent* to the facts in the case.

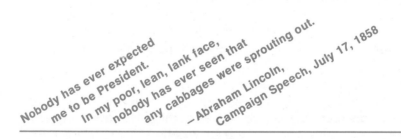

Nobody has ever expected me to be President. In my poor, lean, lank face, nobody has ever seen that any cabbages were sprouting out.
—Abraham Lincoln, Campaign Speech, July 17, 1858

Just-Folks-Ism. "I'm too simple and stupid to do anything dishonest," says the demagogue, raising his right hand to swear and putting his left into your wallet. (How's that for name-calling? Did our "demagogue" work?) Because I'm just like you, with roots in the same soil, I can't be bad. After all, Abe Lincoln split rails as a youth and was raised in a log cabin—as he carefully pointed out in his campaigns.

Red Herring, or Get-'Em-Off-the-Scent-Ism. Criminals used to drag a smelly red herring over their tracks to confuse and divert pursuing bloodhounds. Shysters in persuasion drag irrelevant issues and appeals past your noses, too. They try to divert you from the real issue or proposition by discussing how much money an opponent makes, their opponent's recent divorce or child-custody case, the exclusivity of the neighborhood in which an opponent resides, etc. Or they turn proudly to their own war record, or their record as a God-fearing and upright citizen who is a "good provider and taxpayer."

Red-herring persuasion tactics need not be personal attacks, however. Answering charges that policemen had maliciously beaten demonstrators during a political convention, a big-city mayor declared: "Those outside agitators were spitting on the police and calling them filthy names. What would you do in their place?" (In their place, we might have beaten the demonstrators, too—and have been *equally* guilty of malicious abuse of power.) "Besides," continued the mayor, "they're fine family men. They wouldn't do something like that." (Hitler loved and raised dogs, too. And dog-lovers can't be bad, can they? In case you missed it, we've just tried to refute the mayor's argument by dragging a red herring or two across the trail of *his* argument.)

Glittering Generalities, or Snazzy-Abstraction-Ism. As we repeatedly emphasized throughout Part Three of this book, the more specific and concrete a statement is, the greater its vividness and clarity. The opposite also is true. When persuasive "swindlers" wish to gloss over the weaknesses or holes in their arguments and "products"—when they want to disguise their actual thoughts or cover up the truth—they conceal them in meaningless, but high-sounding generalizations and decorate them with the prettiest words and the emptiest phrases. And sometimes, when a meaningful phrase uttered in valid circumstances becomes popular, expect the persuasive con artists and hustlers to pick it up and exploit it to the fullest and always out of context. Typical of such distorted and overused catchphrases are "Make the World Safe for Democracy," "Peace with Honor," "The Welfare Rip-Off," "Detente," "Stamp Out Food Stamps," and "The Military-Industrial Complex." Beware of slogans which because of overuse or intentional distortion have become meaningless, and watch out for those catchphrases which had little meaning to begin with.

You're-Either-For-or-Against-It-Ism. Sometimes called the "either/or fallacy," this shows up in the arguments or appeals of persuaders accustomed to oversimplifying complex issues. For them, ideas or positions have only two sides: right or wrong. Sometimes, to be sure, issues *are* clearly drawn; but for most issues, the lines tend to blend or overlap. Although most issues have many shadings and colors, the "fer-it-er-agin-it" people want to throw a bucket of paint against the wall and call it the whole picture. "America—love it or leave it," they say. (But should we "love" pollution, political chicanery, a ballooning crime rate, an out-of-control cost of living? Can't we stay and try to lessen America's problems?) "Register criminals, not guns." (Are these opposites?) "Guns don't kill, people do." (With what? Potato chips?) Such persuaders, we suspect, suffer from an "I'm OK—you're not OK" attitude.

The-First-Thing-Caused-the-Second-Ism. The human mind seeks to explain everything, to seek causes for events. But because one thing precedes another in time, the former doesn't necessarily cause the latter. Many parents raised their children by the advice of Dr. Spock, and teen-age alcoholism is increasing. Is the good doctor, therefore, responsible for the prevalence of teen-age drunks? Rome fell to invaders after crime increased within the Empire. Crime is increasing in the United States, so should you make sure your old fallout shelters are freshly stocked?

That's-What-You-Said, You-Dirty-Dog-Ism. By leaving out a word or two or by ignoring the context of the original remark, verbal con artists can distort or even completely reverse the meaning of the original speaker's utterance. Here's a statement by that well-known communist, Abraham Lincoln, taken from his First Annual Message to Congress, December 3, 1861: "Labor is prior to, and independent of capital. Capital is only the fruit of labor, and could never have existed if labor had not first existed. Labor is the superior of capital, and deserves much higher consideration."

"Move over, Karl Marx!" your persuasive swindler might shout in loud accusation, and would be sure *not* to explain that Lincoln also said in that same speech: "Capital has its rights, which are as worthy of protection as any other rights." In your role either as an ethical persuader or a typical listener, discovering intentionally incomplete quotes, quotes taken out of context, and deliberate misquotes is admittedly difficult work. To counteract this tactical fraud, you must either know the original quote, or spend the time and effort to find it. But don't be a sucker—*spend* it.

In sum, then, with the potential for use and abuse of emotion as a persuasive weapon so great, you can readily see why you *should* anticipate your listeners' emotions. You can also see why you *should* use emotionally laden appeals—use them sensitively, skillfully, but sparingly, not to supplant appeals to reason and logic, but to *augment, support,* and *balance* them. Respect your audience's intelligence, and they will respect you. Provide them with sufficient information and evidence to change their attitudes or move them to action, but don't try consciously to bait your persuasive line to hook their fears or anxieties or guilts without weighing the consequences. No cause, no matter how pure, justifies the use of impure means.

REASON: THE SECOND BIG GUN
IN YOUR PERSUASIVE STRATEGY

Your emotional appeals may make your audience *want* to accept your arguments, but you mustn't disappoint them with flimsy ones. To be convincing, your arguments must be logical and well grounded in evidence. However, before we inspect the "big gun" of reasoning, and before we attempt to define and examine "reasonable" or "logical" arguments, we should quickly review what we said in Chapter 11 about *evidence* and when to use it.

Persuasion is effected by arguments, when we demonstrate the truth, real or apparent, by such means as inhere in particular cases.
—Aristotle, *Rhetoric*

What evidence is

Evidence can be just about anything that supports an idea or helps establish a point: your own experience, an example—real or hypothetical—a statistic, a comparison, a photograph, a chart, the name of a person or a whole list of persons supporting your claim, a quote from the Bible or Martin Luther or Martin Luther King or Alexander Hamilton or Alexander Solzhenitzyn or Karl Marx or Groucho Marx or Adam Smith or Adam and Eve or any of the McCarthys—Joseph, Eugene, or Charlie.

In Part Three, as you hunted for your materials for your *informative* speeches—in books, in your own past, in conversations with others—you first of all challenged the validity of the discovered information and its sources for *you.* Now, as you "research" your *persuasive* speech, you should also question the validity of the discovered evidence for *you* (your credibility and persuasive purpose), for the convincing *case* you are developing, and for your *audience.* You aren't, it's true, proving your case in a courtroom, but you are courting your audience's approval and agreement. Will the audience think your experiences typical? Will your statistics impress them? Will your audience respect your sources, or even recognize them? Will your quotes bring mild approval, vigorously affirmative nods, or worshipful bows? How many of your intended statements will your audience accept at face value, and how many will need proof? Some of your claims the audience will accept without question and without objection. For your audience, they aren't controversial; they seem true, or at least plausible. When, however, you say something you expect your audience to quarrel with or doubt, you'll need evidence to prove it. So determine what materials you'll need to establish each point, painstakingly search for it—and *find* it.

2 Small-Group Speaking
Analyzing the Validity of Evidence

Look through a newspaper article, a magazine article, or a textbook for one statement you feel lacks convincing evidence. Analyze the reason or reasons: It names no supportive sources; you don't recognize the sources if it names them, or you don't respect them; it provides no testimony or no examples; it explains its point inadequately; it doesn't answer your objections. Bring the entire article or book to class, and read the statement aloud to your group, along with whatever evidence, if any, the author or writer supplies to support it. Then, in a two-minute speech, try to persuade your listeners why you find the evidence unconvincing. The members of your group will discuss whether they agree or disagree, supplying their reasons and—in effect—telling you how persuasive you've been in making your case. If there is disagreement, you should discuss what it stems from. Do some members of the group simply accept the statement because it sounds plausible? Do some respect or recognize the sources you didn't? Do some disagree with your objections?

What reasoning is—and is not

What is reasoning? It's a *process,* like building a house. You lay a foundation, a row of bricks on top of that, another row on top of that, until you're finished. Reasoning means establishing the truth or falsity of one idea, then showing how that idea proves or disproves the next, and so on, until you've developed an entire case to support your thesis.

Logic—induction and deduction—has often been viewed as synonymous with reasoning. However, a study by William J. McGuire, who has published numerous articles on persuasion, seems to indicate that the classical forms of logic apply to your thinking/reasoning process less than twenty-five percent of the time.[5] Moreover, many studies of persuasion suggest that the credibility of the speaker's sources—*how reasonable they seem*—is probably more important than how "logical" the argument is in the classical sense. Equally important, if not more so—at least in terms of how your audience perceives an argument—are such factors as how carefully you formulate and draw your conclusions, and how carefully you supply adequate evidence. Therefore, let's look closely at a number of *characteristics* of what might be termed contemporary "logical arguments." Then we can perhaps distill certain key elements of the reasoning process in a compact and workable *model.*

Some characteristics of logical arguments

1. *Logical arguments,* as we've indicated, are based on evidence whenever possible. If you can supply a fact or a figure or a quote to support a statement, do it.

2. *Logical arguments* carefully qualify their conclusions where contradictory evidence exists. If you can think of instances when your statement isn't true, say so. If you think your statement probably—but not certainly—is true, then say so, too.

3. *Logical arguments* state their assumptions (since evidence proves a conclusion reached because of an idea people only assume to be true). They establish, in terms of the Declaration of Independence, the truths they hold self-evident. Prior to the mid-eighteenth century, few people assumed that all people were created equal and entitled to life, liberty, and the pursuit of happiness, so Thomas Jefferson, John Adams, and the other authors of the Declaration made clear that they did.

4. *Logical arguments* attempt to define and explain the causes of a problem before offering a solution, unless you can safely assume the audience already knows the problem and what causes it.

5. *Logical arguments* anticipate counter-arguments and refute them. To cite the Declaration of Independence again, Jefferson knew he would be accused of being a radical, of going to war over trivialities, so he listed "a long train" of King George's "abuses and usurpations" to show that, although the revolutionaries were "prudent" and peace-loving, they could not bear such injustices.

6. *Logical arguments* will concede a point or two to the opposition. Thus, not only will you *seem* fair, but you'll also *be* honest, especially if you know the other side is right.

7. *Logical arguments* attempt to explain their structure, just as you did in your major informative speech at the conclusion of Part Three. They show the relationship between ideas. They move by clear, one-at-a-time steps, and erect signposts along the way so listeners can follow the development of your idea or proposition.

Key elements of a persuasive argument: A reasoning-from-evidence-to-conclusion model

To pull together the essence of what we've just said about "logical arguments," consider the diagram shown below. It illustrates one commonly used kind of *reasoning process.* In its original form, the model was designed by Stephen E. Toulmin, a British mathematician and professor of philosophy. However, because the terms he used are rather specialized, we've modified the design somewhat and — in a few instances — substituted terms which, we feel, better suit the purposes of our discussion here. Our modified version of Toulmin's model looks like this:

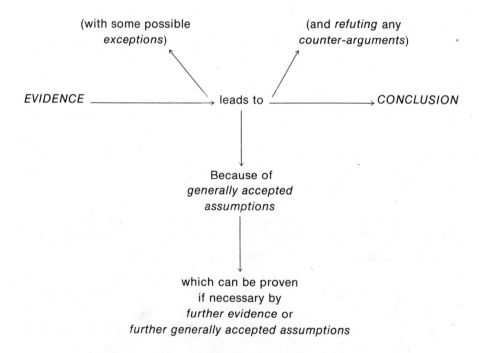

REASONING FROM EVIDENCE TO CONCLUSION: A MODEL[6]

Notice in particular how this model accounts for most of the *elements* in an argument: evidence, assumptions, conclusion, exceptions, and refutation of counter-arguments. Suppose your conclusion—the point you wish to persuade your audience to accept—is: "Required courses should be abolished in colleges." You offer as evidence statistics showing that ultimately few students retain much information in courses outside their specialties or their sphere of interests. Thus:

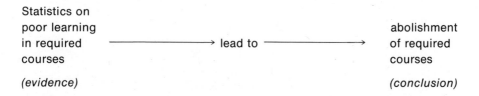

However, since you want to explain how you reached that conclusion, you show the relationship between the evidence and the conclusion by adding your *assumption* that people learn best only what they want or realize they need to know; thus:

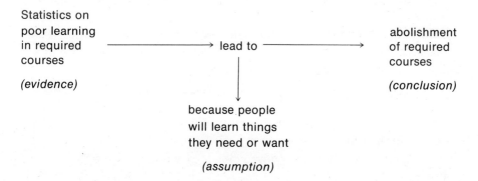

If, however, your audience doesn't accept your assumption, you might supply *additional support* for it. Now the model looks like this:

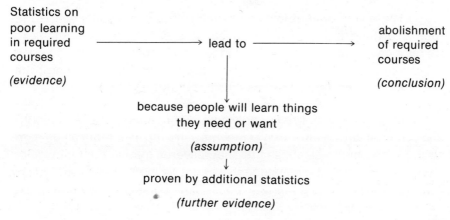

But you realize that there are *exceptions*. Some students—geniuses and highly motivated persons—retain much of anything they learn. Such exceptions fit into the model like this:

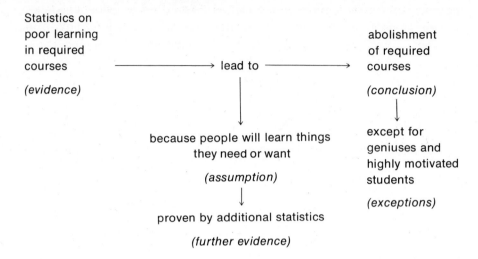

Statistics on poor learning in required courses

(evidence)

⟶ lead to ⟶

abolishment of required courses

(conclusion)

because people will learn things they need or want

(assumption)

except for geniuses and highly motivated students

(exceptions)

proven by additional statistics

(further evidence)

Fine. A neat, logical argument—which, for example, persuades your fellow students who hate physical science anyway. But the board of governors of your college or university might reply:

1. Then *motivate* the students better, so they fit in with the exceptions.

2. Then make students realize they *need* writing courses, mathematics, foreign language, etc.

3. How do students know what they want until they've experienced it?

4. What do we do with all the professors we've hired to teach the required courses, and how can we staff our college with professors when we can't predict what students will want to learn?

These would all fit into the counter-arguments you'll need to refute. And good luck with them, because *each* of your refutations requires a new conclusion, new evidence, new assumptions, etc. In short, each refutation requires a new run-through of the reasoning-from-evidence-to-conclusion process illustrated in the model.

We'll show you, briefly, how you might construct a refutation of one counter-argument—that students should be motivated more strongly. You might establish first that research into student motivation has documented that most students cannot be motivated as strongly by *external* factors as by *internal* ones. You conclude, therefore, that

teachers cannot very effectively motivate students. The "Refuting Counter-Arguments" section of the model now looks like this:

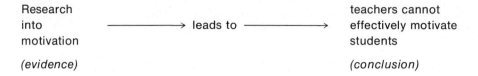

Research
into   ─────────────→ leads to ─────────────→   teachers cannot
motivation   effectively motivate
                                                                      students
(evidence)   *(conclusion)*

If your audience needs further explanation of how your evidence
warrants this conclusion, you could explain that teachers as external
forces cannot provide internal motivation. Thus the model shows:

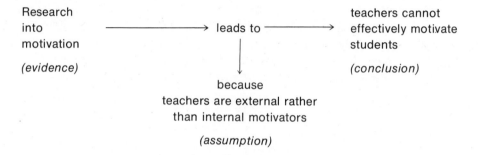

Research
into   ─────────────→ leads to ─────────────→   teachers cannot
motivation   effectively motivate
                                     │   students
(evidence)   │   *(conclusion)*
                                     ↓
                                because
                       teachers are external rather
                          than internal motivators

(assumption)

If you think of exceptions—like the very talented, dynamic teachers—you might also acknowledge them; and you might also supply
some evidence that teachers often are *external* motivators.

<big>**3**</big> Discovering for Yourself—and with Your Small Group
Structuring Your Argument in a Reasoning-
from-Evidence-to-Conclusion Model

Using as a basis the case you are preparing for your major ten-to-fifteen-minute persuasive speech, try to fit its essential argument into the
models shown on pages 238–241, putting the essence of it on paper. See
if your conclusion and evidence are clear, and if you can state your assumptions which link them together. Consider the exceptions and the
counter-arguments. Then, in your small group, discuss your model and
seek possible suggestions for clarifying it further. Also, be especially alert
to other exceptions you might include, and possible counter-arguments
to anticipate from your classmates. Discuss how you intend to refute
those arguments. Instead of working with your entire group, you might
decide to work in pairs or groups of three to save time. Or, as another
variation, your instructor may ask you to hand in your model so he or she
can comment on it.

And so ends our inspection of the two "big guns" in your persuasive strategy arsenal: using emotion and reasoning. We've looked at the problem of what *emotions* to anticipate, which to encourage, and the essentials of using emotional appeals to advance your persuasive purpose. We've also posted some warnings against a number of swindles and perversions in evoking emotional responses in listeners. Then, turning our sights on the process of *reasoning,* we've explored when to use evidence and what characterizes a "logical" argument; and, finally, we've provided you with an evidence-to-conclusion "model" of reasoning into which you may easily fit many of your persuasive propositions and proposals. This model, while it should help you see more clearly the reasoning process, is not the be-all-and-end-all. It ignores appeals to emotion and the function of speaker credibility as a persuasive force, and it doesn't tell you in what order to present your arguments. These matters—especially the *organizing* and *structuring* of the persuasive elements of your speeches—will, therefore, be our principal concerns in the next chapter, where we consider putting your strategy into action.

Reference Notes

[1] Drawn and adapted from Leon Festinger, *A Theory of Cognitive Dissonance* (Stanford: Stanford University Press, 1957).

[2] Phyllis Schlafly, "On Women's Rights and the E.R.A.," speech delivered at Wilbur Wright College, Chicago, Illinois, April 16, 1975.

[3] George Orwell, "Politics and the English Language," *Shooting an Elephant and Other Essays* (New York: Harcourt Brace Jovanovich, Inc., and London: Secker & Warburg, 1950), p. 84.

[4] William Jennings Bryan, "The Cross of Gold," in *A Treasury of the World's Great Speeches,* ed. Houston Peterson (New York: Simon & Schuster, Inc., 1954), p. 642.

[5] William J. McGuire, "A Syllogistic Analysis of Cognitive Relationships," *Attitude Organization and Change,* M. J. Rosenberg and others, eds. (New Haven, Conn.: Yale University Press, 1960).

[6] Stephen E. Toulmin, *The Uses of Argument* (New York: Cambridge University Press, 1958), especially "The Layout of Arguments," pp. 94–105. Our alterations in Toulmin's terminology are as follows: We use the term *evidence* where Toulmin uses *data.* We use *generally accepted assumptions* where he uses *warrant.* We use *further evidence* or *further generally accepted assumptions* where he uses *backing.* We use *exceptions* where he uses *qualifiers.* And, finally, we use *refuting any counter-arguments* where he uses *rebuttal.*

19 Organizing and Delivering Your Persuasive Speech

For this, your major, climactic engagement on the field of public speaking, you've brought up your two heaviest pieces of artillery, emotion and reason. You've trained them on your persuasive target. You've selected the best and most appropriate speech materials to fortify your position. You've thoughtfully considered the bearings of your listeners' needs, attitudes, and beliefs. You've anticipated some emotional cross fire, and you've tried to calculate the trajectories of the emotional and rational appeals you intend aiming at your listeners. Now . . . put all of this ammunition and strategic expertise into the clearest, most telling, and most moving array. *Assemble, organize,* and *structure* them confidently and convincingly. Maximize their "firepower" and go into action.

This is no easy matter. You want to establish credibility with your listeners early, of course, so they will respect, or at least not reject, you as a source of persuasion. You want to be clear, too, for no audience will be persuaded by an argument they don't understand. Thus, your thesis and your major supporting points should be apparent, as should the signposts that help your listeners follow the movement and direction of your speech—the internal summaries and restatements. But, on the other hand, in some persuasive strategies you may not want to state your thesis at the beginning or even hint at your intentions. You would merely be alerting a hostile crowd to mount their defenses, or even launch an attack, before they've heard you out.

Therefore, to help ensure eventual victory, you should plan to save your best ammunition—emotional and factual—for the moment when your audience is most inclined to surrender their prejudices and misconceptions. At their point of least resistance, your listeners will be most strongly influenced to accept or at least consider your thesis.

How do you organize a persuasive speech, then? We can't offer you any easy formula; but in this chapter we can discuss some options open to you as you develop a plan, evaluate it, discuss it, and improve it until you know where you're going and why you're going there. We'll begin by introducing four steps that you can take—specific, successive tasks that you can try to accomplish in effecting your persuasive strategy. Then we'll examine two methods of arranging and sequencing the steps: (1) through a *climax organization* and (2) an *anticlimax organization.*

PLANNING YOUR STRATEGY ONE STEP AT A TIME

In the broadest terms, you can divide your persuasive strategy into the following steps:

1. *Establishing your credibility*—proving that you are trustworthy, likeable, and believable.

2. *Establishing the problem*—defining it and demonstrating that it is a problem.

3. *Presenting your solution to the problem* — describing and explaining your solution, comparing it to others, demonstrating its superiority, and refuting anticipated objections to it.
4. *Moving your audience to act on your solution* — demonstrating and picturing how they will benefit from acting, showing that the desired action is practical and physically and socially "safe," and that benefits justify the possible risks.

Establishing your credibility

As a persuasive speaker, you must be concerned with your *believability.* Your thesis, your evidence, your arguments — all must be believable. But above all and preceding all else, make *yourself* believable, and your whole case will gain force. As you begin, try first to create some *rapport* with your listeners. If you sense resentment, attempt to dissipate or reduce it. Establish your credentials: your *persuasive credibility.* You can accomplish this, in large part, by *(a)* knowing yourself, *(b)* knowing your materials, *(c)* knowing how to command yourself and your materials, and *(d)* knowing how to command listener respect and attention.

Knowing who you are. For your classmates, your audience for the persuasive speeches you'll be giving, this should present few difficulties. They know you; they know some of your interests. They know your strengths, and they probably respect you for what you are, even if you're very different from them. And you've reciprocated — from an "I'm OK — you're OK" position. Therefore, your credentials as a decent human being are well established. You'd be silly at this point to alter your behavior, your appearance, or anything else about you. As you begin, ask your classmates only that they allow you an opportunity to make your case.

Knowing what you know. But even with a friendly, receptive audience, you'll need to establish your credentials to speak on your subject. You've chosen your subject out of your interest and belief in it, and probably because you've had some experience with it. Let your audience know the "inside" story of your interest or experience: Relate a personal anecdote, or briefly summarize what you've read or studied, or single out a striking or startling encounter with some aspect of your topic.

Knowing how to command what you know. We remind you again that you should be as confident as you are knowledgeable. Prepare a *spectacular* case: erudite, clear, well illustrated, without exaggerations, and careful in its conclusions. If you seem unprepared, unsure, or confused, you won't exactly look like a pillar of strength to rest your argument on. Know your speech plan and your speech thoroughly; rehearse it; feel comfortable with it. Your audience, whether they know you well or not, expect and can excuse some nervousness. But they don't and shouldn't expect you to be inept or lacking control either of your subject or yourself.

Knowing how to command respect and attention.   If you know — and respect — yourself, if you know — really know — what you're expected to know about your subject, and if you're in command of your speech materials and yourself, you'll command the respect and attention of almost *any* audience. Oftentimes, out in the real world, you'll address members of your club, your community organizations, your church, your work group, your street gang, your circle of friends. Relate to them in much the same way you relate to your classmates. If, however, in the real world you're to speak to a group you've never met, you must try to predict their probable attitudes toward you and your subject. Then speak to magnify the positive attitudes, combat the negative ones, and eliminate the neutral or indifferent ones. Doing this and establishing *common ground* with your listeners, you'll likely find yourself quickly on *safe* and *solid* ground as a persuasive speaker.

Admittedly, you will also find barricades on the road to rapport with an audience of strangers. Generally, people can more easily dislike or hate a speaker they don't know if they can *stereotype* him or her as an outsider, an "alien," not a real human being. The speaker (especially in persuasive situations) is a commie with red eyes and horns. The speaker is a millionaire with no feelings and a fat wallet. He or she is a moral degenerate with seedy clothes, smelly armpits, and a disrespect for all that's holy and decent in a God-fearing, upright, uptight society. Exaggeration aside, for a negative or hostile audience especially, you are something of a threat — as is anybody or anything that's unknown. In the beginning at least, you're a scapegoat for their anxieties and fears. They may see you as an outrageous lout who has been slinging many arrows and at whom they would now like to sling a few of their own. In short, you're the resident baddy; and your first job is to rid yourself of that role — *pronto.*

Let your audience know right away that you aren't a faceless member of the evil crowd. Show them that you're a *real* person, *human* and *humane:* smile, poke a little fun at yourself, wink, chat about your past, your future (you hope!). Show them how like them you are, what backgrounds you share, what experiences, what attitudes, what beliefs, what values you hold in common and toward your subject. If you, too, oppose the campus radicals, tell them. If you, too, resent the depersonalized atmosphere of big, computer-run schools, say so. If you, too, think there must be *some* required courses, let them know it. Find some common ground, as we've urged; then lead them into new territory. And, above all, be yourself: charming, intelligent, reasonable. Relax to whatever extent you can. Assume you're OK, and so is your audience. They're people, too; not the enemy. Joke a bit if you want. It rarely hurts, and can cool a great many hotheads.

Knowing how to use "protective coloration." One small concession you can make to raise your credibility with the audience is something we call "protective coloration." It's a part of the natural law of self-preservation in nature, a way to blend in and become a part of your surroundings. Some rabbits grow white coats in winter; octopuses change hues as they move along the ocean floor. With the proper protective coloration people, too, can — on occasion — reduce their visibility as easy prey for attack. As speakers, it's true, you'll usually want to stand out; but sometimes it's not good strategy to stand out *too much.*

During the 1968 Democratic presidential primaries, a number of young people opposing the Vietnam war decided to work in the Eugene McCarthy campaign. Their slogan was "Get Clean for Gene." They cut their hair, dressed conservatively, and generally made themselves look different from the yippie stereotype so many people associated with the antiwar movement. With this kind of protective coloration, they could blend in more easily and readily with the political environment; they made themselves and their persuasive position less vulnerable to opposition and attack; they made opposition to the war more respectable and defensible; and they were able to influence the political process. With their protective coloration they were obviously able to "rub people in the right way."

In sum, in order to establish your credibility with an audience, be confident, thoroughly in command of yourself and your materials; stress the ground and background you hold in common with your listeners; and use protective coloration — especially in negative or hostile situations.

Establishing the problem

Even a hostile audience may agree with your *definition* of a problem; college professors, for instance, may accept your contention that many students lack motivation. These same professors, though, may not accept your interpretation of the *causes* of the problem — that too many unnecessary required courses destroy student motivation. Therefore, before you can discuss your interpretation of the causes, you may need to address yourself to each of the probable interpretations held by your audience (e.g., poor environments, lack of student maturity, a society which stresses only the "practical" goals of education at the expense of "higher" goals, etc.). You can concede, and possibly demonstrate, that each of these causes may *partially* explain the problem (thus stressing your agreement with your audience and reducing their possible resistance to your interpretation). Yet, at the same time you can show that your listeners' interpretations don't satisfactorily explain the *whole* problem (thus preparing the way for your interpretation). Being able to predict and understand your audience's attitudes and beliefs about the existence and real nature of the problem is a crucial second step in your strategic plan.

Presenting your solution to the problem

Here, again, you may need to address yourself first to possible solutions already advanced by others or which, for one reason or another, may be a part of your listeners' thinking. So, as before, you acknowledge their *partial* validity, yet stress their weaknesses before you introduce your own solution. Then, having proposed your method of solving the problem, you must refute known or suspected objections to it. In presenting your solution you might, for example, assure your college-professor audience that eliminating required courses would benefit everyone, that teaching motivated students would be a joy, and that students permitted to choose courses based on their own priorities and preferences would be more intellectually inquisitive, and—prompted by curiosity and a genuine desire to learn—would be more willing, even eager, to enroll in many of the previously required courses. Note that the audience's "benefits" skillfully embedded in these assurances are actually appeals directed to your listeners' emotional and intellectual needs and satisfactions. In this step of your persuasive strategy, understanding your audience's needs and how best to appeal to them is your major task.

Moving your audience to action

Convincing an audience to act upon your solution or proposal, to put it into action, requires considerable skill. Although many people in your audience may not feel happy with the status quo or the present situation, they will be reluctant to change it. This especially will be the case if the proposed change personally inconveniences them, if it involves sacrifice, or if there is a substantial risk—particularly a financial risk. People don't like to lose money unless they have to, and they certainly don't want to endanger or lose their jobs. Whenever possible, therefore, in inducing your audience to act on your idea, show or prove that it is *workable*. Demonstrate that it will involve little or no inconvenience to their daily lives, that resulting sacrifices (if any) will be minimal, that the cost will not be great—even less extensive than if they do *not* put your solution into effect promptly. Further, show that the risks to

ESTABLISH CREDIBILITY   ESTABLISH PROBLEM   PRESENT SOLUTION   ACT ON SOLUTION

". . . But you gotta' admit, Joe, when Art Schmutz gives a persuasive speech, he takes all the steps to build an ironclad case!"

their jobs, their families, and their pocketbooks will be far less than it will be later if they fail to take positive action now. In short, in this concluding step of your strategy, you must drive home to your listeners the benefits, present and future, that your solution surely will produce — that the action you are urging is basically reasonable, practical, positively beneficial, and non-threatening. When you sense the need or inevitability of compromise, *make* it — but on your terms if you can. For example, in calling for action on eliminating required courses from the college curriculum, you could explain how those professors whose jobs are seemingly threatened will remain on the staff in another capacity.

The four-step sequence we've just suggested for developing a strategy for your persuasive speech is but one of many. You can discover or devise others. This sequence or "battle plan," however — establishing your credibility, establishing the problem, presenting your solution, and moving your audience to act on that solution — usually offers, we feel, a good workable basis for producing effective results. In certain circumstances, one or more of the steps may prove unnecessary; in other cases, they'll be irrelevant.

In the section that follows, where we begin consideration of the first of two major methods of organizing and structuring your actual arguments, we provide a detailed analysis of an address by Newton Minow to show you specifically the practical application of the four-step sequence, along with the strategic concerns and tactics characterizing each step.

ORGANIZING YOUR PERSUASIVE SPEECHES

Aside from establishing your persuasive credentials with your audience, everything you present is one or both of two things: (1) *groundwork upon which you will build your thesis* — be it merely that a problem exists, or that a solution exists, or that your audience must act on your solution; and (2) *the systematic softening of your audience's resistance to that solution.* To accomplish these tasks, let's examine two approaches to structuring persuasive speeches: organizing your arguments in *climax order* and organizing your arguments in *anticlimax order.*

Climax order, or clearing away the defenses before giving it your best shot

Climax order is the arrangement of your key ideas, propositions, arguments, and appeals *according to their increasing importance, strength, or strategic value*—or, as Webster phrases it, "arranged in ascending order of rhetorical forcefulness." As we are using the term, it means the straightforward, logical, step-by-step *buildup* to the concluding and most potent point of your speech. *Anticlimax order,* as we'll develop it later, is the reverse of this.

As John Wilson and Carroll Arnold note in their book *Public Speaking as a Liberal Art:*

> There has been much discussion and experimentation seeking to determine exactly how climactic arrangement persuades. The best conclusion seems to be that structuring . . . in this fashion *can* add persuasiveness, but that under some circumstances creating an anticlimactic structure in which the strongest thought comes first rather than last can yield at least an equal persuasive force.[1]

The climax is an emotional moment near the end of your speech, when you fire your heaviest gun, when—insofar as you're concerned—you've settled the issue one way or another. In your speech, that should be the moment when you most directly reveal your thesis, or you appeal to your audience to act on it. At that moment, your audience's resistance to your persuasive efforts should be lowest. You can, of course, infuse your speech with other high points or lesser, "internal" climaxes if you're whipping up your listeners emotionally. But the key climax, the really big one, should be the revelation—or at least the most powerful restatement—of your thesis. Generally, that big moment when a hostile, suspicious, or apprehensive audience's resistance to your thesis is lowest will not be in the beginning. Too many obstacles in their beliefs and knowledge about you and your argument must be cleared away first. Therefore, the most common form of persuasive-speech organization is to start out slowly, pick up momentum, and build to a climax; hence the name, *climax order.*

An example of a climax-order persuasive speech

In 1961, as newly appointed head of the Federal Communications Commission (FCC), Newton N. Minow addressed the very people he had been appointed to regulate: The National Association of Broadcasters.[2] The previous year had seen several scandals involving rigged television quiz shows and bribes to disk jockeys in exchange for playing certain recordings, and many broadcasters were apprehensive about possible changes in their traditionally cozy relationships with the FCC. Minow did, in fact, intend to clean up the broadcasting industry, to make the broadcasters live up to their own code of ethics. He announced his plans during this speech and requested the networks' voluntary cooperation to achieve them. Naturally, with such a nervous, suspicious, and potentially hostile audience, he needed first to dispel their fears and objections to his proposals. Consequently, he moved carefully from establishing his audience's trust in him, to establishing the problem, to proposing a solution, to calling for action—each time balancing a potentially threatening remark with a reassuring one. For the following analysis, we've used textual commentary and a series of excerpts from the speech itself to suggest the climax order of its structure, and we've inserted labels to call your attention to the four progressive steps in the speaker's persuasive strategy.

[*Step 1: Establishing Credibility*]

Mr. Minow realized that humor disarms hostility and makes a speaker appear more human. So he began his speech lightheartedly. He'd waited this long to speak publicly, he said, because he wanted

> . . . to do my homework and get my feet wet, but apparently I haven't managed to stay out of hot water. I seem to have detected a certain nervous apprehension about what I might say or do when I emerged from that locked office for this, my maiden station break.

After more kidding about the rumors concerning what he might say this evening, Minow assured the broadcasters that he was on their side, that they had his "admiration and respect." Nonetheless, he added, in his first hint at his thesis, "That doesn't mean I would make life any easier for you."

[*Step 2: Establishing the Problem*]

Having attempted to lessen the tension with humor and avowals of goodwill, Minow began to define and analyze the problem in broadcasting: *mediocrity.* He noted that as the public's representative, the broadcasters' "health and product are among my chief concerns." He found their financial health excellent, but had some doubts about their product. Quickly reassuring his audience, however, he carefully defined the FCC's role, "to enforce the law in the public's interest," but not to censor the media. Besides, he added, many television programs were of high quality already.

Nevertheless, he went on to say, the problem was that not enough shows were of that quality. As he put it, "When television is bad, nothing is worse." He asked the television executives to see for themselves, to watch their stations without distraction for an entire day. What they would find, he insisted, would be a

> . . . vast wasteland . . . a tedious parade of game shows, violence, audience-participation shows, formula comedies about totally unbelievable families, blood and thunder, mayhem, violence, sadism,

murder, Western badmen, Western good men, private eyes, gangsters, more violence, and cartoons. And, endlessly, commercials—many screaming, cajoling, and offending. And, most of all, boredom.

Can't you do better? he asked, in effect. True, he conceded, television's problems are great: the pressure from competition for high ratings, the huge costs of producing shows, the pressures from advertisers, the public's own bad taste. These were, he admitted, great obstacles. Nonetheless, he saw no convincing evidence that the broadcasters genuinely were attempting to overcome them.

[Step 3: Presenting the Solution]

Contending that unless television created "more diversity, more alternatives," it was liable to lose its own audience, Minow declared that he felt the networks should change their offerings for their own good. Serious and straightforward now, he said that as FCC head he would "like to see television improved," and enumerated the "fundamental principles" he would follow in looking for that improvement: (1) his belief that the public owns the airwaves and that the broadcasters "owe" the public better programming, (2) his willingness to ignore and forget the recent scandals in broadcasting, (3) his belief in "the free-enterprise system," (4) his interest in aiding "educational television" to create more competition, (5) his strong opposition to government censorship, and (6) his intention to be vigilant in ensuring that "the public's airwaves" aren't squandered. To put these principles into action, to achieve a solution, he proposed public hearings each time a broadcasting license was to be renewed. His solution to the problem of protecting the public's ownership of the airways and ensuring quality programming would be to let the *public* decide whether its interests and needs were being served.

[Step 4: Moving the Audience to Action]

As he neared the climax of his speech, Minow momentarily softened the tone of his remarks. He was not threatening the broadcasters with non-renewal of their licenses; he was merely asking that they voluntarily "make a conscientious, good-faith effort to serve the public interest." He asked his listeners to consider the needs of their communities and satisfy them. Under these circumstances, no one need fear losing a license. He reiterated his conviction that television had achieved many great things. Then he concluded with his most powerful pronouncement—the *climactic statement* of his thesis—which briefly summarized his arguments while repeating his assurances in words that paraphrased a portion of President Kennedy's Inaugural Address:

Ask not what broadcasting can do for you—ask what you can do for broadcasting.

I urge you to put the people's airwaves to the service of the people and the cause of freedom. You must help prepare a generation for great decisions. You must help a great nation fulfill its future.

Do this, and I pledge you our help.

As the Minow example illustrates, in a persuasive speech the climax order aims at reducing systematically, step by step, an audience's resistance to your proposed solution or your call for action. In using it, you first carefully establish your assumptions and the reasoning behind them, and you allay your audience's misgivings and objections. Then you urge your proposal.

Anticlimax order, or firing
your heaviest cannon first

In some situations, you may decide to begin your speech with a powerful barrage, with a flat-out firing of your strongest ammunition and assertion of your thesis. This is the *anticlimax order.* Your persuasive thesis—your most important and strategically valuable idea— comes *first,* followed by your evidence, assumptions, exceptions, and refutation of counter-arguments.

The Shock Tactic.　You may decide that a shock treatment would be effective in neutralizing opposition. Clarence Darrow, the famous controversial trial lawyer, was generally blunt and aggressive—and successful—so powerful was his personality and credibility. On one occasion, he addressed the inmates of Chicago's Cook County Jail. Immediately he raised his point (and quite a few eyebrows) with these opening words:

> If I looked at jails and crimes and prisoners in the way the ordinary person does, I should not speak on this subject to you. The reason I talk to you on the question of crime, its cause and its cure, is because I really do not in the least believe in crime. There is no such thing as crime as the word is generally understood. I do not believe there is any sort of distinction between the real moral condition of the people in and out of jail. One is just as good as the other. The people here . . . are in jail simply because they cannot avoid it on account of circumstances which are entirely beyond their control and for which they are in no way responsible.[3]

The Direct Onslaught.　As another use of anticlimactic order, you may decide that the urgency of the situation requires a quick and direct approach to your audience. You want to persuade listeners to act and

"The difference between the two basic strategies for a persuasive speech is that they fire their 'ammo' in different order."

act quickly, so you begin by saying, in effect: "Don't fool around; this is serious. Here — precisely — is what I propose." You tell your audience that circumstances won't permit delay or evasiveness. For example, in a television address to the American people on January 13, 1975, when the United States economy seemed near collapse, President Ford chose to be direct, hoping to spur citizens and Congress to immediate action. Here are his blunt opening remarks:

> Without wasting words, I want to talk with you tonight about putting our domestic house in order. We must turn America in a new direction. We must reverse the current recession, reduce unemployment, and create more jobs. We must restore the confidence of consumers and investors alike. We must, without delay, take firm control of our progress as a free people.[4]

Reinforcing Your Reinforcers. Sometimes, too, when you know that many in your audience strongly agree with you, that they support you, you may fire a strong opening shot and then lead them in an applause-filled charge that may help persuade the few non-believers. In this case, you are more of a cheerleader than a persuader. (Many political speeches are more the product of cheerleading than of true persuasion.) At other times, when your audience not only supports but is also overheated about your subject, you may decide to waste no words in order to cool them down. Seemingly, they want a solution more far-reaching or drastic than you are proposing. Abraham Lincoln faced such an audience in 1858 when accepting his party's presidential nomination. His supporters strongly opposed slavery, and many were ready to go to war to end it. Lincoln shared their beliefs, but he couldn't condone a war. So he opened with this famous thesis statement:

> "A house divided against itself cannot stand." I believe this government cannot endure permanently half slave and half free. I do not expect this Union to be dissolved—I do not expect the house to fall—but I do expect it will cease to be divided.[5]

Advancing from Signpost to Signpost. Finally, if your audience obviously trusts and respects you, and feels no strong resistance to your thesis, you may greatly increase their understanding of your argument by stating your thesis early and then proceeding to develop it, point by point. In this case, the thesis creates more of a rational and "intellectual" effect, with little emotional impact. It serves essentially the same function as the thesis in a speech to inform; it is mainly your point of departure, the first signpost on your journey to and through the needs, attitudes, and beliefs of your listeners in relation to your topic. A student, trusted and respected and aware that her audience felt little, if any, resentment against her proposal, chose to launch her speech with this statement:

> We can't allow the criminal acts of inner-city children to continue. We must stop such acts at their source—by strengthening the fabric of the family—and increase our law enforcement against those people whose families cannot stop them from committing crimes.

The speaker, as she continued, made it clear that she would not ignore the opposing arguments despite her confidence that the audience was on her side. She would assume that her classmates knew the counter-arguments, but didn't believe them. Her refutation, therefore, would be a reminder, a tidying-up device, a way to wipe out opposing arguments completely.

1 Discovering for Yourself
Deciding Upon a Strategy

Decide whether to use climactic or anticlimactic order for your major persuasive speech, and then experiment with several possible organizations both in your mind and on paper until you arrive at one you think will best fit your purposes, your subject, your credibility, and your classroom audience. Give yourself plenty of time to experiment. You may even decide, after careful analysis, to switch from climactic to anticlimactic order, or vice versa.

2 Small-Group Speaking
Rehearsing Your Speech

In your small group, give your speech in rough-outline form, explaining in general terms what your strategy will be, how you'll use evidence, and so on. Or, if time permits, present your entire speech to your group. In either case, group members can offer both support and suggestions for possible improvements.

3 Discovering for Yourself
Continuing the Preparation for Your Speech

The day, the night, the hour before you give your speech to the entire class, try it out completely in private and/or—if possible—for a friend or relative. Be thinking about it constantly before you face the members of the class, too, to keep yourself well prepared and to allow for any last-minute brainstorms while still maintaining communication connections with your listeners.

4 Public Speaking
Delivering Your Persuasive Speech

Now give your persuasive speech to the class as a whole. And good luck.

Thus, you see your choices between *climax order* and *anticlimax order.* The option you choose will, of course, hinge upon what exactly you want to achieve in your speech and which of these two possible structures would most effectively ensure its fulfillment. Then experiment with the elements, modifying them as necessary, until you feel you have finally organized and structured them in a way that best suits your persuasive intentions. The choice between climax order and anticlimax order need not be a rigid, either-or matter. Many speeches, in fact, combine elements from the two, with one order predominating. Be less concerned with "formal" or technical structuring than you are with developing a strategy that will get your solution or proposal accepted and acted upon as you'd wish it to be. And always, as we've urged in this chapter, establish your credibility to the extent that you must; establish the problem you wish to solve; establish, if possible, the significance and urgency of your proposed solution; then call for action on it.

Reference Notes

[1]John F. Wilson and Carroll C. Arnold, *Public Speaking as a Liberal Art,* Third Edition (Boston: Allyn and Bacon, Inc., 1974), p. 236.

[2]Newton M. Minow, "The Vast Wasteland," in *Equal Time: The Private Broadcaster and the Public Interest.* Copyright © 1964 by Newton M. Minow (New York: Atheneum Publishers, 1964), pp. 48–64. All excerpts subsequently quoted are from this source.

[3]Clarence Darrow, *Address to Prisoners in Cook County Jail,* 3rd Reprint (Chicago: Charles H. Kerr and Company, 1913).

[4]From a television address to the American people, January 13, 1975. Reprinted in *The New York Times* (January 14, 1975), p. 20.

[5]Reprinted in *A Treasury of the World's Great Speeches,* ed. Houston Peterson (New York: Simon & Schuster, 1954), p. 491.

259

20 Preparing for Your Job Interview

In a sense, the final exam for a speech course occurs after college ends and your job begins. The real test comes as you communicate to achieve your goals and satisfy your needs in the world outside the classroom. We remind you of Abraham Maslow's hierarchy of needs. At each level, the work you do greatly influences your sense of fulfillment. Satisfying the lower needs—from survival to security—depends largely on your ability to earn a wage or salary. Satisfying the higher needs—from belonging, to recognition, to self-esteem, to self-actualization—depends largely on how you and others feel about the work that earns your income. In short, your job must provide you with rewards both financial and psychological.

No paychecks or pleasures will come your way, however, unless you can get the job you choose. Hence, the importance of a successful job interview. Though not a formal, uninterrupted presentation, the interview nevertheless requires you to speak to a given listener or series of listeners about a given topic—essentially the same one you've discussed throughout your speech-course work: your *experiences* and *ideas.* The habits and practices you've developed throughout the course also apply. You'll have to consider your purpose. You'll have to consider your listeners' expectations, their needs, values, beliefs, and biases. Then you'll have to adapt your presentation to all of these considerations, doing research to strengthen weaknesses in your knowledge, deciding on a protective coloration, formulating answers to possible questions in advance, thinking about questions you'd like answered—in general, preparing a strategy. And, most important, because you're well prepared, you'll be able to speak with confidence. You'll be the best self you can be.

Blessed is he
who has found his work;
let him ask
no other blessedness.
—Thomas Carlyle
Past and Present

In the pages ahead, let's examine what you should *know* as preparation for the interview: your purpose, the physical circumstances or setting for the interview, your listener's (interviewer's) expectations, needs, and biases. Then, let's examine what you should *do* to prepare: investigate the background of the company, organization, or agency you hope to work for; think about questions you're likely to be asked, the probable answers you'll provide, the questions *you'll* want to ask; and, finally, the making of your resumé—a compact and concise account of your qualifications and a summary of your working career to date.

WHAT YOU SHOULD KNOW ABOUT THE INTERVIEW

Your purposes and your prospective employer's purposes

Job interviews aren't intended solely to give the employer an opportunity to scrutinize you. They also give you a chance to scrutinize your hoped-for employer. The company—its *interviewer*—will use the interview to evaluate your intellectual, social, temperamental, moral, and physical qualifications for the job. This is the kind of information only personal, face-to-face contact can provide. You, as the job applicant and *interviewee,* will evaluate (as best you can) the nature of the work or job or position, the working conditions, the "image" of the company, your opportunities for possible advancement, and perhaps the people you will have to work with if hired.

Therefore, both you and your prospective employer have not only to *exchange information* — to speak to inform — but each of you also has something to *prove:* you, that you can handle the job and that (given your aspirations) it's worth handling; your employer, that you are worth hiring, that you have the potential to handle the job capably and competently. Of course, the interviewer has less to "prove" than you do; he or she needn't be very persuasive when the available job or position carries high prestige and salary, or when applicants are many and jobs few. But your reputation as a go-getter and a prince or princess charming in school, in a previous job, or in both may enhance your persuasive attractiveness, too. You may, for instance, find an organization's representative interviewing you right in your college. Or, once you've worked on a job, you may find another company luring you away with promises of a bigger salary, a bigger office, and a more impressive title.

The physical circumstances

Interviews can occur just about anywhere: in an office, a school auditorium, a country club, or — as with a friend we know who applied for a sales job with a leather-goods firm — in the back room of a factory next to a vat of chemicals. Often, for white-collar jobs, part of the interview includes having lunch. Wanting to see you at your best, the interviewers may take you to a restaurant where you can chat informally in less intimidating surroundings. No matter what the situation, however, relax; but don't lose self-control. At an early lunch, if a martini makes your conversation *too* informal, pass up the drink. Be on top of the situation, not under the table. The photos on the facing page illustrate just a few of the many contexts in which a successful job interview can take place.

Your listeners' expectations

Typically, the company's representatives will begin the interview by providing you with information about the job. Most of it will be up-

THE JOB INTERVIEW can take place almost anywhere . . . in either *formal* or *informal* settings.

beat, glorifying the company and the virtues and advantages of the position you're applying for. But some will be less pleasant. You may learn that the job offers little chance for advancement, or that it requires a one-year training period, constant travel, a great deal of night work, or putting up with a tyrannical supervisor. Most companies would rather you know the disadvantages of the job beforehand. You're less likely to quit, disillusioned, within a short time; and they're less likely to have to repeat the interviewing and costly training process.

As the interviewers talk, they will be observing your reactions, and then asking you questions. In general, all this is designed to determine your suitability for the job, which includes: (1) *your stability and reliability*—whether you can be counted on to perform what the job entails; whether you will stay with the firm, arrive at work on time, miss very few days for problems not related to sickness; (2) *your confidence and sensitivity to others*—whether you will learn and adjust to the job quickly; whether you will handle yourself well in dealings with associates, superiors, subordinates, and clients; (3) *your intelligence and thoughtfulness*—whether you will learn quickly, and not make foolish errors or hasty decisions; (4) *your ambition*—whether you will work hard, show potential to grow and rise within the company; (5) *your leadership ability and,* conversely, *your ability to accept the leadership of others*—whether you will perform your role in the company smoothly, coping with difficulties, resolving conflicts, knowing when to give orders, when to ask for advice, how to take charge, how to raise objections, how to be quiet, and stay at work; (6) *your concept of the job*—whether you know what's expected of you; whether you have considered how to meet these expectations; whether your ideas are workable.

Your listeners' needs and biases

All this may sound like a gestapo interrogation, but it won't be—most of the time. Generally, the interview will be cordial, with the company's representatives encouraging you to relax, be yourself, but expecting you to be sharp. Interviewers aren't necessarily hostile, just critical. They represent a much larger audience: the entire management group, the board of directors, the stockholders, the employees on every level, and the clients the company serves. If they're not interested in the company's success, certainly they are interested in their own. The quality of the people they hire reflects the quality of their own judgment and determines, in part, their future with the company. They won't want to make errors, though like any other human beings, they can't avoid their own subjectivity, biases, prejudices, and *Parent* and *Child* "tapes."

PREPARING YOUR STRATEGY FOR THE INTERVIEW

Deciding on your physical appearance:
"Protective coloration"

Part of your preparation for the interview, therefore, involves maximizing your first impression. Your dress, posture, and hair style may affect the interviewer's judgments of you. Aspiring cooks slinging hamburgers or aspiring lawyers slinging words must consider the most appropriate "protective coloration." And so should you. The old dress code of white shirt and tie for men and dress or skirt and blouse for women has loosened, but not completely. So when in doubt, go conservative. If you want to go casual, go neat-and-clean casual. A torn tee shirt and a toothpick dangling from your lip may have impressed the hard guys in your old neighborhood; but unless you're applying for a position as Minister of Defense with a street gang, your interviewers may not be charmed.

Conversely, when you arrive for the interview, don't let the interviewers' "protective coloration" deceive you. That crew cut, narrow tie, and gray suit don't necessarily imply that the person across the table from you trusts no one under sixty-two. Be as open-minded about the interviewers as you'd like them to be about you. If you take and maintain an "I'm OK—you're OK" attitude, you are much more likely to gain the information you need to decide whether you fit the job and the job fits you.

Researching the company's background

Most importantly, your preparation should focus on the topic for discussion: your qualifications for the job and its suitability for you. Never walk into a job interview ignorant of what the company makes or does, whom it serves, and what the job entails. Do some research. Even if the interviewer tells you everything you need to know immediately, you shouldn't be encountering most of it for the first time. Your remarks and questions will be sharper when you've considered them beforehand. Read any pamphlets, annual reports, or other materials the company supplied you with earlier. Or ask a reference librarian for directories which provide information about the company. Useful directories to consult include *Moody's Manuals, Standard and Poor's Corporation Records, Thomas' Register of American Manufacturers, Dun and Bradstreet Reference Book, Fitch Corporation Records, Poor's Register of Directors and Executives, College Placement Annual, College Placement Directory.*

Anticipating the questions you'll be asked

Think about the questions you'll be asked, too. That person who was interviewed next to a vat of chemicals for the leather-goods sales position didn't get the job because he couldn't answer an obvious question: What stores in Michigan would be most interested in buying this company's products? He couldn't even explain where to look for such information.

The specific questions to anticipate depend, of course, on the nature and particulars of the job and your background. The kinds of questions, however, will fall roughly into four categories. You can expect some *closed questions* to elicit simple, factual information: Did you take a course in statistics? How long have you lived in the area? When could you start work? Most of the questions will be *open-ended,* requiring you to structure the answer and decide how long it should be. The interviewer may follow up your replies to such questions with *probing questions* that require additional information and explanation from you. Occasionally, too, an interviewer may ask you some *leading questions* which you can answer in only one way: You agree that labor unions cause more harm than good, don't you? Some of the questions will be personal — about your family background or where you grew up. Though by law no employer may deny you a job on the basis of your religion or politics, a question may stray — innocently or otherwise — into such areas, too. Probably the best answers to these questions are those that are honest, but guarded; for example: "I'm not all that interested in politics right now."

Generally, the greater the salary, prestige, and responsibility associated with the job, the less the interviewer will talk, and the more you will. You may hear very little about the job before the questioning begins; and the questions will be open-ended and tough, to test your intelligence, confidence, competence, and imagination. Nonetheless, regardless of the question, you should observe a few common-sense rules in making your reply: (1) It should be complete, showing what you know without showing off. (2) It shouldn't be a bluff; if you don't know the answer, say so. (3) It should relate directly to the question and not stray into irrelevant matters, especially your own personal problems: how badly you need work, your difficulties in recovering from your recent divorce, your terminal lumbago. Occasionally, interviewers won't question you about some of your strong points — things in your training or experience you'd like them to know about. Therefore, you may want to consider how you can manage to mention these strong points in the course of the interview, either by including them in response to questions, or by formulating your own questions, for example: "Would you like to hear about my work experiences as an accountant?"

Discovering for Yourself and Small-Group Discussion

Preparing Tentative Answers to Typical Questions Asked in an Interview

As practice in anticipating and formulating answers to questions you might be asked, look at the list below. Add a number of questions of your own. Then outline, in general terms, what your answer to each might be. Consider whether your answer should be lengthy or short. Prepare to *discuss* and *compare* your outlined answers in your small group, and to talk about your conceptions of the particular employee traits each question seems designed to reveal.

1. Why are you interested in working for us?
2. What do you expect to be doing ten years from now?[1]
3. How much salary do you want?
4. Why are you applying for this position?
5. Why are you leaving your present job?
6. What are your goals?
7. Do you think your education prepared you well for this job?
8. What can you offer the company?
9. What kinds of people do you like to work with?
10. Tell me what you know about our firm.
11. Tell me about yourself.
12. How do you determine or evaluate success?
13. What kind of job are you looking for?
14. How do you feel about moving to another part of the country in case the company should want to transfer you?
15. How do you feel about our two-year training program?

---

2 Discovering for Yourself and Small-Group Discussion

Preparing Your Questions for an Interview

Since the job interview also helps you decide whether you want to work for the company or organization interviewing you, you should think about some questions *you* should ask. Although the questions depend upon your specific needs and the specifics of the job, the following list should provide some general possibilities. In considering each of these possibilities, consider under what circumstances you would ask it. Would you avoid asking some of them and, if so, which ones? When during the interview would you plan to ask each of the questions? Would you rephrase any of the questions? Why? And how? Again, as in Exercise 1, *discuss* and *compare* your probable questions in your small group; and talk about your intentions and desires for particular employer traits and job characteristics as they are reflected in each of the following questions:

1. What will be my responsibilities in the job?
2. What are the prospects for promotion with the company?
3. What kind of fringe benefits does the company offer?
4. How long a vacation do I get?
5. Do you have a set salary or wage schedule?
6. How much overtime will I be expected to work?
7. What kind of public transportation is available for getting to work?
8. Will I have an expense account?
9. Can you tell me about the community and the city?
10. What kind of person is my immediate supervisor?
11. What kind of person are you looking for in this job?
12. What exactly does this job entail?
13. Do you mind if I wait a week before telling you whether I want to take this job? (I have an interview scheduled with another company.)
14. Will you show me around the offices and the plant?
15. Are you interested in my experiences in summer work, or in my extracurricular activities?

Preparing a resumé

The questions in Exercises 1 and 2 were, of course, rather general; more specific ones would depend on the nature of the job and your qualifications. In many cases, interviewers learn of your specific qualifications and decide whether to grant an interview from a *resumé* you send out when you request an interview. The resumé, also called a *vita,* includes basic data about yourself and your educational and employment history. Although it follows no set form, it should be clear, complete, and brief because potential employers want a quick overview of your background and skills.[2] Don't leave out anything important, however; a resumé should be as complete as your qualifications. You should type it and, if you wish, photocopy it to send to various potential employers. If you haven't solved the mysteries of spelling, grammar, and punctuation, give it to someone who has — for proofreading. One careless error can prejudice an employer against you, despite your otherwise sterling qualifications. Someone we know, for example, a hotshot Phi Beta Kappa, applied for his first teaching position — in English, no less — yet misspelled the same word on every resumé. He was puzzled as to why he received so few favorable responses to his letters of application until, in an interview, the department head informed him of his error.

"Sir," the chairperson sneered, "*dossier* is spelled with an 's,' not a 'c.'"

Devastated, the applicant returned home, looked in the dictionary, and there it was—spelled with *two* "s's."

Because your resumé is one of your most valuable assets in job-seeking situations, be careful not to prejudice your case by providing carelessly prepared information.

In your resumé, include specific information about who you are and where you can be reached: your name, address, telephone number, birth date, marital status, and whatever else is pertinent. Next, list under separate headings whatever positive information you can provide about your schooling, jobs, activities, special experiences, recognitions, and awards. List summertime jobs or part-time jobs you've held. List the school, church, and community organizations you've belonged to. Your work as a day-camp counselor six years ago, although it may seem trivial to you, may illustrate to a possible employer your potential for leadership. Finally, include the names, titles, and addresses of two or three people who can serve as personal references. Your mom and dad may love you and think you're wonderful, but omit them as references.

In your resumé, by all means make yourself look good; but don't decorate your past history with phony tinsel. No employer treasures dishonesty. A woman we know wrote that she previously had worked as "Assistant Manager for a radio station." When she appeared for an interview with the representative of the potential employer, the interviewer naturally wondered why someone with that background and experience would want to apply for a new job as a secretary.

"Well," the applicant confessed, "I wasn't *exactly* Assistant Manager."

"What were you, then?" inquired the interviewer.

"Assistant *to* the Manager."

"In what capacity?"

She paused. "I was her secretary."

She didn't get the job.

The illustration on the following page includes an example of a typical resumé.

When applying for a job, send a copy of your resumé, along with a short cover-letter requesting an interview, to whatever companies, agencies, etc., you find advertising a position in newspapers, professional journals, or through your school's placement service. If you find nothing in your field through these advertisements, check with school counselors, friends, or anyone else who might know of an opening. Look through the yellow pages of your phone book or the business directories in your library. Then write or telephone those companies. Don't give up fishing for a job when you can't get a nibble immediately. Unlike your resumé, your cover-letter should be retyped each time you send one out. Companies don't like form letters any more than you do.

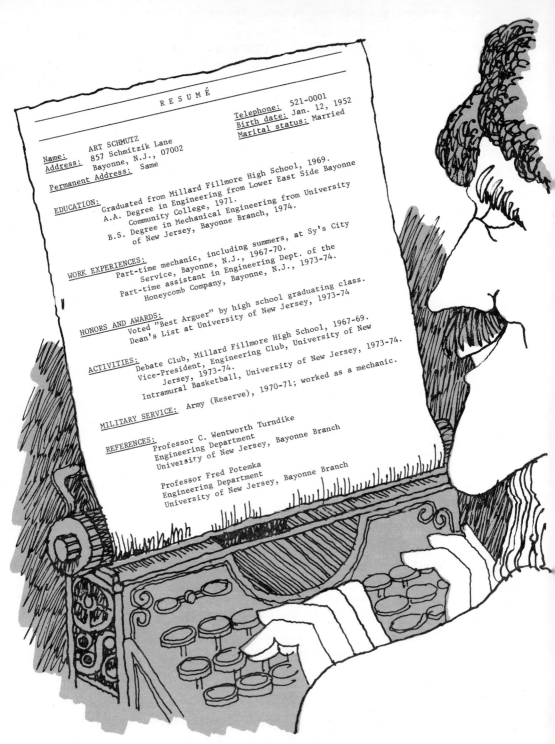

RESUMÉ

Telephone: 521-0001
Birth date: Jan. 12, 1952
Marital status: Married

Name: ART SCHMUTZ
Address: 857 Schmitzik Lane
Bayonne, N.J., 07002
Permanent Address: Same

EDUCATION: Graduated from Millard Fillmore High School, 1969.
A.A. Degree in Engineering from Lower East Side Bayonne
Community College, 1971.
B.S. Degree in Mechanical Engineering from University
of New Jersey, Bayonne Branch, 1974.

WORK EXPERIENCES: Part-time mechanic, including summers, at Sy's City
Service, Bayonne, N.J., 1967-70.
Part-time assistant in Engineering Dept. of the
Honeycomb Company, Bayonne, N.J., 1973-74.

HONORS AND AWARDS: Voted "Best Arguer" by high school graduating class.
Dean's List at University of New Jersey, 1973-74.

ACTIVITIES: Debate Club, Millard Fillmore High School, 1967-69.
Vice-President, Engineering Club, University of New
Jersey, 1973-74.
Intramural Basketball, University of New Jersey, 1973-74.

MILITARY SERVICE: Army (Reserve), 1970-71; worked as a mechanic.

REFERENCES: Professor C. Wentworth Turndike
Engineering Department
University of New Jersey, Bayonne Branch

Professor Fred Potemka
Engineering Department
University of New Jersey, Bayonne Branch

". . . Not bad for a kid who could never build a sandcastle . . ."

3

Preparing a Resumé for a Job Application

Look in the want-ad section of a newspaper or a professional journal in your field, then choose one job listing you'd like to apply for now or after you complete your schooling. You may not at this point know exactly what that job is, but don't worry. You'll change your mind and your occupation more than once. So pick something that looks good and promising to you now. Perhaps you can talk to counselors, instructors, or people outside school for additional advice on what to include in your resumé. Also, you might check your college catalog for the degree requirements in your vocational field or hoped-for career.

Then write a resumé including all the credentials you now have, or think you will have, when you apply for the job. If you choose an accounting position, for example, include references to your part-time work as a bookkeeper, the course work you've completed in accounting and other business-related fields, and your membership in the Business Club. Include the activities you've participated in and/or honors won.

4

Role-Playing a Job Interview

Now, using your resumé as the basis, try role-playing a job interview. With a classmate, ideally with someone you've come to know and trust, exchange the resumés you prepared in Exercise 3, and tell each other the kind of job you'd like to apply for. Then, outside of class, prepare a list of questions—based, in part, on the resumé you've received—that you will ask your classmate in your role as the interviewer. Since you will also role-play the person applying for a job, prepare a list of questions you'd like to ask in that role.

In the following class period, conduct the interviews. Take notes on each other's performance, deciding whether the questions and responses exchanged between you were appropriate, and singling out the ones in need of improvement. Subsequently, your instructor may choose several of you to conduct your interviews before the whole class—to serve as examples and to spur whole-class discussion.

In sum, when you prepare for a job interview, you must be *thorough.* Generally, you must write a resumé; decide on the appropriate details of your physical appearance; investigate the background of the company, organization, or agency in question; anticipate and formulate answers to questions from the interviewer; and decide on the questions you want to ask. In the interview itself, you should be ready to discuss yourself, your qualifications, and your work experiences positively, confidently, and honestly. Plan carefully to succeed—and you will.

Reference Notes

[1]New York Life Insurance Company's excellent booklet, *Making the Most of Your Job Interview,* claims that this question is a "favorite." The booklet also lists eighty questions frequently asked in job interviews, supplied by Frank S. Endicott, Professor of Education, Emeritus Director of Placement, Retired, Northwestern University. Many of the other questions in our list are based on this booklet.

[2]Some school placement services may, on request, supply you with the necessary forms for a resumé, including places for letters of recommendation from a number of people, generally your college instructors. After you have completed the form and gathered letters of recommendation, the placement service will reproduce them in small booklet form, and will send copies of it (usually for a small fee) to the prospective employers you specify.

21 Communicating on the Job

You've made it. You've been hired. You're ready now to put all your training to use, to apply your ideas, to innovate, to prove to your employers that they chose a real go-getter. Unfortunately, it isn't that easy. The world you're about to walk into has already been created, a world with rules — written or unwritten — about production, procedures, and protocol which the other employees have learned, practiced, and expect you to learn, too. It's a world with people, also — people who feel important or unimportant, happy or unhappy, people whom you must work shoulder to shoulder with. If you get along with the person who owns the shoulder next to yours, you'll most likely keep your job and your mental health. If you learn to function within the power structure, you're most likely to win friends and promotions. If you learn to lead your subordinates effectively, you're most likely to maintain friends and the company's profits.

Let's examine your role as both a subordinate and a leader, then. First, let's look at your behavior as a subordinate dealing with your peers, individually and in groups. Next, let's look at your dealings with clients. Finally, let's explore your responsibilities and behavior as a member of management, both in treating subordinates and also in directing or participating in managerial meetings.

If you do your fair day's work,
you are certain to get your fair day's wage
—in praise or pudding,
whichever happens to suit your taste.
—Alexander Smith,
On the Importance of a Man to Himself

OBSERVING THE "RULES" AS YOU BEGIN YOUR JOB

Entering any new job, your first task is to find out the written and unwritten rules. As you meet people and learn procedures, do more watching and listening than talking. Possibly, there is a logical reason for inefficient procedures, duplication of effort, or silly rules that hurt production. Possibly, there isn't a logical rule; but the people involved like the procedures and are too stubborn to change. You don't know yet, so wait a while — perhaps a long while — before you revolutionize the company.

Rule one: Everybody is important. You may walk into a company where all your co-workers are pleasant, well-adjusted, cooperative, and efficient, and where everyone is treated as equals. But we doubt it. Even in supposedly equal positions, some people are "more equal" than others. Expect to find that some people hold more power or exert more influence because of their experience, their age, their relationship with management, or the force of their personalities. Expect to find others resentful or jealous of those with power. Expect to find a relative of the boss who knows all the answers, or a person who has been with the firm thirty years and who seems old-fashioned and slow-moving. Expect to find conflicts and cliques among the employees. And expect to learn to deal with them all.

Rule two: Don't ignore the chain of command. You may have great ideas for saving the company money or making everyone's work easier. But your immediate supervisor may not be receptive to great ideas. Your supervisor may be authoritarian, inflexible, and — in your view — not terribly bright. Nevertheless, he or she does occupy the position above you, and does make the decisions. Bypassing that person and going further up the chain of command can insult or threaten your superior and cause both of you difficulties. Nevertheless, it's sometimes necessary. Before you take the risk, however, observe the next rule.

Rule three: Be diplomatic. Don't push your suggestions on others. Instead, let others think that the ideas are partially theirs. Be humble. Think about a strategy which will persuade your superiors, and which will allow them to save face. Begin, perhaps, by asking your superiors for help, then state your solution in the most tentative of terms, with "I wonder if we might . . . ."

Rule four: Be willing to compromise. Your solution, obviously, is the best for the company, but not if other people don't want to accept it. Try to resolve a problem to everyone's satisfaction. Discuss the issues and not the personalities of the people involved. If anyone challenges you or seems irritated — treating you as if you're a not-OK *Child* — respond with your *Adult.* Returning the hostility simply escalates the conflict and increases the difficulty of finding a compromise. You can't avoid occasional conflict, but you can minimize it.

Regarding the exercises in this chapter . . . . *For the thirteen exercises in the balance of this chapter, you and the other members of your small group are required to play various roles in on-the-job situations — first in situations with peers; then in situations with clients; then in superior-subordinate relationships; and, finally, as members of a managerial problem-solving team. In each case, you and the others with whom you will be working will need to create the specific details characterizing the relationship. Above all, get involved with the role-character you're portraying. For each of these exercises, analyze the issues, prepare the persuasive strategy, and anticipate the responses of the other people in their roles.*

1 Working with Another Member of Your Group
Role-Playing an On-the-Job Conflict

Situation: The head secretary has been with the firm for twenty-four years. Although she uses outmoded techniques of filing and accounting, she acts as if she's perfect, criticizing all the new employees and driving them into resigning or quitting. A new employee, a graduate of a secretarial-training program, knows techniques that are more efficient and would like to implement them. She asks the head secretary to discuss the possibilities. *Roles:* Ms. Walchak, head secretary; Ms. Adams, only recently employed by the firm.

2 Working with Another Member of Your Group
Role-Playing an On-the-Job Conflict

Situation: A new employee in the actuarial department of an insurance firm finds that a more experienced employee — but one with the same job description as hers — is checking and criticizing her work. She resents the interference, but the experienced employee feels that he has a responsibility to the firm to supervise new employees. The newcomer requests that the two meet to try to resolve their differences. *Roles:* Ms. Peters, the new employee; Mr. Boone, the experienced employee.

3 Working with Other Members of Your Group
Role-Playing an On-the-Job Conflict

Situation: Three employees in an advertising agency must work together on a large project. One employee is often late in getting to work, takes frequent coffee breaks, constantly socializes with employees in other departments, and does very little work. The other two persons involved in the large project, in order to compensate for the deficiencies of the third, find themselves saddled with more than their share of the work. One, extremely resentful, asks the others to meet and decide on a method of allocating the work equitably and fairly. *Roles:* Mr. Stantley, the inefficient worker; Ms. Buzhard, the resentful worker; and Mr. Chan, the third worker.

Role-Playing to Reduce an On-the-Job Conflict

Situation: A gym teacher in a junior-high school must teach four sixth-grade classes for one period each day. An older man, he is an authoritarian and frequently punishes students for "misbehavior" that three of the four sixth-grade home-room teachers find "trivial." The four teachers request a meeting with the gym teacher to discuss the issue. *Roles:* Mr. Bowen, the gym teacher; Ms. Olner, a new teacher who is very popular with the students, and is not a strict disciplinarian; Ms. Ford, an older "traditional" teacher who, basically, sympathizes with Mr. Bowen; Mr. Conley, a "long-haired" teacher with five years' experience, and who also is not a strict disciplinarian; and Ms. Kennedy, a teacher with eight years' experience who tends to be "moderate" about discipline.

DEALING WITH CLIENTS

Most of the time, your relationships with clients will be pleasant, stimulating, even fun. But you'll be confronted with occasional dilemmas, too. Here again, your most successful strategy will be to take into account the issues, and try to see them through the needs, beliefs, and attitudes of the client in question. Try to plan your strategy in advance, and adapt it as the situation demands.

Role-Playing an Interaction with a Client

Situation: The sales representative for a high-priced, high-quality women's clothing company—just beginning in business—enters a store to try to open a new account. The buyer for the store tends to invest the store's money in proved big sellers. *Roles:* Mr. Lewis, the sales representative; Ms. Wine, the store's buyer.

Role-Playing an Employer-to-Employer Relationship

Situation: Federal laws against "blackballing" employees prohibit one employer from counseling another not to hire the first employer's ex-employee. An employee quits a job as a computer operator after three months' work and applies to a new firm. The Head of Personnel of the prospective employer of the applicant must call the Director of Computer

Operations of the former employer to check the applicant's references. *Roles:* Mr. Kowalski, Head of Personnel, employing firm; Mr. Stevens, Director of Computer Operations for the former employer.

---

7 Working with Another Member of Your Group
Role-Playing an Interaction with a Client

Situation: The president of a company which is a major client of an accounting firm requests that an accountant illegally backdate a document so that the company in question can save some money in federal taxes. *Roles:* Mr. Andalman, president of the requesting company; Ms. Gomez, the accountant.

LEADING OTHERS IN THEIR WORK

If you're hired or promoted to be a manager, an assistant manager, a supervisor, a department head, a junior or senior partner, a president or a vice-president, you'll be responsible for the productivity of other human beings. Essentially, you'll be directing small groups in cooperative and problem-solving tasks, just as you've done occasionally in your in-class activities. Of course, the most successful managers and supervisors are enthusiastic and fair, and respect the people they supervise.

Conversely, poor supervision often damages worker productivity. Any group naturally forms cliques and develops a sense of cohesiveness. That, usually, is desirable. But employees also can easily band together against a superior they dislike, doing the minimum amount of work or even sabotaging the work or product.[1] Don't expect your job to be easy, therefore. You'll meet with suspicion and resentment. Your old friends will treat you differently because you must treat them differently. You must direct them, criticize them, occasionally discipline them. Some, with strong feelings against management, will reject you. Others will try to exploit their friendship with you. Whether your style of leadership is authoritarian, democratic, or laissez-faire (terms we used in Chapter 2), you'll be forced to do a balancing act between the demands of productivity and the human concerns of your subordinates. Keep in mind, therefore, what studies on the subject have found to be effective leadership traits:

(1) Stand up for subordinates when you deal with superiors. You'll win their loyalty.

(2) Try to ensure that subordinates get along with each other.

(3) Praise subordinates' work, as well as criticize it. Don't be a nay-sayer only.

(4) Listen to subordinates' ideas, and act on them when they make good sense.[2]

(5) Take an interest in subordinates as individuals; don't see them just as workers.

(6) Don't supervise subordinates so closely that they are led to feel you don't trust them. Explain a task clearly, then let them carry it out.[3]

To these six traits, we add two more that we feel will increase your effectiveness as a leader of other workers:

(7) Be personally enthusiastic about the job, and be willing to work hard yourself. Set an example for your subordinates.

(8) When you criticize or discipline subordinates, do so fairly and even-handedly. Don't play favorites or single out enemies.

8 Working with Another Member of Your Group
Role-Playing a Superior-Subordinate Work Relationship

Situation: An accountant with a major accounting firm makes frequent errors and has been responsible for the firm's loss of two important clients. A junior partner, a close friend of the error-prone accountant, must tell him that unless his work performance improves during the next six months, he will be fired. *Roles:* Mr. Harrison, the junior partner; Mr. Abrams, the accountant.

9 Working with Other Members of Your Group
Role-Playing a Superior-Subordinate Work Relationship

Situation: A delivery company acquires a new truck. A supervisor must meet with the drivers to decide who will use it, and how the other, older trucks will be assigned to the drivers. *Roles:* Joe, twelve years with the company, a good worker, now driving a two-year-old truck; Mary, two years with the company, a good worker, now driving a seven-year-old truck that runs poorly; Paul, one year with the company, now driving a battered truck because he's had two accidents; Melvin, twenty years with the company, not a hard worker, now driving a five-year-old truck in need of repairs; Frieda, three years on the job, an indifferent worker, driving a badly damaged truck because Paul smashed into it; Howard, the supervisor.

"Guys . . . meet Lola, your new foreman."

10 Working with Other Members of Your Group
Role-Playing a Superior-Subordinate Work Relationship

Situation: The owner of a small, light construction firm wants to hire a new foreman—a woman. He must explain his intentions to a crew of all-male employees. *Roles:* Mr. Dobetter, the owner; Mr. Wietecha, with the firm seventeen years; Mr. Subeck, with the firm one year; Mr. Atkins, with the firm five years; Mr. Pawley, with the firm six years.

CONDUCTING AND PARTICIPATING IN MANAGERIAL MEETINGS

Often, members of management or management teams must meet to discuss problems and plan new policies. As the person responsible for conducting such meetings, you must be sensitive to the task and the feelings of the people involved. You must see that the discussion addresses and resolves the issues. Similarly, you must see that the participants react to the issues and not to each other's personalities. Here are four specific "know-how's" that can help you increase your communicative effectiveness in managerial meetings:

Preparing an agenda. One way to structure a discussion is to prepare an agenda, a brief outline of what will be covered in the meeting. If time allows, prepare and distribute copies of the agenda prior to the meeting so the participants can study it. You might, in fact, ask certain of those who will be present to speak on particular items on the agenda. However, once the meeting is under way, don't follow the agenda automatically if the discussion reveals problems you hadn't anticipated, or if it follows productive routes you hadn't envisioned.

Using a problem-solving sequence. John Dewey, in *How We Think,* describes the steps in the thought process of an individual trying to solve a problem.[4] These steps in what he calls "reflective thinking" you can usefully apply to group problem solving as well. Although Dewey specifies only five steps, he implies a sixth—a step which we have included as the first step in the following sequence: (1) defining a problem and analyzing its causes, (2) establishing what the solution should accomplish, (3) suggesting possible solutions, (4) weighing the effectiveness and practicality of each solution, (5) choosing one solution, and (6) deciding on how to implement the selected solution. Dewey says that every human being doesn't follow every step in every problem-solution attempt; he or she may devote more thought to some steps than to others, or omit certain steps entirely. A group engaged in a problem-solving discussion should be just as flexible.

Managing potential conflict. Feelings wound easily in group decision making, especially if people assume they haven't been allowed to participate fully, or that others are manipulating the discussion to achieve their own goals, or that they must compete with other members of the group. As the person conducting the meeting, you should anticipate and attempt to minimize such potential sources of conflict. Allow everyone the opportunity to contribute, or to decline to contribute. Look for compromises between positions. Try to create face-saving routes for group members to follow. Read their nonverbal messages and respond to them.

Working as a participant in a managerial meeting. By definition, each group requires that all its members participate and that all work to achieve common goals. Therefore, get involved in and try to facilitate the decision-making process. Ask questions and make suggestions to help carry the group through the agenda. Volunteer information, initiate compromises, smooth over conflicts. You're a member of management and a leader, too, so take leadership responsibilities.

11

Role-Playing Participation in a Managerial Meeting

Note: For this exercise, and also for Exercises 12 and 13 which follow, the person conducting the meeting should prepare an agenda and distribute copies of it to the other participants—preferably before the meeting convenes.

Situation: A television manufacturing company pays its employees on a piecework basis (i.e., a specific sum for each set the employee assembles). The sets require careful handling; and because production is slow, wages are low and morale poor. Employees are beginning to ignore quality controls in order to increase their productivity. The company president calls a meeting to resolve the problem. *Roles:* Mr. Ender, the company president; Mr. Wolinsky, production manager; Ms. James, president of the employees' union; Ms. Jacobson, quality-control manager; Mr. Thompson, head accountant.

12

Role-Playing Participation in a Managerial Decision-Making Conference

Situation: Three years ago a coat manufacturing company lost a great deal of money on the "maxi-coat," which quickly went out of fashion. Now the European designers are touting a buttonless coat tied around the waist by a belt. The president of the company calls a meeting to decide whether to produce the coat, in what quantity, how much to spend for fabric, how much to pay each seamstress per garment on a piecework basis, and—in order to be competitive in the market—what the selling price of the garment should be. *Roles*: Mr. Schultz, company president; Ms. Randall, head designer; Mrs. Grazioli, president of the company's seamstress union; Mr. Campbell, sales manager; Mr. Groffman, head of production.

13

Role-Playing Negotiation of a Management-Labor Contract

Situation: Despite rising inflation, a small food-canning company has maintained its prices on its products so as to be able to compete with larger competitors. Now the employees are demanding a ten percent cost-of-living increase which will, in turn, produce a four percent increase in the price of the company's products. The vice-president of the company convenes the first negotiating session. *Roles:* Ms. Greene, company vice-president; Mr. Dolan, head accountant for the firm; Mr. Johnson, production manager; Mr. Mancuso, president of the workers' union; Ms. Washington, vice-president of the union; Ms. Randolph, union secretary.

Thus ends your attempt at role-playing in the business world. As a newly hired employee, you've tried to recognize each person's importance, observe the chain of command, be diplomatic, and be willing to compromise. You've prepared strategies for resolving potential conflicts among your peers and with your clients. As a member of management, you've attempted to be sensitive to the demands of productivity and the concerns of the people you supervise. As a leader of or a participant in problem-solving meetings, you've attempted to prepare an agenda and to arrive at a solution which can be implemented. In each role, you've planned your strategy, basing it on the requirements of the situation and the other people involved. Overall, you've attempted to apply to the business world what you've learned throughout this course in speech communication. Fully prepared, in command, you've attempted to be clear, persuasive, and the best self you could be. You've attempted to speak with confidence in real life—which should be, and must be, your goal and ours.

Reference Notes

[1] *Modern Management,* the Bureau of National Affairs, Inc., Washington, D.C., August 15, 1955, p. 2.

[2] Robert E. Schwab, "Motivation and Human Relations Principles," *Personnel Series,* No. 155, American Management Association, Inc., 1953, pp. 31–34.

[3] Rensis Likert, "Motivation: The Core of Management," *Personnel Series,* No. 155, American Management Association, Inc., 1953, pp. 3–7.

[4] John Dewey, *How We Think* (Boston: D. C. Heath and Company, 1933), especially pp. 106–117.

Appendix

285

I. A STUDENT SPEECH FOR ANALYSIS

For this exercise in speech analysis, we have chosen a speech by Ralph Zimmermann. In 1955, as a senior at Wisconsin State College in Eau Claire, Wisconsin, Mr. Zimmermann won first place in the men's final contest of the Interstate Oratorical Association for his speech, "Mingled Blood."* The following year he died from the illness the speech describes. Although the speech contains a few flaws, it exhibits many traits of effective speaking which we have emphasized in this book.

As you read the text of the speech, analyze it on the basis of the specific points we have discussed: the strength of the introduction; the adequacy and appropriateness of speech materials, whether derived from other people directly or from printed pages; the choice and integration of personal anecdotes; the organization—the structure—of the speech; the quality of the language; the relation of the speech materials to the audience; the use of internal summaries and transitions; the effectiveness of the conclusion. The paragraphs are numbered for your convenience.

Bring your written analysis to class and, using it as a reference, participate in a class discussion evaluating the speech.

"Mingled Blood"

by Ralph Zimmermann

I am a hemophiliac. To many of you, that word signifies little or nothing. A few may pause a moment and then remember that it has something to do with bleeding. Probably none of you can appreciate the gigantic impact of what those words mean to me. /1

What is this thing called hemophilia? Webster defines it as "a tendency, usually hereditary, to profuse bleeding even from slight wounds." Dr. Armand J. Quick, Professor of Biochemistry at Marquette University and recognized world authority on this topic, defines it as "a prothrombin consumption time of 8 to 13 seconds." Normal time is 15 seconds. Now do you know what hemophilia is? /2

It is by no means a 20th-century phenomenon. Ancient writings reveal the Jewish rabbis, upon the death of firstborn sons from bleeding after circumcision, allowed the parents to dispense with this ceremony for any more sons. Family laws of ancient Egypt did not permit a woman to bear any more children if the firstborn should die of severe bleeding from a

*"Mingled Blood," by Ralph Zimmermann. Reprinted from *Winning Orations* by special arrangement with the Interstate Oratorical Association, Randall Capps, Executive Secretary, Western Kentucky University.

minor wound. How odd it seems to link the pyramids of the 4th dynasty with prothrombin consumption of 1955. /3

Hemophilia has had significant influence on the pages of history. Victoria, the queen of an empire on which the sun never set, was a transmitter of this dread ailment. Through her daughter, Alice, it was passed to the Russian royal family and Czarevitch Alexis, heir apparent to the throne of Nicholas II. Alexis, the hemophilic heir apparent, was so crippled by his ailment that the Bolshevik revolters had to carry him bodily to the cellar to execute him. And through Victoria's daughter, Beatrice, it was carried to the sons of the Spanish monarch, Alfonso XIII. While this good queen ruled her empire with an iron hand and unknowingly transmitted this mysterious affliction, my forebears, peasants of southern Germany, worked their fields, gave birth to their children, and buried their dead sons. Hemophilia shows no respect for class lines. It cares not whether your blood be red or blue. /4

For hemophilia is a hereditary disease. It afflicts only males, but paradoxically is transmitted only by females. The sons of a victim are not hemophiliacs, and do not pass it on. However, all of the daughters are transmitters. Of the transmitter-daughter's children, half of the girls may be transmitters like their mother, and half of the sons may be hemophiliacs. Thus the net spreads out and on. Theoretically, it follows strict Mendelian principles. But because it is a recessive characteristic, it may lie dormant for generation after generation. As far back as my ancestral line can be traced, there is no evidence of hemophilia until my older brother Herbert and me. The same is true of 50 per cent of America's bleeders. /5

And there are many of us. Medical authorities estimate that there are some 20,000 – 40,000 hemophiliacs of all types in the United States. Clinically we divide into three groups: classic hemophilia AHG, and two other less common types of hemophilia, PTC and PTA. I am a classic hemophiliac — the real McCoy. /6

What does it really mean to be a hemophiliac? The first indication comes in early childhood when a small scratch may bleed for hours. By the time the hemophiliac reaches school age, he begins to suffer from internal bleeding into muscles, joints, the stomach, the kidneys. This latter type is far more serious, for external wounds can usually be stopped in minutes with topical thromboplastin or a pressure bandage. But internal bleeding can be checked only by changes in the blood by means of transfusion or plasma injections. If internal bleeding into a muscle or joint goes unchecked repeatedly, muscle contraction and bone deformity inevitably result. My crooked left arm, the built-up heel on my right shoe, and the full-length brace on my left leg offer mute but undeniable testimony to that fact. Vocal evidence you hear; weak tongue muscles are likely to produce defective L and R sounds. /7

Childhood and early adolescence are the danger periods of a hemophiliac's life. As recently as November, 1950, *The Science Digest* reported that 85 percent of all hemophiliacs die during that period. While the figure is exaggerated, it tends to indicate this salient point: if society can keep a hemophiliac alive until after adolescence, society has saved a member. During those years, society is given a responsibility it too often refuses to accept. /8

You might ask: But what can I do? What do you expect of me? The answer lies in the title of this oration: mingled blood. For all that boy needs is blood, blood, and more blood. Blood for transfusions, blood for fresh frozen plasma, blood for serum fractions. Not Red Cross Bank Blood, for stored blood loses its clot-producing factors. But fresh blood directly from you to him in a matter of hours. Your blood, dark and thick, rich with all the complex protein fractions that make for coagulation — mingled with the thin, weak, and deficient liquid that flows in his veins. Blood directly from you to the medical researcher for transformation into fresh frozen plasma or anti-hemophilic globulin. During those years, his very life is flowing in your veins. No synthetic substitute has been found — only fresh blood and its derivatives. /9

Because medical science had not advanced far enough, and fresh blood not given often enough, my memories of childhood and adolescence are memories of pain and heartbreak. I remember missing school for weeks and months at a stretch — of being very proud because I attended school once for four whole weeks without missing a single day. I remember the three long years when I couldn't even walk because repeated hemorrhages had twisted my ankles and knees to pretzel-like forms. I remember being pulled to school in a wagon while other boys rode their bikes, and being pushed to my table. I remember sitting in the dark empty classroom by myself during recess while the others went out in the sun to run and to play. And I remember the first terrible day at the big high school when I came on crutches and built-up shoes, carrying my books in a sack around my neck. /10

But what I remember most of all is the pain. Medical authorities agree that a hemophilic joint hemorrhage is one of the most excruciating pains known to mankind. To concentrate a large amount of blood into a small compact area causes a pressure that words can never hope to describe. And how well I remember the endless pounding, squeezing pain. When you seemingly drown in your own perspiration, when your teeth ache from incessant clenching, when your tongue floats in your mouth and bombs explode back of your eyeballs; when darkness and light fuse into one hue of gray; when day becomes night and night becomes day — time stands still, and all that matters is that ugly pain. The scars of pain are not easily erased. /11

Once a hemophiliac successfully passes through the dangerous period, his need for blood steadily decreases and his health improves. The nightmare of youth is gradually hidden behind a protective curtain of objectivity that is seldom raised. In contrast to my childhood days, I can look back on more than three years of college with joy and a sense of achievement. I've had some good breaks. I've been in debate and forensics for four years and had a variety of satisfying experiences. I've been lucky in politics. My constituents, the student body at our college, elected me President of Student Government. Like so many other American youths,

I've worked my way through college as a clerk in a hardware store. On warm weekends, while not a Ben Hogan at golf, I have shot an 82. And back home, a girl wears my wedding band. /12

For today, except for periodic transfusions, my life is as normal as anyone else's, and my aims and ambitions are the same as anyone else's. But now a different type of social relationship needs to be found. Because a hemophiliac is so totally dependent on society during his early years and because his very existence is sometimes then precarious, society now tends to lag in recognizing the change. It sometimes fails to realize that this hemophiliac's life is no longer in serious question and that now his right to aspire to any new height should not be frowned on by a society still vividly remembering the past. Now he seeks neither pity nor privilege. He wishes to be regarded not as a hemophiliac, but rather a human being to be evaluated like any human being. /13

I cannot change that part of my life which is past. I cannot change my hemophilia. Therefore, I must ask you to help those hemophiliacs that need help. For I remember too well my older brother Herbert, so shattered in adolescence by hemophilia that his tombstone reads like a blessing: "May 10, 1927–April 6, 1950, Thy Will Be Done." And I ask you to help hemophiliacs because one day my grandson may need your blood. But I also must ask you to recognize a hemophiliac for what he is today; to realize that past is prologue, that weakness sometimes begets strength, that man sometimes conquers. And so I pray: /14

"God give me the courage to accept the things that I cannot change; the power to change the things which I can; and the wisdom always to know the difference between the two." /15

II. A SELECTED LIST OF USEFUL SOURCE-INFORMATION AND REFERENCE BOOKS FOR THE PUBLIC SPEAKER*

Indexes to Books and Periodicals.

Agricultural Index, 1916–1964. In 1964 it became *Biological and Agricultural Index.* Subject index to a selected list of periodicals, bulletins, documents.

Annual Magazine Subject Index, 1908–   . Subject index to American and English periodicals.

Art Index, 1929–   . Author and subject index to fine arts periodicals and museum bulletins.

Bibliographic Index, 1938–   . Subject index to bibliographies in books and periodicals.

Biography Index, 1946–   . Subject index to biographical material in books and periodicals.

Dramatic Index, 1909–1949. Index to articles and illustrations concerning the American and English theater.

Education Index, 1929–   . Subject index to educational periodicals, books, and pamphlets.

Engineering Index, 1884–   . Subject index to technical periodicals; transactions and journals of engineering and other technical societies; reports of government bureaus, engineering colleges, research laboratories.

Reference Works

Architecture: *A History of Architecture on the Comparative Method* (Fletcher), 17th ed., 1961.

Art: *Encyclopedia of World Art,* 1959–1968, 15 vols. *Encyclopedia of the Arts* (Read), 1966. *Lives of the Painters* (Canaday), 1969, 4 vols. *McGraw-Hill Dictionary of Art* (Myers), 1969, 5 vols.

Biography (American): *Dictionary of American Biography,* 1928–1937, 20 vols. and index; supplements 1944, 1958. *Who's Who in America,* biennially since 1899. *Who Was Who in America,* Vol. I, 1897–1942; Vol. II, 1943–1950; Vol. III, 1951–1960 (*Who's Who* subjects who died during those years). *Who Was Who in America,* Historical Volume, 1607–1896, 1963.

Biography (British): *Dictionary of National Biography,* 1885–1901, 63 vols. and first supplement (2 vols.) with other supplements through 1950. *Who's Who* annually since 1849.

Biography (General): *Current Biography,* monthly since 1940, with annual cumulative volume. *International Who's Who,* 1935–   . *World Biography,* 5th ed., 1954.

Business: *Encyclopedia of Banking and Finance* (Munn), 6th ed., 1962.

*From Porter G. Perrin and Wilma R. Ebbitt, *Writer's Guide and Index to English,* 5th ed. (Glenview, Illinois: Scott Foresman and Company, 1972), pp. 399–406.

Chemistry: *Encyclopedia of Chemistry* (Clark), 2nd ed., 1966. *Thorpe's Dictionary of Applied Chemistry* (Thorpe and Whitely), 4th ed., 1937–1956, 12 vols.

Education: *Encyclopedia of Educational Research* (Harris), 3rd ed., 1960. *The Encyclopedia of Education* (Deighton), 1971, 9 vols.

Government and Political Science: *Cyclopedia of American Government* (McLaughlin and Hart), 1914, 3 vols. *Political Science: A Bibliographic Guide to the Literature* (Harmon), 1965, supplement 1968. *United States Government Organization Manual,* 1935–   , annual.

History (General): *An Encyclopedia of World History* (Langer), 4th ed., 1968. *The Cambridge Ancient History* (Bury et al.), 2nd ed., 1923–1939, 12 vols. of text and 5 vols. of plates. *The Cambridge Medieval History* (Bury et al.), 1911–1936, 8 vols. *The Cambridge Modern History* (Ward et al.), 1902–1926, 13 vols. and atlas. *The New Cambridge Modern History,* 1957–   , 14 vols.

History (American): *Dictionary of American History* (Adams), 1940, 5 vols.; supplement, Vol. 6, 1961. *Encyclopedia of American History* (Morris), rev. ed., 1965. *The Oxford Companion to American History* (Johnson), 1966.

Music: *Grove's Dictionary of Music and Musicians* (Blom), 5th ed., 1954, 9 vols.; supplement, Vol. 10, 1961. *The International Cyclopedia of Music and Musicians* (Thompson, rev. Sabin), 9th ed., 1964. *Harvard Dictionary of Music* (Apel), 2nd ed., rev., 1969. *The Oxford Companion to Music* (Scholes), 10th ed., 1970.

Psychology: *Encyclopedia of Psychology* (Harriman), 1946. *A Dictionary of Psychology* (Drever), rev. ed., 1964.

Quotations: *Bartlett's Familiar Quotations* (Bartlett), 14th ed., 1968. *Dictionary of Quotations* (Evans), 1968. *The Oxford Dictionary of Quotations,* 2nd ed., 1953. *The Home Book of Quotations, Classical and Modern* (Stevenson), 10th ed., 1967. *The Home Book of Bible Quotations* (Stevenson), 1949. *The Home Book of Shakespeare Quotations* (Stevenson), 1937.

Religion: *New Catholic Encyclopedia,* 1967, 15 vols. and index. *Universal Jewish Encyclopedia,* 1939–1944, 10 vols. *Encyclopedia of Religion and Ethics* (Hastings), 1908–1927, 12 vols. and index. *New Schaff-Herzog Encyclopedia of Religious Knowledge* (Jackson), 1908–1912, 12 vols. and index; reprinted 1949–1950, 13 vols. *Twentieth Century Encyclopedia of Religious Knowledge* (Loetscher), 1955, 2 vols., an extension of *New Schaff-Herzog Encyclopedia of Religious Knowledge. Dictionary of the Bible* (Hastings), rev. ed., 1963.

General Science: *Dictionary of Scientific Terms* (Speel and Jaffe), 1965. *Harper Encyclopedia of Science* (Newman), rev. ed., 1967. *Hutchinson's Technical and Scientific Encyclopedia* (Tweney and Shirshov), 1935, 4 vols. *The New Space Encyclopedia,* 1969. *Van Nostrand's Scientific Encyclopedia,* 4th ed., 1968. *Dictionary of Scientific Biography* (Gillispie), 1970, 2 vols. *McGraw-Hill Encyclopedia of Science and Technology,* 3rd ed., 1971, 15 vols.

Industrial Arts Index, 1913–1957. In 1958 it became two separate indexes: *Applied Science and Technology Index* and *Business Periodicals Index.* Subject index to a selected list of engineering, trade, and business periodicals.

International Index to Periodicals, 1907–1965. In 1965 it became the *Social Sciences and Humanities Index.* Author and subject index to periodicals from various countries; devoted chiefly to the humanities and the social sciences.

Nineteenth Century Readers' Guide to Periodical Literature, 1890–1899. An index to periodicals, with supplementary indexing, 1900–1922.

Poole's Index to Periodical Literature, 1802–1881. Supplements cover years through 1906. Subject index to American and English periodicals, many of which are no longer published but are still important; precedes coverage of *Reader's Guide.*

United States Government Publications, Monthly Catalog, 1895–   . A bibliography of publications issued by all branches of the government.

Indexes to Specialized Materials

Vertical File Index, 1932–   . An annotated subject-and-title catalog of pamphlets, booklets, leaflets, and mimeographed materials.

Books in Print, 1948–   . Author, title, series index to books currently in print in the United States.

Cumulative Book Index, 1898–   . An author, subject, and title index to books printed in English.

Essay and General Literature Index, 1900–   . Author-and-subject index to essays and articles in collections and miscellaneous works.

Song Index, 1926; supplement 1934. Author and title index to more than 19,000 songs in collections.

Index to Plays, 4th ed., 1963. Author, title, and subject index to plays in collections or separately published.

Play Index, 1949–1952, 1953–1960, 1961–1967. Augments but does not supersede the *Index to Plays.*

Social Sciences: *Encyclopedia of the Social Sciences* (Seligman and Johnson), 1930–1935, 15 vols. *International Encyclopedia of the Social Sciences* (Sills), 1967, 16 vols. and index.

Yearbooks and Almanacs

World Almanac and Book of Facts, 1868–

Information Please Almanac, 1947–   .

Britannica Book of the Year, 1938–   . Annual supplement ot the *Encyclopaedia Britannica.*

Facts on File, 1940–   . Weekly digest of world and domestic news, with index.

The New York Times Encyclopedic Almanac, 1969–   . New comprehensive annual.

Statistical Abstract of the United States, 1878–   . Summary statistics on the industrial, social, political, and economic organization of the U.S.

Reference Shelf, 1922–   . Reprints of articles, bibliographies, and debates on topics of current interest.

A REFERENCE CHART OF ACTIVITIES AND EXERCISES IN THIS BOOK

Index

A

Abstractions, words as, 67–68
Accuracy of word choice, 71–72
Action, moving audience to, as step in persuasive strategy, 245, 248–250, 253–254
Activities, List of, 293–296
Adaptability, vocal, 81, 189–190
Adapting to the unforeseen, 188–191
 illustration, 189
Adapting your speech
 to differences in the occasion, 191–193
 exercises, 193–194
 to questions, 191
 to the unforeseen, 188–191
Addison, Joseph, 51
Adler, Mortimer J., 43
Adult, as ego state, 17–18
 -to-*Adult* relationship in communication, 47, 128
 "tapes," 15, 17–18
Agenda, preparing an, 281
Allen, Woody, 177
Analogy. See *Comparison*
Analysis
 of audience, 147–155

 exercises, 152, 155
 illustration, 149
 of speeches, 286–289
 See also *Transactional Analysis*
Anecdotes, 56–64, 99–112
 coupling, to make a point, 107–112
 illustration, 109
 to develop or illustrate a point, 102–106
 exercises, 105–106
 to humanize speech materials, 175
 to introduce a point, 101–102
 to introduce a speech, 168
 to make a point, 100–106
Angle of speech, 165–168
 exercise, 168
 illustration, 166
Anticlimax order of persuasive strategy, 244, 250, 254–257
 illustration, 255
Appeals, emotional
 examining, *exercise,* 230–231
 illustration, 229
 misusing, 231–235
 using, 228–231
Aristotle, 159, 202, 228, 235
Arnold, Carroll, 251

C

Carlyle, Thomas, 261
Carmichael, Stokely, 61
Carroll, Lewis, 66
Carson, Johnny, 188
Challenging your materials,
136–146
   exercises 138, 139, 141, 145
Charts. See *Visual and auditory aids*
Cheerleading
   as function of persuasion,
   255–256
   as function of speech criticism,
   42, 51–52
   See also *Critic* and *Criticism*
Chesterfield, Lord, 244
Child, as ego state, 16–17
   and core beliefs, 223
   OK, 21
   "tapes," 15
Clarifying ideas with gestures,
87, 89
Clarity, as goal of speaking
   through language, 65–75
   organizing for, 164–172
   with your voice, 76–84
Class format, 27–41
   photos, 30–31
Classifying, defining terms by,
68–69
Cleaver, Eldridge, 63
Clients, dealing with in job
situation, 277
   exercises, 277–278
Climax order of persuasive strategy,
250–254
   illustration, 255
Closed question, 48, 266
Cognitive dissonance, 198–199,
229–230
   illustration, 198
Common ground, establishing, 151,
246
Communicating on the job,
273–283
   exercises, 276–280, 282–283

Communication. See *Speech communication*
Communication journal, student's
   contents of, 38–40, 117–119
   excerpt from, 10
   interests-inventory as part of, 38,
   117–119
      illustrations, 38, 39, 118
   keeping a, 37–40
Comparison of known with
unknown for clarity, 73–74
   exercise, 74
Conclusion, as element in logical
argument, 237–241
Concreteness of language, 70–71
   with details, 59–62
   exercise, 70–71
Confidence
   gained through experience, 27
   See also *Self-confidence*
Conflict, as factor in persuasion,
199
Conflict resolution
   on the job, *exercises,* 276–277
   in small group, 33–36, 41, 281
Contrast, use of for clarity, 73–74
Core beliefs, 221, 223–224
Cosby, Bill, 57
Counter-argument, as element in
logical argument, 237–241
Coupling anecdotes, 107–112
   exercise, 111
Credibility, establishing, as step in
persuasive strategy, 244–246, 252
Credibility tests
   for examples, 143
   for facts, 138–139
   for statistics, 140–141
   for testimony, 142–143
Critic, 51–54
Criticism
   acceptance of, 53–54
   and listening, 51
   negative, 52
   positive, 51–53
   of speeches, 51–54
   as supportive behavior, 52–53

D

Darrow, Clarence, 148, 254
Defining terms, 68–69
   exercise, 69
Delivering your speech, 188–191
   exercise, 193, 258
Details
   arrangement of, to create tension,
   106–107
   in storytelling, 59–62, 100
     exercise, 62
Dewey, John, 281
Diagrams. See *Visual and auditory
aids*
Dialogue, in storytelling, 61
Dinwoodie, S. David, 102–103, 106
Dissonance, 198–199, 227,
229–230
   illustration, 198
Distractions, handling, 190

E

Ebert, Roger, 127–128
Effective speaker, traits of, 180–182
Ego states, 15–18
   Adult, 17–18
   Child, 16–17
   in communication transactions, 19
   illustration, 16
   Parent, 15–16
   See also *Transactional Analysis*
Einstein, Albert, 73
Ekman, Paul, 87
Emblem gestures, 87, 89
   exercise, 87
   photos, 88
Emotion
   exercise, 230–231
   as factor in persuasion, 227–235
   illustration, 229
   misusing appeals to, 231–235
   using appeals to, 228–231
Empathy, as factor in listening, 45
Emphasizing with gestures, 87, 89

Encyclopedias, as source of speech
material, 129
Endicott, Frank S., 272*n*
Ending a speech, 171–172
Establishing credibility, as step in
persuasive strategy, 244–246, 252
Establishing problem, as step in
persuasive strategy, 244, 247–248,
252–253
Esteem needs, 213, 216–217
Evaluation of speeches, 43–44,
286–289
Evidence, 235–236
   as element in logical argument,
   237–241
   exercises, 236, 241
Evidence, 142
Examples
   defining terms by, 68–69
   as supporting material, 143
Exceptions, as element in logical
argument, 237–241
Exercises, List of, 293–296
Extemporaneous speaking, 58
   storytelling, *exercise,* 59
Eye contact
   duration of, 12
Eyewitness reliability, 139
   exercise, 139

F

Facial expression
   as "mood music," 91
   as nonverbal communication, 12
Facts, 136–146
   credibility tests, 138–139
   exercise, 138
Fader, Daniel, 103–105, 106
Fairbanks, Grant, 84*n*
Fear, appeal to, 229–230
Feedback, 91–95
   exercises, 92–95
   illustration, 93
Feelings, 34
Festinger, Leon, 198–199, 230

and perception of spoken language, 12–13
  exercise, 13
and restatement capability, 45
  exercise, 45–46
to your own voice, exercise, 83
Little, Reginald K., 183n
Logical argument, 235
  characteristics of, 237–238
  elements of, 239
  models of, 238–241
    exercise, 241
Lounsbury, Thomas Raynesford, 174
Love and belonging needs, 213 216
Luft, Joseph, 22

M

Macrorie, Ken, Preface
Manuscript speaking, 58
Maps. See Visual and auditory aids
Maslow, Abraham H.
  hierarchy of needs, 212–220
    illustration, 215
Materials, speech. See Speech materials
McGuire, William J., 237
Meetings, conducting in job situation, 280–283
  exercises, 282–283
Memory, and perception, 12–13
Mencken, H. L., 217
Message, 12
  adaptation of and to, 12–13
  affected by relationships with others, 13
  affected by state of mind, 14
  nonverbal, 12, 14
    exercise, 14
  senders and receivers, 12
  verbal, 12
Metaphors
  in storytelling, 59, 62–64

  exercise, 64
"Mingled Blood," sample speech, 286–289
Minow, Newton N., 251–254
Mirror question, 48
Model
  of beliefs, 221
  of cognitive dissonance, 198
  of hierarchy of needs, 215
  of Johari Window, 23, 24
  of logical argument, 238–241
  of Transactional Analysis, 16, 18, 20
Models. See Visual and auditory aids
Movies. See Visual and auditory aids
Moving audience to action, as step in persuasive strategy, 245, 248–250, 253–254
Mumbler, as survival strategy, 4–7

N

Needs of audience
  exercises, 218–219
  as factors in persuasion, 212–220
  illustration, 215
Negative or hostile audience, 210–212
  photos, 210
Neutral or indifferent audience, 210–212
  photos, 210
Newman, Robert P. and Dale R., 142
New York Times Index, 131
Noise
  external, 12
  internal, as psychological/emotional distractions, 14
Nonverbal communication, 12, 85–98
  of attitudes and feelings, 90

observing, *exercises,* 14, 90
photos, 88
as reinforcement of message,
   exercise, 89–90
space as factor in, 95–97
in understanding communication,
44
See also *Body language* and
Gestures
Notes
in interview, 126
keeping, 131
organizing, 132
tape-recording, 134

O

Occasion, adapting to differences
in, 191–193
OK Seat, *exercise,* 26, 32–33
Open Area, of awareness, 22
Open-ended question, 48, 266
Openness, in interpersonal
communication, 22
Organizing speech materials,
156–172, 243–257
   for clarity, interest, usefulness,
   164–172
   to develop thesis, 157–163
   exercises, 162–163, 168, 172,
   256–257
   illustrations, 170, 249
   for persuasive speech, 243, 257
   questions to aid, 161–162
Orwell, George, 60–61, 231
Ostrich, as survival strategy, 4–8,
43
   illustration, 8
Outline of speech, 157–159
   illustration, 186

P

Pappus, Archimedes, 95
Parent, as ego state, 15–16, 21, 47

Participation
in group interaction, 33–34,
28–29
in managerial meetings, 280–283
   exercises, 282–283
Patterson, Alexander, 142
Pause, 12
Pause-fillers, 77–80
   exercise, 77
Penfield, Wilder, 15
Perception
focus of, 12
and memory, 12–13
and the speech communication
process, 12–13
of spoken language, *exercise,*
13–14
Periodicals, as source of speech
material, 129–131
   exercise, 133–134
Peripheral beliefs, 221–222
Personality
conflict, in groups, 34
three dominant attitudes in,
16–18
Persuade, speeches to, 118
analyzing audience for, 208–225
choosing strategy for, 226–242
choosing subject for, 205–206
gearing up for, 205–207
illustrations, 229, 249, 255
organizing, 243–258
Persuasion
illustrations, 229, 249, 255
what it is, 196–202
what it is not, 203–205
   exercise, 204
Pettas, Mary, 84*n*
Physical appearance for job
interview, 265
Physical circumstances
of speech, 95–97, 191–193
of job interview, 262
Physiological-survival needs,
212–213
Pitch, of voice, 12
Pity, appeal to, 228–229

Planning, speech. See *Organizing speech materials*
Point of speech, 100–106
   restatement of, 190–191
Positions, speaking and listening, 95–97
   exercise, 96
Positive audience, 210–212
   reinforcing, 255–256
   responses, 225
   photos, 210
Prejudgments, avoidance in listening, 44
Presenting solution to problem, as step in persuasive strategy, 245, 248, 253
Presummary, 169–170
Printed matter, as source of speech material, 127–131
   exercises, 133–134
Probing question, 48, 266
Problem, establishing, as step in persuasive strategy, 244, 247–248, 252–253
Problem solving
   in the small group, *exercise,* 40–41
   sequence for, 281
Producer, as survival strategy, 4–8
Protective coloration, 247, 265
Public distance, 96
Public speaking, 10–11, 59, 99–112, 164–170, 173–182, 193–195, 205–206, 257
Puchalski, Mark C., 172*n*

Q

"Quasi-courtship" ritual, 86
Questioning
   as a communicative skill, 42, 46–51
   to avoid misunderstandings, 46–47
   types of, 48–49
Questions

adapting to during and after speech, 191
Adult-to-*Adult,* 49
brevity in answering, 49
interpreting for real meaning, 49
in job interview, 266–267
   exercises, 267–268
listening to and answering, 49–50
types of, 48–49

R

Rakove, Milton C., 169
Rapport, 245, 246
Rate, of speaking, 12
Rationalization, 199–202
Reactions of audience, anticipating, 211–225
Reader's Guide to Periodical Literature, 130–131
Reason, as factor in persuasion, 235–242
   illustration, 229
Reasoning from evidence to conclusion, 238–241
   exercise, 241
Recording information about speech materials, 131–132
Recordings. See *Visual and auditory aids*
Reference books, as source of material, 130–131, 290–292
   exercise, 133
Refutation, as element in logical argument, 237–241
Rehearsing your speech, 184–188
   exercise, 187, 257
Reinforcing ideas with gestures, 87, 89
Renshaw, Domeena, 49–50, 157–158, 179
Resolving conflicts in a small group, 35–36, 33–34, 41
Restatement
   as a communicative skill, 45, 49

exercise, 45 – 46
  of point of speech, 190 – 191
Resumé, preparing a, 268 – 269
  exercise, 271
  illustration, 270
Robinson, James Harvey, 199
Rogers, Carl R., 34
Rokeach, Milton
  system of beliefs, 221 – 224
    illustration, 221
Role-playing on-the-job situations,
  exercises, 276 – 280, 282 – 283
Rosetti, Christina Georgiana, 91
Roth, Philip, 151

S

Safety needs, 213, 214 – 215
Sample speech, 286 – 289
Scanzoni, John, 153
Scheflen, Albert E., 86
Schlafly, Phyllis, 230 – 231
Schmutz, Art, 1 – 8, 11, 39, 46, 59
Schwab, Robert E., 283*n*
Secretary, group, 37
Self-acceptance, 12
Self-actualization needs, 213,
217 – 218
Self-awareness, 21 – 26
  and the OK Seat, *exercise,* 26
  for persuasive credibility,
  245 – 247
  as revealed through the Johari
  Window, 22 – 25
Self-confidence, 10
  acquired through speaking
  experiences, 27
  and adopting a "Why not?"
  attitude, 21
  for persuasive credibility,
  245 – 247
  and self-awareness, 21 – 26
Self-sharing
  for persuasive credibility,
  245 – 247
  through storytelling, 57 – 58

Self-understanding, 10 – 26
  by the Johari Window, 20 – 25
  for persuasive credibility,
  245 – 247
Sellin, Thorsten, 142
Sensitivity
  to feelings of group members,
  35 – 36
  to group task, 35
Setting of speech, 95 – 97, 191 – 193
Shakespeare, William, 77, 201
Sharpe, R. D., 157
Skills, speechmaking, 180 – 182
  illustration, 181
Slang
  avoidance of, 72
  in storytelling, 62 – 63
Slides. See *Visual and auditory aids*
Small-group approach, 27 – 41
  photos, 30 – 31
Solution to problem, presenting, as
step in persuasive strategy,
245 – 248, 253
Sophistication, audience, 231
Sources of speech materials
  books, 129
  challenging, 136 – 146
  encyclopedias, 129
  interviews, 124 – 127
  list of, 290 – 292
  periodicals, 129
  reference books, 130 – 131
Space as nonverbal factor in
communication, 95 – 97
Speaker, recording your progress
as, 38 – 40
Speaking publicly, 10 – 11
  See also *Public speaking*
Speech communication
  and self-awareness, 22 – 25
  and self-confidence, 21, 25
  as transaction, 12 – 20
    illustration, 20
Speech evaluation, 43
*Speech Improvement: A Practical
Program,* 84*n*
Speechmaking, 41